Embracing the
Human Jesus

Embracing the Human Jesus

A Wisdom Path for Contemporary Christianity

David Galston

POLEBRIDGE PRESS
Salem, Oregon

To Barbara

Cover and interior design by Robaire Ream

Library of Congress Cataloging-in-Publication Data
Galston, David, 1960-
  Embracing the human Jesus : a wisdom path for contemporary
Christianity / David Galston. -- 1st ed.
      p. cm.
  Includes bibliographical references and index.
  ISBN 978-1-59815-105-3 (alk. paper)
1. Jesus Christ--Historicity. 2. Jesus Christ--Humanity. 3. Q hypothesis
(Synoptics criticism) 4. Bible. N.T. Gospels--Criticism, interpretation,
etc. I. Title.
  BT303.2.G35 2012
  232'.8--dc23
                                                        2012025148

Table of Contents

List of Abbreviations

Gen	Genesis
2 Sam	2 Samuel
Isa	Isaiah
Jer	Jeremiah
Ezek	Ezekiel
Zech	Zechariah
Prov	Proverbs
Eccl	Ecclesiastes
Dan	Daniel
Matt	Matthew
Mark	
Luke	
John	
Thom	Gospel of Thomas
Rom	Romans
1, 2 Cor	1, 2 Corinthians
Col	Colossians

Except where indicated otherwise, New Testament quotes are from the Scholars Version (SV). Hebrew Bible quotes are from the New Revised Standard Version (NRSV).

Acknowledgements

There are many people I wish to thank, who have made possible the journey this book represents. My deepest gratitude goes to the people of Eternal Spring United Church who became and are now known as The Quest Learning Centre for Religious Literacy. There is a need on my part to tell some of their story.

The Quest Centre began as a mission project of the United Church of Canada, and originally it took the name of Eternal Spring. It was, from the start, an experimental community trying to "do" Christianity in a postmodern and increasingly non-religious context. In 2001, the community faced the prospect of needing a new minister, and, holding to its vision of being a different kind of church, I was appointed its leader. I had said in the interview process that I wanted to try to start a historical Jesus community. The idea of a historical Jesus community was eagerly received only until what the historical Jesus meant was understood. Almost immediately people left the community. But a core of people remained, and from this core the community developed to take on a new identity. Eventually, the goal was not to be a church but to be a learning center, which is why the name and status of the community was changed. I need to thank this community very deeply for not bailing out when we began, for giving me a lot of space to experiment with the historical Jesus in church, for putting up with my indecisions before I am able to write something out, for receiving the liturgies of the historical

Jesus with both critical eyes and welcoming hearts, and in general for holding a spirit of openness, curiosity, and compassion.

Within the community there are individuals who extend their generosity to me in the spirit of learning through the criticism of my thoughts. Though I could name several people here, I do want to mention Mary Goldsberry and her ability to keep me honest. I was taught the apocalyptic Jesus model in seminary; it is, of course, the most popular model in Christian history. And at one point I rejected the model almost categorically, but Mary objected. This led to a series of talks we did in the community on arguments for and against the model. She argued the point in favor very well, and I learned from her presentation. The consequence was my awakening to the need to study the position again, and Mary offered a helpful bibliography. I still find the position less attractive than the model of wisdom because it seems very difficult to turn parables into apocalyptic allegories. The parables are very stubborn in this way. Nevertheless, it is evident that virtually all scholars, even those who emphasis apocalypticism, do not deny that along with apocalypticism there is also wisdom in the voice of the historical Jesus. I thank Mary for pushing me to be clearer about this point and to think about wisdom as momentum within the historical Jesus, but not so exclusively as to close my mind to other options and other scholars.

I wish to thank Larry Alexander, Cassandra Farrin, and Char Matejovsky of Polebridge Press. Larry is the publisher of Polebridge, and he first approached me about this book idea after I had presented a talk in relation to *When Faith Meets Reason*, a book to which I contributed an essay. Larry suggested that I could probably write a book on the topic of the historical Jesus and Christianity. Of course, since I register as a strong "N" (iNtuiton) on the Myers-Briggs scale, I quickly picked up the idea and become very excited about it without realizing how much work would actually be involved. I thank Larry for guiding me after the excitement through the actual work and for being able to tell me frankly where I needed to re-think and re-write the content. I thank Cassandra for reading every chapter carefully and editing the text. She was a faithful e-mail correspondent and along the way never let her need to critique and correct the text to interrupt her encouragement of the writing. I have known Char for several years and have always enjoyed her friendship. She has helped and encouraged me in many endeavors related to the Jesus Seminar, and it is no different this time around. I thank Char for her editorial skills, acumen, and support that have made this writing possible.

Several scholars that I have met through the Jesus Seminar have influenced my thinking and changed my mind on many occasions. I want to mention the late Robert W. Funk, who befriended me and who always treated me with great kindness. He opened several opportunities for me to present some ideas either in writing or in a lecture format. On occasion he would e-mail me some ideas he was working on or ideas he thought I should consider. I was always astounded that he considered me a friend, and I miss him very much. He once wrote to me that I needed to write a book called The Re-turning of Nicaea, indicating that we can't, of course, go back to the fourth century but can only start from where we are. I tried to write that book, but it eventually became this one. I hope this book is something that Bob would have liked.

Don Cupitt is a second scholar who I want to mention and thank very much. Over the years, he has faithfully sent to me each of his publications as well as other books that he has thought I should have. He has been both a critic and inspirer of my thinking and my endeavors, which is truly the sign of a wonderful friend. I have read almost everything he has written—it is hard to keep up with the massive amount of writing he is able to produce—and each book has opened up the world to me. I hope in this book that Don will happily be able to see some of the impressions of his own thinking.

There are a few other scholars I want to thank for their consistent friendship and inspiration: Lloyd Geering, Brandon Scott, Bob Miller, Dominic Crossan, Stephen Patterson, and Jack Lightstone. I have always benefited from conversation with them and from their writings.

The people of the SnowStar Institute of Canada also need to be thanked. I started this Institute with two friends, Chris Kraatz and Del Stewart, as a forum for free and progressive thinking in religion. We have benefited as an Institution from a close and cordial relationship with the Westar Institute. In the context of SnowStar, I have had the opportunity to present some of my thinking and to receive the critiques of its members. It has been a great joy in my life to be part of the SnowStar community, and I thank the people of SnowStar very much.

Finally, my family members, who have supported me through the writing of this book, hold my innermost gratitude. My partner, Barbara, remained patient and offered constant love those many times I was not present in family matters. Christopher and Andrew, my step-children, who have taught me a lot about parenthood, about letting things be, and about how to be a kid again have helped to remind me that writing is a creative exercise and not just work. To my students at Brock University who sit in my office and listen to me as I wander way off topic but who nevertheless have helped keep my interest in theology and philosophy alive, I offer thanks. And to the members of the Brock Ecumenical Chaplaincy Committee who have supported me both as a chaplain and as an academic, I owe a great deal of thanks. To Jean Little, author and friend, who helped with the title of this book, I owe a "little" thanks.

Introduction

When I was in seminary I remember a New Testament class in which our teacher said that there was only one sentence in the Bible that Jesus certainly said. When the class eagerly asked which one, our teacher said that he forgot. Of course he was joking. His point was that no one really knows whether or not Jesus said anything attributed to him in the Bible. Then, on another occasion, he was asked if there was anything we could say with certainty about Jesus. His answer was that it was certain Jesus died. And with this plain truth we could also say certainly that he was born.

In seminary I was taught the neo-orthodox gospel,[1] where the question of whether Jesus lived or not, or what he said or didn't say, does not count for much. The point in neo-orthodoxy is that, in Jesus, the Christ-event is encountered. In Jesus, the Word of God breaks into history from outside as the Incarnation. The only thing that matters is the judgment of God on humanity by way of the Word of God descending upon us. To use the metaphor from Jeremiah, which I will refer to again in these pages and which Karl Barth[2] loved so much, the Word of God as Christ-event hits humanity like the hammer that breaks the rock into pieces. Neo-orthodoxy was a great and powerful theology during the time of the Second World War when Christianity was in danger of losing its independence by accommodating itself too closely to political ideologies and nationalism, especially that of Nazi Germany. In such a context, the Word of God breaking

1

in from the outside was the critical, counter-cultural act of prophetic witness. In as much as I have become highly critical of
neo-orthodox theology, I remain an admirer of this aspect of its
voice.

The background of neo-orthodoxy is significant to this book
for a few reasons. The main one is that, from the point of view
of neo-orthodoxy, the historical Jesus does not matter. In fact,
it is best to have an obscure and unrecoverable Jesus for the op-
erations of neo-orthodox theology. The historical Jesus crashes
the neo-orthodox party because, in neo-orthodox circles, what
matters is the confession of the Word as revelation. The historical Jesus does not really have anything to do with confessing the
Christ. A human being who is not God incarnate is not, by
definition, the Word of God. So, it becomes bothersome if the
historical Jesus is given more authority than Jesus Christ, God
incarnate, who is two natures in one person.[3] Only Jesus Christ
as the event of the Incarnation can break in from heaven as the
Word of God. A strictly human Jesus, however, can only be the
same as anyone else.

A second problem is that neo-orthodoxy has no way to critique itself. It is subject to the very problem it sought to overcome, which is the problem of adapting the gospel to cultural
norms. We see neo-orthodoxy today in the voice of those fundamentalists who deny evolution, reject biblical criticism, stand
firmly against same-sex marriage, eagerly advocate war against
one's enemies or perceived enemies, and defend to an absurd
level the right to bear arms. All of this is done in the name of an
uncompromising gospel that breaks into history from the outside. The consequence of neo-orthodoxy on the cultural level is
fundamentalist arrogance and narrow-mindedness, exactly the
things that Karl Barth would abhor. But since there is no self-
criticism (that is, no sense of relativity) built into neo-orthodoxy,
its theological claims can defend any position, however ridiculous, that advertises itself as "counter-cultural."

My interest and, finally, conviction that the historical Jesus in fact does matter and can open a different path to Christianity comes out of my experience of disillusionment in neo-orthodox circles. Inside those circles, I was a witness to how the neo-orthodox mantra of the judgment of God based on the independence of the Word could be employed to justify social prejudice and basic attitudes of antagonism. It seemed to me, as it still does, self-evident that the Bible and tradition, too, are products of culture, and that cultural assumptions always color our interpretation of whatever we think the Word of God is. I escaped neo-orthodoxy because I escaped the supposition that the Bible is something more than a human document (or even a symbol of something more) and because I escaped the idea that religion is something more than a human creation. In learning to unlock these two escape hatches, I owe a great debt to Robert Funk and to Don Cupitt.

The problem, though, in a post-neo-orthodox world is what to do with a Jesus who was human like anyone else. The great models of theology, both classical and modern ones, were built on the idea that in Christ the essential truth of God meets the existential reality of humanity. This is a very important point to understand even though, sometimes, it becomes hard to explain. The essential truth of anything, in classical thinking, is the virtue of the thing. It is what the Greeks called *areté*: what a thing aims to be. We can say in English that the essence of a thing is its excellence. For ideas like justice to be properly practiced, the law must work according to its excellence. For a society to be properly governed, the different components of society must function according to their excellence. Excellence is a code word in antiquity for saying that a thing, including a human being, is performing according to the way it was meant to perform.

In classical theology, the problem of essence and existence is expressed in the contradiction between the excellence of God, which is unsurpassable, and the existential mediocrity of human beings. Human beings cannot be essential (that is, perfect in excellence) as God is; we cannot be so because, unlike God, we exist in time. Knowledge comes to us not purely but only packaged through our senses. So we are never perfect. In fact, we are always in sin. This troubling relationship between the essential excellence of God and the existential sin of human beings created Christian theology and still defines it. Christianity could develop both as a philosophy and as a religion on this foundation. The great doctrines of Christian theology also find their home here. The doctrines express the essential qualities of God (like grace and power) in relation to the existential needs of human beings (like forgiveness and salvation). There are doctrines about human nature and doctrines about divine nature, and the two meet in the Incarnation of Jesus Christ. Jesus Christ is the manifest appearance of the essential in the existential. He is the excellence of God in the mediocrity of humanity: he is the manifest virtue of what we are meant to be but exactly what we cannot be. Here again, though, as these doctrines are worked out in Church councils and among Christian theologians, the historical Jesus absolutely does not matter. In fact, Jesus as a strictly historical person interrupts the process because, as human like anyone, he cannot be the essential appearance of God. It seems that the historical Jesus means the end of Christianity, which is why, perhaps, many theologians are terrified of him.

My journey with the historical Jesus started with lunch with Robert Funk in the year 2000. I did not tell him at the time that I was having trouble with the neo-orthodoxy I was taught in seminary and that I could not, after my work in Foucault and philosophical theology,[4] see much point in going forward with the classical understandings of systematic theology. Funk never thought the historical Jesus was necessarily an answer to the troubles of modern theology. He did think, though, that the consequences of biblical scholarship were not being translated very effectively into theology and that the Jesus Seminar needed philosophers of theology to think about these problems. Hence, by the conclusion of our lunch, I was a Fellow of the Jesus Seminar and involved in thinking about the historical Jesus and Christianity. I wanted initially to try to re-think Christian doctrine—which is what a theologian is supposed to do—on the basis of the historical Jesus, yet I discovered that the immediate question was not doctrine but practice. My theological habit is to default to the doctrinal questions, but the historical Jesus, if he is taken seriously, had no idea about such matters. He was, rather, about a lifestyle that we can see in the fragments, as Funk said, of a vision. Those fragments, I became convinced, involve being in the world differently. There is not a bunch of religious beliefs that one needs to associate with the historical Jesus, but there is a practice of life that can be drawn out from him and awakened in our time as if a kind of momentum to his teaching. To be sure, as many are quick to point out, the historical Jesus is embedded in first-century Judaism, and he can only be understood in that context, but there is a momentum to his movement that does not have to be sealed in antiquity. All religious movements grow and change over time in relation to contemporary settings, and the momentum of the historical Jesus can do the same. It does not have to be exactly what Jesus thought; it can be in the spirit of what he was about. That spirit, I eventually came to believe, along with many others who participated in the Jesus Seminar, was the spirit of wisdom found in parable.

In spite of this academic background to the question of the historical Jesus, it turned out in my case that because I started focusing on the question of practice rather than belief, the place to explore this emphasis was in church rather than in the academy. In the academy, everything is theoretical; questions are debated, and there is a lot of consternation about what is right and what is wrong, who is in and who is out. But in the setting of a group of everyday people looking for spiritual direction, the merits of Theory A versus Theory B do not often count for very much. What counts is whether or not Theory A or B speaks to life and helps an individual develop in maturity as a human being. To stand in front of a group of people and proclaim that I think Theory A (or Theory Q in my case) is right is to invoke the collective stare of eyes that are asking "so what?" The answer to "so what?" involves translating the theory not just to a practice but as a practice in life. I still do theology with the historical Jesus, but in my struggle with this "enigmatic" figure (as Albert Schweitzer called him) I found that theology is not the point. In so far as the historical Jesus is taken seriously in church, the point is lifestyle, not belief.

The struggles involved in the formation of this book were certainly academic ones, and I hope these struggles, along with my option to follow the route of wisdom, are clearly presented. However, the emphasis in the end is a community practice. I am fortunate to belong to a community of the United Church of Canada that was constituted as an open experiment. It started as a community meant to explore new options in Christianity in light of the changing religiosity in Canada and the Western world. I came to the community with the idea that Jesus needs to be given back his humanity and that this basic act of honesty can shift the center of community practices. The result of that experiment, which is still ongoing, is this book. It is an effort to articulate Christianity on the platform of the historical Jesus. My hope is that such a platform might find a home, in whatever shapes it may take, in the practices of other communities who similarly seek to take the historical Jesus to church.

Notes

1. Neo-orthodoxy is a theology that emerged in the first half of the twentieth century emphasizing the Word of God as judgment in relation to human beings. It is important to note that, in this theology, the judgment of God is grace and that "Word of God" does not refer to the Bible. The Word is the transcendental power of God to which the Bible bears witness.

2. Karl Barth (1884–1968) is generally regarded as the founder of neo-orthodoxy and certainly its principal theologian.

3. The confession of historic orthodox Christianity from the Council of Chalcedon is that Jesus Christ is of two natures, fully human and fully divine, unconfused and concurring in one person.

4. This endeavor was published as *Archives and the Event of God: The Impact of Michel Foucault on Philosophical Theology.*

Why the Historical Jesus Is a New Path

Though it is highly unlikely that the Jesus of history ever thought himself the founder of a new religion, the fate of history has made him such. In his new religion, Jesus is God incarnate, begotten of the Father, born of a virgin, and a person of the Holy Trinity. It is an impressive resume. The historical Jesus, on the other hand, was a human being crucified by the Romans as a state criminal. Getting through the former Jesus to find the latter is the challenge now known as the quest for the historical Jesus. In the late nineteenth century, the quest rose to unprecedented heights such that, as if by attrition, it arrived in the twentieth century as a controversy and then landed in our age as a crisis. When a founding figure of a movement like Christianity turns out to be someone quite different from the one depicted by traditional ideas of the movement, a clash occurs—not only between contemporary thinking and the tradition, but also between the founder and the tradition. This is what happens when the historical Jesus meets Christianity. There is cause for something far more than a revision. There is a call for a new direction, a demand for a new path. Updating the old model will not do. The time has come to imagine a new one. This is our crisis.

The crisis in no small measure arises from a plethora of new information. Even as the quest for the historical Jesus reached new heights in the late nineteenth and early twentieth centuries, it remained esoteric and basically restricted to academic halls, but through the twentieth century and now into our time, debate about the historical Jesus has become widely disseminated. It is difficult in Christian circles to find those who have not heard about the Jesus Seminar, or Progressive Christianity, or various scholars either for or against conclusions about Jesus. In many ways, the historical Jesus has performed a new miracle: he has turned obscure biblical scholars into the celebrities of Christianity. Still, even though there are many books dedicated to discovering the human Jesus behind the confessional curtains of Christianity, a great task remains. How does one take the historical Jesus to church? Can it be done?

To those who reject the divine Jesus of tradition, the problem of church can be described as a kind of roadblock. Engaging the question of the historical Jesus means admitting to the fact that Jesus was human like anyone. It means understanding that the divine titles used for Jesus, like Son of God and Savior of the World, are those of ancient politics. Similarly, miraculous birth narratives and resurrection accounts are mythologies: good stories that may even have good points but never actually happened. Attuning oneself to the question of the historical Jesus means developing a mature, critical mind that no longer believes biblical narratives literally—narratives that, in any case, were not intended "literally" to begin with. So, one who has seriously engaged the historical Jesus has, in effect, crossed a bridge. But now a roadblock appears. Once an individual or a community has accepted that Jesus was human like anyone, it becomes increasingly impossible to engage realistically in Christian worship and language. True, many among such folk continue to go to church because friends remain there. Or perhaps such a person does not go to church, and never did, but now there is an even better excuse. The point is, when and if a person awake to the historical Jesus enters church, the Christian language and tradition sound foreign, as if they are now exactly what is no longer believed. The roadblock is met. The individual may be in church but is not really *into* church. The game is played only because others play it, too. Alternatively, such an individual decides to leave the church to join Bishop Spong's alumnae association.[1] When an individual takes the historical Jesus seriously but the historical Jesus is found nowhere in church—and, in some cases, is even exiled from it—then it is an either/or situation: either take leave, or grin and bear it.

Staying in the game and taking leave hardly constitute inspiring choices. But what other avenues are there? The current way to be in church is to worship Jesus as if he were Augustus Caesar. Every Christian service invariably employs the old Roman imperial language about Jesus as the Lord, Savior, Son of God, and Redeemer. Like Augustus, he brings peace to the world and carries the name of God on earth.[2] Just like Caesar, too, all these titles place Jesus in the transcendental realm of heaven where we need not distinguish between myth and history. To confess Jesus as Lord is to make him abstract, inspiring, and ideal, but it is also to fundamentally deny his humanity. How strange that to confess Jesus is to deny Jesus, yet this, in a nutshell, is the problem of the historical Jesus and Church. Perhaps it is time to give Jesus a break. In the words of the late Robert "Bob" Funk, Jesus deserves a "demotion" not only for the sake of his memory but also for the sake of our future.[3]

What makes it difficult to find a way around the roadblock of traditional Christianity is the way "change" and "church" mix like oil and water. Commonly in church communities, change is relegated to that small number of "radical" folk who gather, sometimes secretly, to study biblical criticism and historical Jesus research. Change consequently does not happen; the church only tolerates the idea of change provided it remains the idea of the minority. Largely, the church goes on as usual. Meanwhile, ministers, priests, or pastors who accept the results of biblical criticism and historical Jesus research are not sure what to do with them. Clergy are trained for Christian service based on printed liturgies, hymns, and prayers, along with sacramental practices. The job of a Christian seminary, after all, is to produce a Christian leader. Understandably, there is no training on how to create a historical Jesus community that may turn out not to be Christian. For clergy there is also the question of job security. The ecclesiastical penalties for telling the truth might be too high. As the historical Jesus found out, to be perceived as a troublemaker is to put retirement at risk.

In the rejection of change, secular society at large proves to be a strange bedfellow with the church. Society generally, and candid atheists in particular, expect Christianity to be "Christianity" despite advances in science. Casual visitors to church want to see "authentic" Christians doing real Christian stuff. As Richard Dawkins observed in his documentary, *The Root of All Evil,* "If you want to experience the medieval rituals of faith, the candle light, the incense, music, important-sounding dead languages, nobody does it better than the Catholics." A professed atheist once visited my congregation because he had heard it was "progressive"; at the conclusion he expressed disappointment that we were "not Christian." When I questioned further, he explained that on those rare occasions he goes to church, he wants to see "church" and be reassured about why he left! Sometimes well-rehearsed programs, like Christian worship, despite how predictable and unbelievable they become, remain psychologically secure and reassuring—even when the reassurance is about why we do not participate. There is something attractive to conservatism in this respect. Though it comes at the cost of intellectual honesty and self-critical regard, it does provide an easy sell. Comfort is not only popular; it is also a basic human need. Change, on the other hand, even when desperately needed, is ridiculously difficult to achieve. Change is helped along, though, if there is a vision of the desired end. Against an instinctive fear that cries, *It can't be done,* is the possibility of finding creative paths that take the historical Jesus to church. The first step is to learn why we need to take the historical Jesus to church in the first place.

Saving Jesus
from Christianity

Christianity is the tragedy of Jesus. It is the story of how his teaching slipped through his hands to become, for early Christians, disguised confessions about Augustus Caesar and his glory. When Christians today confess that "the Lord is great" and "God rules over the earth," or that "in Christ God created all things in wonderful beauty and order,"[4] the lines resonate with confessions about Caesar, who was similarly praised for bringing peace to the world and ruling over the lands and seas. They resonate with images of King David, who was the messianic paradigm of biblical times and Israel's once and future King. Indeed, they resonate with virtually all royal figures of history whose power-hungry drives or divine generosities forced confessions or invoked praises for their greatness. If there is any doubt about this, we need only read the dedications found in the prefaces of books past. In the intended *The Great Instauration*, Francis Bacon addressed James VI as "Our most serene and mighty Prince and Lord," called himself a "most bounden and devoted" servant, and acknowledged James as a king "surpassing all others in wisdom and learning."[5] Soren Kierkegaard had to gain permission from Christian VIII to write his Masters thesis in Danish rather than academic Latin, and we can read how his thoughtful and humble petition holds the tone of a "sinner" defending his acts and seeking divine grace.[6] Galileo Galilei dedicated his *Dialogue Concerning the Two Chief World Systems* to the Grand Duke of Tuscany. Galileo even suggests that all the effort of his work really belongs to the munificence of the Duke in the same way Christians might claim theirs is really the work of Christ.[7] With little surprise, we encounter familiar ecclesiastical language employed to laud nobles from the commoner's position of supplication. It is of little surprise because this is where the language originated. Christian church language is the language of laud and supplication directed upstairs to nobles. God is a patrician, not a plebian.

There is little said in church that is not also appropriate for kings, royals, or other culturally deemed saviors who remind us of the ancient cult of Caesar, the latter being the setting of the birth of Christianity. The gospel writers took the imperial garments of Caesar and inadvertently, if not intentionally, slipped them over Jesus. The problem of the historical Jesus begins with the recognition that while an imperial Jesus became the *sine qua non* savior of the world, this imaginative figure never actually lived. Yet, by the time Christianity arrived in the European Middle Ages, this Jesus who shared royal language with kings, princes, and landlords, and who granted pardon or received faith, was the standard fare. Perhaps, when looking back on the Middle Ages, it is understandable how Jesus was cast as the greatest of feudal lords, but is it inevitable that such an image should remain as the immovable object of the Christian heritage now perpetuated as "tradition"? Is it necessary to repeat medieval ideas even if they are out of date and out of touch, just for the sake of tradition? What if Christianity re-sets itself on a human Jesus and forgoes the royal language?

It is possible that in the beginning Christianity did not mean to create a Jesus Caesar—that is, Christ—for its Lord. It is possible that the first Christians were quick-witted and politically astute folk who employed a form of ancient satire rooted in the teaching of Jesus. In the context of first-century Rome, after all, the imperial language used for Jesus was absurd. The historical Jesus, as Dominic Crossan has pointed out, was obviously not the Son of God. In Roman eyes, he was no more the Son of God than a common criminal could be the President of the United States. In Luke, the birth of Jesus is announced with the sounds of a heavenly host, and the reading or hearing audience cannot help but be impressed with such overt flamboyancy. Never has an omen heralded a new emperor better; never has a mighty general been given such fanfare. But the announcement is made to a few isolated shepherds. It seems like some kind of joke. In fact, in Luke the shepherds don't really do anything besides show up. Once they see Jesus, they disappear from the gospel. Usually such heavenly announcements are reserved for prophets, or perhaps a horde of Roman soldiers who then support their general's quest for the imperial crown. True, shepherds are the great biblical image for caretakers, but they are never the messengers who announce extremely important news about a new leader of government. The full glory of angels making an unbelievable announcement to a few shepherds in a field is so anticlimatic it must have made the average Roman laugh. But then as now, isn't this exactly how political satire works? At the 2006 White House Correspondents' Association gathering, Stephen Colbert, political satirist and host of *The Colbert Report*, announced in front of President George W. Bush that reality has a liberal bias. Pretending to be as conservative as it gets, Colbert's exaggerated comment revealed the flaw of the very extremism he pretends to represents. Since extremism is a form of reality denial, Colbert sarcastically revealed the dangerous nature of views that dismiss obvious facts or seek ways to silence truth. His comment was indeed an invective judgement on the Bush administration . . . but it was also just plain funny. Colbert is a contemporary example of what a gospel writer like Luke might be doing with shepherds who receive the announcement of good news about the birth of a new savior. The setting is at one level funny, but at another level it is given to the poor and it is a gospel for the poor. This satire *par excellence*, amazingly, puts Caesar's good news for the rich in its humble place.

The nature of well-played satire is to be deeply critical of politics and society but at the same time to carry the lightness

of being. Though satire is not the best guide for biblical interpretation—because such judgments can easily become too
subjective—occasionally we can ask if biblical writers did not
intend satire in the various exaggerations they employed. Many
scholars agree that satire is an element in the parables of Jesus,
and it is possible that gospel writers like Luke got the punch line.
Jesus as a misplaced site for language about Caesar raises the
theological question of whether gospel writers deliberately transformed everyday reality into a new kind of good news. That the
"happy" gospel of Jesus should be found especially among the
poor—"How happy are the poor!"[8]—is a strange turnaround to
the common state of affairs. Caesar Augustus is supposed to be
the one with the happy gospel. Bible scholar Dominic Crossan
explains this satirical edge with a flare matched by few others:

> Caesar was running the world, and he controlled the Roman
> Empire and brought peace to the Mediterranean—all of that
> at least makes sense because he is divine. But Jesus? This no-
> body? Who was crucified on a Roman cross? He is actually
> the Lord of the universe? It's either very stupid or you're
> talking about a radically different type of world, a different
> type of God.[9]

Crossan is making his point about Paul, who calls Jesus Lord. An
equal point can be extended to Matthew, in whose nativity scene
Herod, the Roman appointed governor, is told by the Magi that
they are seeking his replacement, and in Luke, described above,
where this magnificent announcement of birth is made to lonely
shepherds in abject poverty. To repeat Crossan's words, it's either very stupid, or something radically different is going on.

If we can see the satire of early Christian compositions not as a
joke but as a serious meddling in Roman imperial affairs, we can
understand certainly why the empire was not amused. However,
if the early Christians got the joke (as well as the message), by
the fourth century the church was no longer able to laugh.
What had been edgy critique and revolutionary vision became

the bulwark of emperors and kings. For a growing number of Christians, it is the realization of the loss of historic Christianity to empire rather than the need for Christian reform that causes the exodus from the church. There needs to be a new way forward that takes the historical Jesus seriously, hears his punch lines, but does not deliver him to empire.

Distinguishing History from Confession

Taking the historical Jesus seriously means saving Jesus from the imperial church and the memory of the Christian empire—the days when everyone was Christian whether they wanted to be or not. This is no easy task. Despite the apparent waning of Christianity in Western experience, the desire to preserve it for nostalgic reasons remains in place. Even among "progressives," the point often is to explain Christianity correctly and to modernize its language but not genuinely to alter its foundational beliefs. The historical Jesus, though, is all about the challenge of alteration. Recovering a human Jesus means recovering someone who is not the Christian Savior or anybody else's for that matter. A positive future for religion rests on a basic turn to honest human existence. No one really comes from heaven, and no king or emperor or great mind is ever anything but human like everyone else. The imperial language used to name Jesus, even when the satire is noticed, still delivers Jesus to a lofty place beyond his humanity and, accordingly, beyond honest hope that might be associated with him.

In modern times the problem of the historical Jesus was never better stated than when Herman Samuel Reimarus (1694–1768) wrote, "We are justified in drawing an absolute distinction between the teaching of the Apostles in their writings and what Jesus Himself in His own lifetime proclaimed and taught."[10] This basic division, which Reimarus placed between Jesus and the Apostles, is the division between history and confession.

When we speak of the historical Jesus, we speak about the lifetime of a human being. When we speak about Christianity, we
speak about confessional or religious beliefs that emerged in
Christian history after the life of Jesus. We can be assured by
reason alone that in his lifetime the historical Jesus did not hold
confessional Christian beliefs. It is not necessary to offer up this
conviction for debate. As plainly as can be stated, and absolutely,
the historical Jesus was Jewish, not Christian. A few centuries
ago, Reimarus already knew that dividing historical events from
confessional beliefs was no easy matter. Barring some astound-
ing archaeological discovery, like letters irrefutably written by
Jesus—virtually impossible given Jesus's social status and illiteracy—ancient Christian confessions about Jesus are pretty much
the only avenue open for traveling back to the historical figure.
It is a very difficult journey. Anyone who has ever undertaken
it knows the destination is never certain and arrival is never final. Even so, given the starting point—which is the conviction
that we are dealing with human beings and human events—and
the unacceptable alternative—here, the untenable doctrines of
Christian confession—there is no other journey available or
worthwhile to the critically minded. We can't undo modern
understandings of history and science to re-enter the ancient
imagination; we can only recognize the distinction between ancient and modern times and then go forward with the honesty
and integrity of our age.

The criticism levelled against those who undertake the quest
for the historical Jesus is usually built on the charge of relativity. After all, one thing our modern and post-modern age has
taught us is that any "method" employed to examine a subject
also constructs the subject. The "method" becomes like a pair
of glasses that colors our view of reality. Problems and solutions
appear within the scope of the method used to interpret them.
In short, if I employ a mechanism to find apples, I will not see
any oranges. How I look for the "historical Jesus," and what I

accept or reject as evidence for him, will determine the picture I come up with.

The difficulty with criticizing historical Jesus research for relativity—that is, for seeing only what you want to see—involves ignoring the fact that there is no other alternative. Because the complaint is too general and too inclusive, it ends up simply describing the condition of all human research and all human relationships. Human beings can only work within the parameters of being human; there is no way to bypass the senses that we have or the models that we use to interpret the world we are in. The complaint is simply a way of sweeping the historical Jesus question under the rug in the faint hope that no one will bother with it again. But such faint hope is no hope at all; rather, it is a hidden expression of fear that seeks to silence inquiry and to protect the *status quo*. Though relativity sounds like a very smart criticism, it is actually a very stifling one that does not make a claim but simply "complains." To be smart, one has to deal with relativity as the fact of the matter, and then try to go forward.

To go forward boldly, it is not necessary to solve every problem of interpretation or to determine a definitive historical Jesus. These tasks are not the problem. They are only part of the journey. The challenge is to move forward with a human Jesus, not to interpret him conclusively. In the end, being human is exactly about the problem of interpreting others: everyone has problems related to interpreting their neighbor or spouse or child. The problem of interpreting Jesus is what makes him human like anyone. A real Jesus is someone we do have to struggle to understand and is someone whom we have to admit we will never understand fully. The seldom mentioned first insight about the historical Jesus is the realization that to struggle to interpret the historical Jesus is exactly what makes the historical Jesus credible. Anything less leads back to the confessions of incredible Christianity.

Christology and Jesus

A second insight involved when viewing the historical Jesus in contrast to confessional Christianity is recognizing that the task is about far more than reviewing the Christian tradition and then simply claiming the opposite. It does rather involve a thoughtful understanding of Christianity and its development in historical context. The struggle engaged is not with Christianity but with history. What once spoke in antiquity with salutary authority is not only no longer credible but also constructed within a world-view that no longer makes sense. Thus, engaging the path of the historical Jesus means leaving behind "incredible" Christianity to embark on a new way that is realistic in our time and foundational for our future. Of course, there may come a day when our sense of the credible will be incredible to another generation. That is par for the course. The point is that we are not another generation, either in the future or in the past. We need to go forward with what enables our life now. In terms of the Christian tradition, this means understanding but naming what is now incredible in order to clear the way for a new direction.

It would be unfair to go forward insisting that Jesus be seen in context and understood historically but not offer the same courtesy of understanding to ancient Christian doctrines and beliefs. To be sure, the turn away from the incredible traditions of Christianity involves "defrocking" the past of its authority and immutability. It involves taking leave of certain doctrinal expressions. But this act is necessary for a positive and constructive reason; it is not engaged purely for the exhilaration of deconstruction. As clearly as possible, a new path needs to be forged with honesty against the background that brought us to this point of departure.

The term *Christology* describes Christian doctrines related to Jesus that, from the outset, make him non-human. There are, no doubt, other troubling subjects in the Christian tradition that seem equally incredible, like creation, miracles, ideas of salvation, and the end of time. However, Christology defines a set of propositions in Christian doctrine that turn Jesus from a regular human being into the second person of the Trinity. Christology, in this sense, is also the problem that blocks the view of a new horizon with the historical Jesus.

Christ is not the last name of Jesus but the status of Jesus as God's anointed one. Christology begins with the naming of Jesus as God's anointed. It is the study of the nature of Jesus as the Christ. After the biblical period of Christianity, Christology became a problem for early Christian theologians because they needed to explain how Jesus could be both a human being and God at the same time. In other words, how could there be a belief in the divine nature of Jesus as the Christ even while preserving his humanity in a monotheistic faith? How can God be one God (the Godhead) while there is another God walking around on earth? It is hard today to understand why this problem existed, since in our world the view of reality is so different. We don't really have an "up there" and "down here" view of the cosmos. We know quite well that there is no ceiling on the universe. But in ancient times there was, which is why there was a need to explain how divine reality from above could be in history here below.

Tertullian (160–220 CE) was one of the earliest writers of theology in Latin, and more than anyone else provided for Western Christian theology the orthodox words to express the simultaneous divine and human nature of Jesus. In his *Against Praxeus*, he used the word Trinity perhaps for the first time with theological intention to explain the unity of Father, Son, and Holy Spirit. He is also credited with using "person" (*persona*) for the first time to translate theological Greek concepts to Latin (the Greek word here was *hypostasis*). Though Tertullian lived well before the Council of Chalcedon in 451 CE, where the orthodox confession of Christianity was definitively stated, he provided the now commonly used expressions for the nature of Jesus Christ: there is one God, but three persons; there is one Lord Jesus, but two natures. Or, to recite the Chalcedonian agreement exactly,

> we all with one accord teach others to acknowledge one and the same Son, our Lord Jesus Christ, at once complete in Godhead and complete in human nature, truly God and truly human, consisting also of a reasonable soul and body; of one substance with the Father as regards his Godhead, and at the same time of one substance with us as regards his humanity; like us in all respects, apart from sin.

To confess Christ in an orthodox way is to confess that Jesus is one person with two natures, fully human and fully divine.

But why couldn't Jesus, for example, simply be a spiritual redeemer who is the full and perfect incarnation of wisdom and who reveals to us our true spiritual self? Why isn't it enough that Jesus be the one who enlightens us and shows us our true Christ nature? Why can't Jesus be the firstborn of creation who reveals the aim or intention of creation as it was originally in the mind of God? This kind of thinking was available to early Christians, and it was expressed in heterodox thinking and in gnostic circles. But the main Christian tradition developed with the rejection of these other avenues of thought. It is sometimes difficult to know why, and perhaps no one can explain definitively.

One reason has to be the imperial language Christianity adopted—Messiah, King, Lord, Redeemer, Savior—which, by default, is not about inner peace. These are words about authorities that have a message from or represent a power "out there" somewhere. What is mysterious, unknown, and out there needs to be mediated through the select few to the masses. The select stand in place of the power that is otherwise absent. Part of the phenomenon of early Christianity was the way in which its imperial language about a kingdom, a glory, and a future state became so convivial to validating political authorities. Eventually, the Christian God displaced the Greek and Roman pantheons with a much more impressive totalitarian language. We can see the act of displacing Roman gods with God even with Paul, who, centuries before the rise of official state Christianity, advises, ". . . there is no authority except God, and those authorities that exist have been instituted by God" (Rom 13:1). Part of what makes Christianity a religion about history and the outcome of history is its messianic language, which makes God a general and a king. Jesus is not just an envoy who conveys wisdom to reveal our inner Christ nature. He is God's absolute representative here to deliver history to its goal. It is this element of necessarily being about history that makes Christianity necessarily about the actions of human beings. Jesus needs to be the full incarnation of God in human form in order to be the unsurpassable revelation of God carrying history through humans to its end or goal. How could such a conclusion be reached except that God is fully engaged and except that there is a cooperative (redeemed) community at hand? It is impossible to understand the Christian insistence on working out how God can be fully incarnate in human form without linking this insistence to classical Christian eschatology or end-time thinking. In end-time thinking, the incarnation serves the purpose of redeeming a community for God in order to facilitate the plan of history. Such a community cannot be brought to God except through the incarnation, which is the act of God's redemption. When Christianity did become the official Roman religion, the pieces of the puzzle readily fit together. Political authority mediates the will of God on earth, and the faithful church guards the sacred truth and buttresses that authority.

Christology, which is expressed through the doctrines of the Incarnation and the Trinity, gave the Church significant political and social language with which it could support governments as well as claim its own divine authority. But it would be a mistake not to see another side. The confession that Jesus is God incarnate also expressed the solidarity of the divine with human beings. If, on the one side of the coin, there were various kings and emperors claiming to represent the divine on earth, on the other side of the coin there were Christian people who identified the divine dimensions of human psychology in Christian doctrine. The Trinity in particular can be perceived as metaphysically difficult; its complexity almost guarantees misinterpretation among many Christian folk. Still, some of the greatest Christian theologians were able to express this doctrine in ways that are fundamentally descriptive of common human experience. It is not difficult to understand how. If the doctrine is accepted as a revelation of God, and if human beings are created in the image of God, then in principle it makes sense that the Trinity ought to be imprinted on the human psyche. It ought to be a location where God participates in human activity. In traditional Christian thought, and particularly in the thinking of Augustine, this is exactly the reasoning: every human relationship involves the imprint of the divine Trinity. In any relationship there are three elements. There is my self-understanding, or my ego, which is composed of my memory of being in the world; then, there is my understanding of the other, or my interpretation of the world, which is based on my intellect or reason; finally, there is the dynamic inter-play between myself and the other, which is founded on my desire (will) for a relationship. In this way, Trinitarian language in Christianity can be descriptive of human psychology, which for Augustine consisted of memory, intellect, and will. This model of the Trinity can be used to think critically about history and human nature. If, for example, I cannot break free from interpreting my relationship to others exclusively on the terms of my self-understanding, then my interaction with others will be built solely upon my own ego. This will surely make me a victim of "self pride" and likely ensures great resentment among my colleagues, friends, and family members. If I happen to hold this quality while being a leader of a powerful nation, and that nation also holds the same exaggerated emphasis on pride, the world community as a whole will be sown with seeds of discord and rancor. It has always been the case that when nations or powerful individuals are guilty of self-serving pride, the prophetic voice of Christianity arises in one form or another through political and social criticism. We can think for example of Martin Luther King, Jr., or the Christian Social Gospel of the late nineteenth and early twentieth centuries. In its Trinitarian understanding, Christianity has, over the centuries, ably engaged on a critical level the culture or government in which it was located, though we might conclude that, regrettably, this has happened far too few times.

What makes the Trinity, the Incarnation, and other doctrines of traditional Christianity difficult for our time is not their lack of insight. It is rather their foundation on forms of thinking that no longer exist. The problem arises most obviously when we consider that, in our age, it is difficult to imagine why Jesus or Caesar or anyone else should be thought both human and divine and why this, in any case, should even matter? Why do we need difficult metaphysical propositions like the Incarnation or Trinity to ground our morality or justify our social engagement when the nature-based arguments of the sciences and social sciences work better, make more sense, and have ample evidence to support them? Why do we need to introduce a divine being into human affairs in order to engage our humanity? Why can't we just be human on our own? Even when an earnest theologian engages scholarship most thoroughly to tell me how radical it once was to call Jesus *Lord* when there was a Lord Caesar in Rome, the natural reaction is to note how interesting those early Christians were, followed by, "So what?" We don't live in ancient Rome anymore. I don't believe anyone, Jesus or Caesar or anyone else, is Lord. The earnest theologian may respond that *lord* means "controller," and that surely I must see how multinational corporations, wealthy nations with big armies, and various landlords do control much of our world and our politics. To this I respond, of course I can see as much! But the language is still wrong. I don't think a multi-national corporation is Lord; I think it is a multi-national corporation. Equally, I don't think it is divine—and neither does anyone else. I know it is a human creation. I know only human beings can change the reality of our social and economic structures. In order to change, human beings have to want to change. They don't have to pray, and they don't have to believe that something or someone is a lord. In other words, with the help of an earnest theologian, I can understand the biblical world and the development of traditional Christian doctrine, but neither the theologian nor I can live in the biblical world or believe that traditional Christian doctrine is credible. We need different options today.

The difference in worldview reflects the shift in the way pre- and post-Enlightenment people think. Biblical people, Jews and Christians as much as pagan Greeks and Romans, understood the world according to archetypes, or original forms. Their way of thinking about things was *archetypical thinking,* an expression derived from the Greek words *arche* (original or first), and *typos* (impression or shape). Archetypical thinking is the belief that things, people, governments, and even religions have pure or unspoiled (original) forms that they are "supposed" to be. The great philosopher Plato is most often used as the supreme example of what archetypical thinking means. Plato defined a theory of the Forms to explain how human beings interpret the world around them. A Form can be thought of as a shape, but it is a perfect shape, the original shape, from which all other shapes derive. A Form is something like the original mold in which various models are cast, except that the models are both ideas and things. Plato thought that there was an original Form of goodness, what he called the Good, which infiltrated all things and was the aim or goal of all things. Everything that exists is intended to exist for the Good. That does not mean that everything is good, for things do miss their mark. For Plato these original Forms also help us understand why we can distinguish between a horse and a donkey. We know the Form of a horse—what is it supposed to be—and the Form of a donkey—what it is supposed to be—so we have the original idea or features of each animal in our minds that allows us to distinguish between them. This is archetypical thinking because it is thinking that assumes that for everything in existence there is an archetype or original form from which it draws its identity. In this way of thinking, there is such a thing as a perfect human being even though in practice no human being can be perfect, and there is such a thing as perfect justice even though in practice such can never be reached. Still, all human beings seek the "Good," that is, perfection, in their exercise of justice, in their love of others, or in their daily duties. In archetypical thinking, being human means being imperfect but seeking the perfect.

In archetypical thinking, everything in the everyday world is an imperfect expression of an originally perfect form. Only great people or divinities approach, or think they do, the loftier heights of perfection. In antiquity, perfection dwells above us, transcendentally, more or less in the sky. When an everyday person saw a statue of Augustus Caesar, with the chariot of Apollo carved on his breastplate, she or he knew the association automatically. In an archetypical way, the god of order (Apollo) was incarnate in the government of Augustus. The closer something was to truth, the closer it was to unchanging, eternal perfection. The closer something was to God, the closer it was to static being. This is why the ideals of traditional Christianity are fixed in doctrines that do not change. It is also why Jesus in traditional Christianity must be a perfect human being without sin.

Today we still use archetypical thinking but no longer by default. I might take my car to a mechanic, for example, to have my electrical system scoped. In this simple act, archetypical thinking is present because both the mechanic and I assume there is a factory default range into which the electrical system in my car is supposed to fall. There is, that is to say, an assumed original or perfect functionality my car needs to meet in order to run well. The mechanism used to measure this, the scope, was itself manufactured with the same assumption: that all cars regardless of make can be read and judged according to the specifications they were meant to hold. But neither my mechanic nor I hold the same kind of assumption that ancient people held in our use of archetypical thinking. First, we do not relate to the vehicle as an imperfect copy of an original and perfect prototype. There no doubt was a prototype model of my car once, but we relate to the vehicle as an object that is a literal thing subject to manipulation, modification, and even improvement through various enhancements. Also, we naturally assume that a prototype is an earlier stage of a product that is not as good as the final or marketable item. We do not relate to the car as a copy of something, and there is no thought about such a thing as one perfect, eternal, and unchanging vehicle out there somewhere. Ancient people did not normally think in the literal way modern people do. To improve upon something like a weapon of war or an instrument of agriculture, ancient people thought of the change as a move closer to perfection, that is, closer to a static ideal. For ancient people, regress—that is, moving backward to perfection—was progress. When I think of improving something, all my thoughts are about going forward. I have no static ideal in mind.

The contrast between ancient and modern thinking, or, more technically, between pre- and post-Enlightenment thinking, is the contrast between archetypical and literal thinking. It is natural for modern people to think in terms of facts. We are used to understanding that things operate according to laws. The world before us is "nature." When and if we do think or speak of God, we normally refer to God as an object outside or up there or in existence. We have a hard time breaking free from literalism in religion, and indeed most people can't do it. We are moderns, and we are literalists; we have scientific minds that seek explanations according to evidence. These basic things, especially among religious fundamentalists who look at the Bible as if it were scientific evidence, are assumptions held by virtually everyone around the world who lives in a technical society. I share "literalism" socially with billions of other people. Literalism is the act of looking at things on a case-by-case basis and, from the evidence, constructing a general explanation.

The problem encountered with the Bible, Christian doctrine, and Jesus Christ is the problem of archetypical thinking. To our post-Enlightenment minds, archetypical thinking is basically wrong. There is no real way anything is supposed to be; there is only the condition in which things are. Change is possible not because things move closer to or further from perfection but because the condition in which things *are* changes. What is now is so because of the history of the condition of existence that preceded now. Human beings exist not because God created us but because we are the consequence of a long history of adaptation to the conditions of existence. Justice is a human ideal, but it is no archetype. It is the creation of our own thinking that emerges from the historic conditions of our social past. What we mean by justice, by love, by forgiveness, and by hope is in our hands. These are the forms of life that we create, that we employ, and that we share with one another, but we and not a god are responsible for them. Love does not exist where people refuse to love. Forgiveness is impossible for someone whose heart is frozen. Justice is never enacted where human beings cannot reimagine the world.

For Christianity, the practical consequence of turning away from archetypical thinking is turning away from Jesus Christ and turning to the historical Jesus, that is, to the person who was human like the rest of us. Jesus no longer needs to be Caesar in order to be noticed, and he no longer needs to be trapped inside the language of an imperial cage. Changing to the platform of the historical Jesus is the end of Christian archetypical thinking, but it is also the start of a journey to an unknown country. Though it is a journey that draws us to locations without the guide of a map, it is at least an honest journey. It is founded on a real human being who really had something to say that offers real life energy and real hope to our literal times.

Notes

1. John Shelby Spong is a retired American bishop of the Episcopal Church and author of several books, including *Rescuing the Bible from Fundamentalism* (1992) and *Why Christianity Must Change or Die* (1999).

2. See Crossan, *God and Empire,* 15–29.

3. See Funk, *Honest to Jesus,* 306.

4. From the Anglican *Book of Alternative Services.*

5. Francis Bacon, *The Works,* 333.

6. Søren Kierkegaard, *The Concept of Irony,* 350.

7. Galileo Galilei, *Dialogue Concerning the Two Chief World Systems.*

8. Luke 6:20

9. Dominic Crossan, BeliefNet.com interview by Deborah Caldwell (2004).

10. See Schweitzer, *The Quest of the Historical Jesus,* 16.

2

Biblical Criticism
Comes of Age

When Jesus is accepted as a human being, the problem of the historical Jesus becomes the same problem encountered with any famous person from antiquity. Like other prominent figures—a politician, a great philosopher, or a hero of war—Jesus is as much a legend as he is a person. In contrast to the archetypical thinking of ancient folk, our modern interest in biography is literalistic. We want to know what really happened in a famous person's life. What back-room deals were made behind the scenes of a major event? What were the key setbacks and turning points? Ancient people were interested in biography because a famous person could represent an archetype; modern people are interested in biography because we can get to know the real person. We may be attracted to a famous person because of their legendary status, but when it comes down to brass tacks, we want to know the facts.

When our ancient ancestors wrote about a famous person, they wanted to show how that person embodied an ideal. How did that person display heroic characteristics, whether in a tragic or comic form? Or, conversely, they might defile their subject to display an anti-hero character devoid of goodness. Whether their subject was good or evil, they sought to render the person ideal. Here is the ideal philosopher or ideal politician; and there is the ideal villain or the ideal cad. Literature and movies today still hold these historic contrasts of good versus evil, but the modern attitude is distinct. The point isn't to show how closely an individual reaches the eternal and immovable divine or demonic ideal but exactly the opposite: to show how close an individual reaches the greatness of being human.

Accordingly, ancient historians need to be questioned constantly. The figures they write about are normally presented in an ideal, virtually fictional, manner. They loved to portray life as drama—whether it happened or not—rather than actual events. They loved to mix in exaggerations of *amartia,* or tragedy, in the story of the hero. Rarely will an ancient historian offer a behind-the-scenes look into the real life of an individual. Any such look is usually to reveal divine characteristics or guidance. It's not that ancient historians are unreliable, for some ancient writers, like Josephus, give invaluable information, but that their purpose for writing is different. In his *Antiquities,* Josephus is not writing a history in the modern sense of engaging a critical investigation of events. He is quick to express his biases, to present his opinions as fact, to condemn groups or persons with little or no evidence, and to offer tall tales as history.[1] Even though Josephus is an important ancient historian, there is a sense in which he does not actually write history at all. He writes "legendary" accounts of things, which allows him to present his own personal and political spin without a second thought. His goal is to give an account of things in the style of an apology or defense acceptable to those of his social class. We could say he was more like a modern politician than historian.

Ancient writers almost always wrote as apologists. Their purpose was to defend the integrity of a class or a people. The epic poems of Homer define and defend the cultural identity of the Greeks. Virgil's *Aeneid,* in similar storybook fashion, rooted Roman cultural identity in a fabled Greek past, an act that boasted of Roman self-esteem. The historian Plutarch's *Parallel Lives* matches great Greek personalities with great Roman ones to show how, in the stretch of his imagination, great heroes hold similar characteristics (especially Greek and Roman heroes). Plutarch admits he is not writing "history," but in this admission it is clear he thinks that history proper is about glorious deeds: what we today call propaganda. The Deuteronomist is the writer who told the story of ancient Israel found in the books from Deuteronomy to 2 Kings. In this history, the writer portrays the Israelite kings Saul and David in all their tragic faults. The presentation is primarily a theological rather than historical account that defines and shapes a specific interpretation of history. Many archaeologists today hold that the Deuteronomic version of Israel's history is largely fiction. Early Christian writing holds the same apologetic intensions and fictional characteristics. Though the Christian gospels contain some historical information, the writing is largely designed to defend Christianity. The writers are not really interested in who Jesus was, which means that many questions about Jesus simply cannot be answered. Whether or not Jesus was married—a modern interest—is irrelevant to the gospel writers. What Jesus learned from John the Baptist is another question of interest to modern people but beyond the pale for gospel writers. How old was Jesus when he died? In some cases it is possible to infer answers to questions like these, but, by and large, the gospels just don't care about such details. The gospels are not biographies.

What does concern early Christians is how Jesus stacks up against the competition. They want to proclaim their beliefs about Jesus, their *kerygma* (proclamation), and they want to defend the new community of Christians. They also want to attract new folks to their following. We have already noted how the titles used to venerate Jesus were the same titles used to venerate emperors, heroes, and pagan gods. *Son of God* most certainly was the title of Augustus Caesar, but Son of God also referred to Dionysus, Hercules, and Alexander the Great. Israel as a people is God's Son, too. It has never been extraordinary to laud

cultural icons with extraordinary titles, and antiquity in particular was very good at it.

This is what creates the problem of the historical Jesus. In
order to uncover the human Jesus it is necessary to wander in
the land of the legendary Jesus. One of the earliest, if not the
first, legendary beliefs Christians held was that Jesus was God's
Anointed, or Christ. In Rom 1:3–4, Paul relays part of an early
church confession of Jesus: ". . . he descended from David according to the flesh; he was declared Son of God according to
the spirit." To say that Jesus descended from David already links
him to messianic mythology, but to say he was declared Son of
God according to the spirit is to confess a belief.[2] Christians
employed the metaphor of being God's chosen to equate the
presence of Jesus with the intentions of God for history. Jesus
shares the status of "the anointed" with several other figures, like
Cyrus of Persia and King David of Jerusalem. Within the context
of the pagan Roman world, the revelation of heaven's intentions is expressed equally well with Horus, Glycon, and Attis of
Phrygia among others. The image of Jesus Christ set against this
background is a legend born from the mixture of Roman imperial theology and Jewish messianic history. The point is, how can
one retrieve a human being from out of that?

It is understandable that many people conclude the historical
Jesus question is hopeless. It is not much different than trying to
recover a historical Moses or a historical Socrates. Probably such
figures existed, but what does that give us? Yet, when a review
of historical Jesus scholarship over the last few hundred years is
considered, it is valuable to remember that scholars from generations ago did reach conclusions that have stood the test of time.
After all, if we are dealing with one bedrock foundation, which
is that Jesus was human like anyone, then it should be expected
that some basic explanations about a very human process will
stand the test of time. It is encouraging to recall that century-
old conclusions continue to be the first considerations when
approaching the study of Jesus. The tide turned, or maybe came

in, on the historical Jesus in the eighteenth century when the scientific study of the Bible made a huge difference in our understanding of antiquity and pushed irrevocably forward the task of finding, in Christian mythology, the remnants of a real person.

During the nineteenth century, German scholars made what is now a common distinction between *Weltgeschichte* (world or factual history) and *Heilsgeschichte* (salvation or confessional history). The first form of history, *Weltgeschichte,* is the scientific study of history undertaken as a critical investigation of events. It can be called the academic study of history. The second form of history, *Heilsgeschichte,* is history understood as significant events that reveal the purpose of history. This second type of history is history interpreted through the eyes of believers in a cause or defenders of a faith. The form of history in the Bible is *Heilsgeschichte,* or confessional history. It is the presentation of history through the eyes of believers. It can be also called apologetic history, for its purpose is to defend a cause. In relation to Jesus, the division between the academic study of history and the apologetic presentation of history draws the line of distinction between the historical Jesus (a human fact) and the church's confession of Jesus (a Christian apology).

In *Honest to Jesus* (1998), Bob Funk, founder of the Jesus Seminar, noted that there are several breakthrough moments in the academic study of the historical Jesus. Funk, in effect, offered a *Heilsgeschichte* or confessional report of the *Weltgeschichte* or scientific development of Jesus research. Funk did not mean that history in some indubitable way has led toward a historical Jesus epiphany. What he did mean was that the introduction of modern, critical scholarship in the study of Jesus is an important story that does inform the meaning of Jesus for today. The academic breakthroughs of past generations slowly build until they become the assumptions of a new generation that no longer looks at the world in the same way. Similar to how breakthroughs in science change the way we understand the universe, breakthroughs in religious scholarship change the way we interpret the Bible. It is the same for historical Jesus research. Original thinking from the past has become the foundation of progress for the present. Despite many efforts to critique, ignore, or reject the basic conclusions of biblical criticism, they have stood both the test of time and the test of critique.

In *The Greatest Show on Earth* (2009), Richard Dawkins makes the point that evolution by natural selection is really not a theory so much as a theorem of biology. He seeks to dispel the notion that religious explanations of the world are as plausible as evolution. Instead evolution is not simply one explanation among various theories; rather, evolution by natural selection must be considered a theorem. That is, it is as close to a fact as we can get when it comes to explaining the amazing and complex varieties of life on earth. Evolution is not on par with something like creationism. Indeed, creation—a religious belief—and evolution—a tested scientific theory—are not even in the same league. Certainly evolution remains subject to criticism and refinement, but it is not a proposition. Evolution by natural selection is simply what is there to be seen. No amount of argument can change that. As a description of what is, it is not a theory but a theorem. Dawkins explains, "Our present beliefs about many things may be disproved, but we can with complete confidence make a list of certain facts that will never be disproved. Evolution and the heliocentric theory weren't always among them, but they are now.[3]

Biblical criticism is not able to offer a "theorem" in the same way that the natural sciences can, but there are landmark conclusions in the history of historical Jesus research that approach something of this status. Biblical criticism always deals with greater degrees of uncertainty than science does because its research is based on ancient texts that already have a long history of variation in the course of their transmission. The gospel texts we deal with are copies from the fourth century or later of earlier originals now lost. We need to assume that what we can reconstruct as Mark reasonably approximates its first-century form. So, biblical scholarship is never a set of facts like science. From the start, it is set on approximations. Nevertheless, certain landmark conclusions in biblical studies are extremely difficult to deny without creating even more problems as a result, as we will see below.

The Seven Pillars

Robert Funk named seven scholarly breakthroughs that he accepted as more or less "theorems" (my word, not his) of biblical criticism. Of course he did not mean that these conclusions were beyond critique. What he meant was that they are extremely difficult to deny without creating even greater problems as a consequence. He called these breakthroughs the "Seven Pillars of Scholarly Wisdom" in *The Five Gospels* (1993). They remain important to review in order to advance along the path of the historical Jesus.

The first pillar, mentioned in chapter 1, was proposed by the German philosopher Hermann Samuel Reimarus: "We are justified in drawing an absolute distinction between the teaching of the Apostles in their writings and what Jesus Himself in His own lifetime proclaimed and taught." This basic division, which Reimarus placed between Jesus and the Apostles, is the division between history and confession. It is a logical and fundamental distinction between what the gospel writers placed in the mouth of Jesus and what the historical Jesus actually said. No matter what scholarship is involved, liberal or conservative, no one claims that the gospels were written during the time of Jesus. Though conservative theologians naturally want to date the gospel as close as possible to the lifetime of Jesus, no one actually dates the gospels in the lifetime of Jesus. The gospels simply are not a verbatim record of what Jesus said; they are a record of what early Christians believed Jesus said. They are the record of early beliefs about Jesus. Reimarus reached this most basic conclusion about the gospels in the middle of the eighteenth century. Like many before him and since, he knew that it would be dangerous to state publicly his conclusions. He wisely left his writings on this subject for publication after his death.

The elaboration of this first pillar came from the mind of David Friedrich Strauss (1808–1874), who did not remain silent, and it cost him his career. Just in his twenties, the author of *The Life of Jesus Critically Examined* (1835) offered to the world what Albert Schweitzer would call "the most absolutely sincere" effort to encounter the historical Jesus. Of Strauss, Schweitzer states, "His insight and his errors were like the insight and errors of a prophet. And he had a prophet's fate. Disappointment and suffering gave his life its consecration."[4] Prior to Strauss and despite Reimarus, the gospels were still accepted as history, though "suspect" history. Before Strauss, scholars attributed less believable events like the miracles of Jesus to the naiveté of ancient people and times. Early scholars like Heinrich Paulus (1761–1851), who was criticized for his anti-Semitism, proposed the idea, still popular today, that Jesus did not really die on the cross but rather recovered over three days in the coolness of his tomb. Another popular explanation Paulus proposed was that Jesus didn't really walk on water but instead mist along the shore had made Jesus appear as a ghost. Such explanations are called rationalisms because they seek to explain by natural reason sensational events in the Bible. However, rationalisms still assume that the Bible is otherwise historically reliable, otherwise why should these anomalies need an explanation?

In addition to Reimarus's differentiation between Jesus and Christianity, the second pillar from Strauss marks the end of rationalism, the search for reasonable explanation to miraculous gospel events. In its place, Strauss established the now more or less standard understanding that the Christian gospels are myth, not history. This does not mean there are no historical events in the gospels. It means that the gospel writers did not write about events with the idea that they were producing a set of facts. Their stories were produced out of mythic worldview: an environment where, as we have seen, the point is the heroic narrative and the ideal savior. They wrote in an archetypical fashion. It is sometimes difficult for modern people to understand, but nevertheless essential to accept, that ancient people wrote well before the Enlightenment, long before there was ever a notion of natural science, absolutely without any idea that $E=mc^2$, and never heard of nor could have imagined Charles Darwin. Strauss was able to say that the ancient view of the world was mythical; that is, it was non-factual. So, to use modern explanations to understand incredible reports from antiquity is to misunderstand antiquity. Ancient people simply could not use modern explanations, and their point was not to address modern readers. Rather, ancient reports need to be seen through ancient eyes. Ancient writing needs to be thought about and understood in the context of the ancient worldview. This is as true for the Bible as any other document from antiquity. After Strauss, a tremendous shift took place in the understanding the Bible. It is no longer possible to use the Bible as evidence for historical events. Now it is first necessary to prove the reliability of a biblical story before the story can be used as evidence. This distinction is the brilliant legacy of Strauss and it marks the second pillar of scholarly wisdom. This landmark accomplishment, however, did not make him a great scholar. It made him an unemployed and unemployable scholar. He arrived on the scene too early when tampering with the Bible had personal and political consequences.

After Strauss, a third pillar of biblical criticism emerged, though we need not relate it to any one particular scholar. It is an idea that over time became essentially undeniable: Mark is the earliest narrative gospel in the Christian Bible and a source gospel for Matthew and Luke. To put it bluntly, Matthew and Luke copied from Mark, and if they copied from Mark, then Mark already existed. So, Mark is the earliest of the canonical

gospels. Even though there is no reason to think that the compilers of the Christian Bible believed Matthew was the oldest
gospel, that Matthew *appears* first generated the impression held
for centuries that Matthew was *written* first. At the same time,
and equally over centuries, it was widely observed that the three
gospels share a lot of common material. The question is why
do they share so much common material? Forty-five per cent of
Matthew is Mark, and 41 percent of Luke is Mark. Going the
other way, Matthew uses 94 percent of Mark, and Luke uses 79
percent of Mark. In addition, not only do the three gospels share
the same stories, they also share the same basic order of events.
Because of this phenomenal agreement, the three gospels are
collectively called the "synoptic" gospels. They are gospels that
can be seen together.

Explaining this synoptic relationship has always been a challenge, dating from as early as Augustine (354–430 CE). Augustine
proposed that Matthew was the first gospel, then Mark created
a compendium gospel (a Reader's Digest version) of Matthew,
and finally Luke copied at greater length from Matthew. Various
modifications of Augustine's proposal were made in the nineteenth century, some of which still persist today. However, by
the end of the nineteenth century Heinrich Julius Holtzmann's
summary presentation of the synoptic problem, and, later,
Burnet Hillman Streeter's influential *The Four Gospels* in 1924,
demonstrated that upholding Mark as the first written gospel
and as a source gospel for Matthew and Luke is the best solution.
There are approximately a dozen arguments that demonstrate
why Mark is best understood as the first gospel.[5] While some still
insist on Augustine's solution or a form of Augustine's solution,
such alternatives create more problems than they solve. Today,
the priority of Mark is virtually universally acknowledged, and is,
rightly, considered a landmark in the history of biblical criticism.

The fourth pillar in biblical criticism follows immediately from
the third, though chronologically it developed independently

and even earlier than the third. The fourth insight is that once Mark is accepted as the source gospel for Matthew and Luke, it becomes necessary to explain the presence of a second literary source that is absent from Mark but shared between Matthew and Luke. Matthew and Luke have common material about which Mark had limited or no knowledge. As early as 1835, Christian Weisse proposed that the common material shared between Matthew and Luke was a lost gospel. He was repeating in a more sophisticated manner what had already been speculated for some time. As early as 1832, Friedrich Schleiermacher called this shared material a *logia* (oracles) collection, believing that when Papias, a second-century bishop, referred to "sayings" of the Lord recorded in Aramaic, he meant an independent collection of oracles available to the gospel writers. Due to Schleiermacher's influence, for many years the material common to Matthew and Luke was referred to as L, for *logia*. In the late nineteenth century and early twentieth century, it was determined that the material was not that to which Papias referred but rather, more properly, a lost sayings gospel. The material is now called the Q Sayings Gospel, or Q Gospel, after the German word *Quelle* (source).

Today, scholarship on the Q Gospel has advanced well beyond the mere identification of the material and estimation of its value. Scholars like John Kloppenborg have been able to present the document as a typical wise sayings (*logoi sophon*) collection that passed through several editorial stages. The conclusions of Kloppenborg and other scholars involved in the International Q Project are still controversial and at times regarded with high skepticism, but very few people deny that there was an independent Q document used by Matthew and Luke as a sayings source for their gospels.[6] Numerous denials of Q through attempted re-configurations and alternative explanations have been tried, but none have dislodged the simple and satisfactory conclusion that this source document existed. The problem with such denials is that they do nothing to change the fact of common material shared by Matthew and Luke. So, whether or not one posits Q, it is still necessary to address the common tradition. Further, to address the common tradition without Q is paramount to creating a lot of new and unnecessary problems. In other words, explaining the common tradition without Q means multiplying problems such that they make currently "plausible editorial procedures" explained *with* Q more difficult and obscure *without* it.[7] To be sure, the Q theorem, if we can call it a theorem, is not absolutely beyond criticism. But there is no better way to understand the common tradition found in Matthew and Luke. The existence of Q, like the priority of Mark, is a basic achievement of biblical scholarship.

A fifth pillar of scholarly wisdom lies in the distinction between the teachings of John the Baptist and Jesus. This statement might initially seem obvious, but in fact it is one of the more controversial conclusions of the Jesus Seminar. The traditional understanding associated with Albert Schweitzer (1875–1965) depicts both John and Jesus as apocalyptic, or end-time, prophets. With some subtle differences, both figures anticipated the immanent end of the world, both warned of the crisis of their time, and both called for repentance. The words attributed to John—"Bear fruits worthy of repentance"—and the words attributed to Jesus—"The kingdom of God is at hand"—are not at odds. Indeed, the reason for repentance is precisely because the kingdom of God is at hand. Added to this is the certain knowledge that John baptized Jesus, which means Jesus was a student of John.

Despite the undeniable attraction Jesus had to John's teaching, Funk claimed that to a growing number of scholars there is a noticeable difference between both the voiceprints and actions of Jesus and John, so much so that Jesus, in a manner of speaking, needs to be liberated from John. But since Jesus was a student of John, there is material from the tradition of John the

Baptist that early Christians had to acknowledge. Secondly, it is likely that some of the students of John became the students of Jesus and brought with them the influence of the Baptist. The need to demarcate Jesus from John was a challenge not always successfully overcome in writings of earliest Christianity. The challenge is evident both in Q and in Mark. In Q, John stands in the tradition of Israel's prophets when he announces the crisis of the present time and warns of an impending disaster. Like Jeremiah, Amos, or Hosea, he holds contemporary society in his sight line. John's gospel is a powerful call to change ethical behavior before it's too late. In line with the reasoning found in the books of Deuteronomy through 2 Kings, the John of Q cries out, "You brood of vipers! Who warned you to flee the wrath that is to come? Bear fruits worthy of repentance" (Luke 3:7–8).

Though many scholars see Jesus as a second version of John minus the practice of baptism, the evidence for this conclusion is not as persuasive as some would lead us to believe. At times the Q document is self-contradictory, but in relation to Jesus and John it does uphold apparently distinctive traditions. These demarcations appear exactly when the lifestyle of Jesus and that of John are presented. If John proclaimed the end-times with colorful exhortations and excoriating calls for renewed ethical behavior, Jesus paled by contrast. Jesus employs parables and aphorisms. Stories about a truant son or a woman baking bread or an absurd garden of mustard does not hold a candle to exhortations about the end of time. Neither does it seem that Jesus, accused of loose living and carousing, modeled very closely his austere and abstinent teacher, John. Whereas the strongest memories associated with John are those of an ascetic, those related to Jesus are of comical quips and enigmatic stories. Somewhat like the relationship between Plato and Aristotle, John and Jesus had a teacher-student relationship that fostered difference.

The apparent contrast between John and Jesus can be thought of as the difference between a prophet and a wisdom teacher.

This distinction is helpful though not absolute since, in both the
Q Gospel and the history of Israel, these two roles are sometimes thought of as one. Both John and Jesus in the Q Gospel
are called children of wisdom (Q 7:35). Yet, Q also refers to
John as a prophet and much more than a prophet (7:26). So,
the categories of prophecy and wisdom can define each other.[8]
Nevertheless, prophetic books like Jeremiah or Ezekiel are distinctive in genre from books of wisdom like Ecclesiastes or Job.
John is certainly the one who typifies a prophet with his apocalyptic pronouncements and practices of asceticism, but Jesus
by contrast typifies a wisdom teacher who speaks in riddles and
keeps mixed company. A division between the figure of John
and the figure of Jesus seems to lay deep in earliest Christian
memory. This difference is not just one of voice but also one
of lifestyle. A majority of Jesus Seminar scholars consequently
concluded that the historical Jesus is not understood with sufficient independence if clad with John in apocalyptic imagery. As
Funk noted, the parables and aphorisms associated with Jesus
sometimes go so far as to mock the kinds of dire warnings John
proclaims. If, on the one hand, John will imagine God's immanent judgment by saying that ". . . every tree that does not bear
good fruit is cut down and thrown into fire," Jesus appears on a
different track when he says, "Why can't you judge for yourself?"
and announces, "The Kingdom of God is already here!" Though
the contrast between John and Jesus remains subject to debate,
Funk and many others are now convinced that a fifth pillar of
scholarly wisdom has been established with a necessary distinction between John and Jesus.

Funk proposed a sixth pillar of scholarly wisdom with the
recognized division between the Synoptic Gospels and the
Gospel of John. This, though, might be a case of redundancy.
Recognizing the Gospel of John as both later and distinct from
the Synoptic Gospels seems part and parcel of recognizing the
significance of the synoptic problem and the priority of Mark and

Q. Meanwhile Funk unfolded a distinctive seventh pillar when identifying the difference between oral and written culture.

Until the printing press, normal cultural experience was predominantly oral. Public communication involved barkers, statues, icons, drawings, and various other symbolic expressions. Public speaking, too, was a fundamental skill, and rhetoric was a significant university subject. When visiting a medieval church in Europe, one easily sees how important art and sculpture were for telling the biblical story to the majority of people. After the appearance of the printing press, and with the rise of liberal democracies, the reproduction of texts became easy, and there was an eager readership awaiting their publication. But the down side of the printed word was less importance for the practical art of rhetoric and less need for the numerous public displays of art and sculpture. Since the printing press, text has displaced rhetoric and literalism, imagination.

The philosopher Plato related rhetoric to performance,[9] what he called *mimesis,* or imitation. He held that the teller of poems is a different character from the philosopher in that the poet recites and publicly acts out art, whereas the philosopher reasons. In a condescending way, Plato thought that the poet aims to invoke emotion from the audience and to indulge in their pathos, whereas such indulgence is beneath the true concern of philosophy. However, the poet in antiquity appealed to the masses. Perhaps to a degree, the performance of poetry in theatre and public squares was like the ancient form of television—more or less widely available and generally entertaining. Poets used paradox, satire, and hyperbole to take the voice of the poem by means of pathos to the masses. The road from the voice to the masses was rhetoric.

In relation to the historical Jesus, his most memorable words show every sign of having been fixed in oral tradition: they bear the marks of rhetorical genius. His parables and aphorisms are creative, comical, and paradoxical. They hold the interest of an audience by employing contrasts, delaying plot resolutions, and offering unexpected conclusions. They hold what in rhetoric is called a "voiceprint," a striking and memorable style. Funk once commented that the historical Jesus is the rhetorical Jesus. It is the voiceprint of Jesus that is a new, seventh landmark of scholarly wisdom in historical Jesus studies. This, I believe, is Funk's accomplishment.

Ancient cultures were oral cultures, meaning that commonly people were illiterate. To be a "scribe" as the Bible identifies, was to be someone trained in writing and recording transactions, letters, and various legal pronouncements. This service was needed practically and daily in ways that are hard for a technical age to imagine. Most writers in antiquity dictated to a slave or a companion who could write, and most intellectuals of antiquity had books read to them by their slaves or students. It is remarkable to think that the greatest scholars in antiquity could flourish even if practically illiterate because servants performed the tasks of reading and writing for them. What the ancient scholar needed was a good memory, not good penmanship.

In an environment like ancient Rome where basically only the trained professionals could read and write, what survived by word of mouth would obviously be those expressions and forms of story most easily remembered. Those forms include fables, poetry, clever aphorisms, and parables. For example, few people in antiquity or in modernity will recall complex lines from Plato's great work, *The Republic*. But almost everyone who refers to that masterpiece orally will immediately recall the myth of the cave. Indeed in philosophy the myth of the cave is basic shorthand for the whole theory of Plato's forms. Jesus Seminar scholar Bernard Brandon Scott has said that we need to think of ancient shorthand images like the myth of the cave as if they were icons on a computer screen. When you mentally "click" on the myth of the cave, you open up the whole theory (program) of Plato. It is in a similar way that the historical Jesus employs parables. They are memorable compact stories offered like an icon, and when we click on the parable we open the program of Jesus.

So What?

When the seven pillars of scholarly wisdom related to historical Jesus research are taken collectively, there are a few guiding principles that temper the journey forward. There are first the obvious conclusions: Mark is the first narrative gospel in Christian history. Mark provides the framework to the story of Jesus that Matthew and Luke followed. But there is no way to independently verify that Mark's order of events (his narration) is historical. In fact, given the cautions of David Friedrick Strauss, we have to assume that it is not. Second, the sayings tradition associated with Jesus can be found mainly in two early documents. One is Mark but the second is the Q Gospel, which is common to Matthew and Luke. Third, there is no way to say that Jesus said exactly one thing or another since his sayings belong to the oral tradition of Christianity. What is written in the gospels is an approximation of what Jesus said in the style Jesus used, that is, in parables and aphorisms. The point for those who seek to follow the historical Jesus is not to determine precisely what Jesus said but to recognize the style or voiceprint of the teaching. Less obvious but equally important is the general caution that biblical criticism provides. While biblical criticism does not answer every question about the Bible or Jesus, it does limit the range of questions and answers that can be raised. A saying of Jesus can't just mean whatever I think it should mean or wish it did mean. Biblical criticism works to ensure that my thinking or another's will not deteriorate into musing of my private imagination but rather remain at least reasonable in relation to antiquity, to the editorial work of gospel writers, and to the genre of the saying under examination. Biblical criticism provides these necessary cautions when going forward with the historical Jesus.

The development of historical Jesus research brought to the fore the rhetoric of Jesus as a launching point to a new understanding. Somewhat like a Mark Twain or a Franz Kafka, the teaching of the historical Jesus as much as his brilliant sarcasm comes through in small packages of sayings and parables. These forms of rhetoric are easily held in memory and, for the disciple, can inform and shape the practice of a lifestyle. Ancient students, and hopefully modern ones, did not just repeat what the teacher said. The point is to integrate the teaching into one's own practice of life. Recalling the sayings of the master created a doorway into a style or way of being with (or even in the presence of) the master for the student. Anyone who picks up on the voiceprint of the historical Jesus need not determine exactly what he said or what he did—such cannot be determined anyway—in order to know what he was about. If there is a way to follow the historical Jesus today, it involves uncovering a lifestyle that lies in the wit and the vision of parable. This now is the task at hand.

Notes

1. Annette Yoshiko Reed places Josephus in the context of ancient *exempla* writing (what I am calling apology) when examining the figure of Abraham.(185–212)

2. For a detailed discussion, see Whitsett, "Son of God, Seed of David," 661–81.

3. Richard Dawkins, *The Greatest Show on Earth*, 17.

4. *The Quest of the Historical Jesus*, 68.

5. A good website for more information is www.earlychristianwritings.com/mark-prior.html.

6. Some scholars, for example, deny the existence of the Q Gospel, which is the common writing found in Matthew and Luke but not in Mark. Mark Goodacre is an example: www.markgoodacre.org.

7. To pursue the Synoptic Problem in greater detail as well as see the critique of alternatives to theories to the Q Gospel, see John S. Kloppenborg Verbin, *Excavating Q*, 11–54.

8. An example is Nathan, the prophet who uses the wisdom form of a parable to pronounce judgment on King David (2 Sam 12:1–4).

9. *The Republic*, Book X, 609.

3

The Jesus Voiceprint

In his inaugural address to the Jesus Seminar, entitled "The Issue of Jesus," Robert Funk described the hazards involved in historical Jesus research. The hazards for those who engage the research have become well known: the accusations of blasphemy, the hostility of the academy, the *ad hominem* attacks on the Seminar scholars. Nevertheless, "we will set out," Funk upheld, "because we are professionals."[1]

The professionals Funk referred to included the trained academicians who first formed the Jesus Seminar, but there is another meaning for professional that is not strictly the property of scholars. Though the word usually identifies members of a vocation or, more often today, a paid athlete, in fact a professional is someone who declares or professes an accepted community standard. A tradesperson for example can be a "professional" if there are certain standards in place that all who belong to the trade observe.

In historical Jesus research, there is indeed a certain kind of professing demanded of those who would pursue spirituality based on the historical Jesus. This is the profession of honesty. The Christian church historically is the body of those who "confess" beliefs and dogmas, but the historical Jesus community is composed of those who "profess" the credible and the sensible.

In Buddhist thinking, the profession of honesty is called Right View, and it is the most basic instruction the Buddhist tradition has to offer. It will help to contemplate Right View briefly. In order for anyone to grow in spiritual, intellectual, and moral maturity, it is necessary in Buddhism to accept only what is honestly credible to ourselves. If we start believing in things that we do not sincerely understand just because others seem to or because an authority figure said so then we will suffer psychologically as a consequence. The psychological consequences can include the loss of personal integrity, the growth of self-hatred (which can surface as aggression), and a general inability to accept others and ourselves freely. In the words of Stevie Wonder, "When you believe in things you don't understand, then you suffer."[2] And in the words of the Buddha, "Believe nothing, no matter where you read it, or who said it, no matter if I have said it, unless it agrees with your own reason and your own common sense."[3] To put this positively, check out things for yourself, make sure you interpret things correctly, and learn for yourself. Instead of jumping to conclusions about a subject or about other people, first ensure you are reading the situation correctly. This is called Right View because it involves a commitment to understanding things as they truly are.

What then distinguishes a realistic picture of the historical Jesus from an unrealistic one—a Right View of Jesus from a distorted one? The answer lies in the criterion of credibility. Whatever conclusion one might end up with about Jesus, it must be a possible Jesus and not an incredible one. A possible Jesus is a Jesus situated in his historical circumstances and who did things and said things that a real person could have reasonably believed or done at that time. An incredible Jesus is the one who came from the sky, who performed miracles by fiat, and who was as dead as a doornail only to magically return to life. Such a Jesus, in whom literalist Christians force belief and whom ortho-dox Christians hold in the "mystery of faith," not only demands the incredible but also justifies it with the dubious category of revelation. Such a Jesus is confessed because the Bible or the Church says so. Yet exactly this is the difference. To leave the confessing of the Church's Jesus and to return to the professing of the historical Jesus is to take off the glasses of deception and return to the eyes of Right View.

To see a credible Jesus means to narrow the evidence employed to picture him. Another way to understand this "narrowing" is to say that the attributes related to the incredible Jesus of the confessing tradition must be placed in brackets and ignored. The first item to bracket is the dogmatic idea of revelation. Revelation is of no help in historical Jesus studies because it is not a category of evidence. In its place, there needs to be a core of realistic data about Jesus that supports a credible interpretation of him. If the picture of the historical Jesus is largely built on legend, then of course the figure will not be a human being but a fanciful creation of our collective imaginations. In the quest for the historical Jesus, we need to get as close as we can to a reasonable and reliable core of teaching.

The core of reliable teaching is sometimes called the "authentic Jesus tradition." The term is admittedly a bit presumptuous, since it implies that narrowing the evidence about Jesus is a simple matter of sorting out self-evidently true events from false ones. In order not to be overly optimistic, and therefore travel once again to the boundaries of the incredible, it is necessary to admit the basic problem that all material related to the historical Jesus comes from antiquity. It is never possible to reach absolute conclusions about antiquity because the sources are fragmentary, varied, and come from a world no modern person has or ever can visit. Ancient times are to us a stranger and an enigma, as Albert Schweitzer *almost* said,[4] that has left to us only piecemeal witnesses. In antiquity people reasoned without the assumptions of modern science and generally interpreted events from what we would regard today as prejudiced and sometimes absurd points of view. Antiquity, because it is so distant and distinct from us, imports its own uncertainty principle: it is never a sure bet that we can understand what went on back then and how it was experienced by the people of that time. Still, we can be certain that whatever happened was possible, not incredible. This simple foundation is the honest profession involved in the search for the historical Jesus.

In addition to the uncertainty involved in understanding antiquity, when it comes to the historical Jesus—and, for that matter, the discipline of history—there is also the problem of methodology. To undertake the study of history is to employ some tools for the job. These tools are called methods, but all forms of method have an inherent problem. A method used to investigate a set of questions shapes the way questions are asked and answered. The method has its own built-in system of bias. There is no way to prevent this problem. The only antidote is to acknowledge the problem exists. This recognition enables a certain level of objectivity because it changes the way questions are asked. Once the problem of method is recognized, it is impossible to ask about the absolute truth. That's no longer an option. The new question is, what makes the best sense of the available data? To use the bracketing metaphor, the question about absolute truth is sectioned off and removed from the table in favor of the more realistic and mature approach of finding a model that best explains the data. Adapting the words of philosopher Paul Ricoeur, we can call this the "model that suits": it is the best model we can come up with given the available data, what we think we know, and what is reasonable to our understanding. Einstein's General Theory of Relativity is a good example. When relativity was proposed, it offered a radically different model of space, but it dealt with the same data available to Newtonian physics. Relativity just makes better sense of the data. Historical investigations are not exactly like technical science but they do hold a similar intention. The point is to find the best way to make sense of the available data.

When the criterion of credibility is taken seriously, the guideline is to employ models that suit the task of making sense of the historical data and that, especially, identify what can be taken from the historical Jesus to church. Once this credible "authentic Jesus tradition" is identified, the point will be to carry forward into the contemporary world the *momentum* of the Jesus movement: grasping the style of the teacher, capturing the spirit of his words, and living out the implications of these words in our own time with our own creativity. The starting point is to recover the fragmentary witnesses to the voice of Jesus.

Narrowing the Evidence

The first and main act of narrowing the evidence in historical Jesus research comes from the employment of source criticism. There are other forms of biblical criticism, like redaction criticism and rhetorical criticism, that will be mentioned, but source criticism is the place to start. A rule of thumb in historical research is that normally a primary source is superior to the secondary source that employs it. This simple directive means that the sources of the Christian gospels rather than the gospels themselves are preferential evidence, at least initially, in the quest for the historical Jesus. An example of source material is Matthew and Luke's use of material from Mark in the writing of their gospels. Mark, therefore, is preferential in historical terms when seeking the earliest formation of the Jesus material. Unfortunately, just because earlier forms of material can be identified, it does not mean that the material is a direct witness to the historical Jesus. However early the source material, it is still material from the early Christian movement. It still includes various beliefs or confessions about Jesus and his super-human status. Nevertheless, earlier material is less developed than later material and does give us some insight into the birth of Christianity and the first traditions related to Jesus. The major conclusion drawn from source criticism has already been mentioned: Q and Mark are the sources for Matthew and Luke.

Meanwhile, redaction criticism comes into play when we recognize Matthew and Luke's manipulation of the material they took from Mark or Q. Matthew and Luke redact the source material in two ways. Either they correct the source, if they think it is wrong, or they enhance the material if they think it is poorly stated, lacking in detail, or fails to make the point they think it should. There are many examples of redaction in the New Testament. An obvious one is how Matthew tries to correct Mark's account of the entry to Jerusalem (Mark 11:1–11). Mark has Jesus entering Jerusalem riding on a colt, but Matthew wants to make sure it is understood that this scene fulfills prophecy, so he backs up the scene with a direct quotation from Zech 9:9. Strangely, Matthew appears not to understand the poetic repetition used in Zechariah and interprets two animals where there is only one. So, at Matt 21:7, even though Matthew thinks he is "correcting" Mark, he presents Jesus entering Jerusalem as if he were part of a circus act, simultaneously riding on two pack animals, leaving the reader to imagine how he does it. This correction is also an embellishment, for by quoting from Zechariah, Matthew is adding material to what he received from Mark. Matthew wants to draw out what he feels Mark only alludes to. But the material is not there in Mark, so Matthew, in effect, replaces original Mark with his new interpretation of Mark. Among other things, Matthew wants to make sure that if his reader does encounter Mark, the reader will do so according to the Gospel of Matthew. For the source critic, it is significant to understand that the story appears in a more primitive, or less interpreted, form in Mark than in Matthew, for Mark is the source of Matthew. For the redaction critic, it is significant to note what Matthew adds to Mark, for the additions reveal how Matthew interprets things and what he seeks to emphasize in his theology. And even though Mark is the source for Matthew, the redaction activity of Matthew is a witness to the way all gospel writers, including Mark, redacted the material they used for the gospels. For every gospel the redaction critic asks, what is the gospel writer's theology that overlays the earlier material the gospel writer has used? Or, in terms important for historical Jesus research, what interpretive material belongs to the gospel writers but not to Jesus?

Rhetorical criticism is a third significant method for historical Jesus research. Around the middle of the twentieth century, scholars like James Muilenburg called upon biblical critics to expand the menu of critical tools by placing more attention on rhetorical criticism. With form criticism particularly in mind—that is, a method that focuses on an isolated portion of text, like a miracle narrative—Muilenburg stated,

> Exclusive attention to the *Gattung* [or, the genre of a selected text] may actually obscure the thought and intention of the writer or speaker . . . . It is the creative synthesis of the particular formulation of the pericope [that is, the selected text] with the content that makes it the distinctive composition that it is.[5]

Muilenburg meant that if we want to understand a gospel like Mark, for instance, we can't just pull the pieces apart and study them separately. We can't say, here is a miracle and over there is a parable and the two have nothing to do with each other. Rather, we need to imagine Mark as a presentation: as a piece of ancient rhetoric that has a persuasive goal. Various criticisms can help us see how the Gospel of Mark or a letter of Paul or any other ancient Christian text is put together, but this act of identifying the parts should not obscure the sight of the whole presentation. The whole presentation is the rhetorical presentation of the theological work.

Muilenburg was right, and biblical scholarship changed in light of his advice. Scholars today do see gospel presentations as rhetorical devices that, as a whole, are theologically motivated. The gospel writers do have persuasive goals. However, oddly, there was a sort of side effect to Muilenburg's insight that he probably did not intend, and this side effect became significant for historical Jesus research. If we take apart the Gospels with the use of source criticism to find the earlier fragments of the tradition, and if we find in these fragmentary sources various forms of speech—like aphorisms and parables—then do the fragments on their own express rhetorical strategies? The answer is yes. In short, there are persuasive presentations detectable in the sources of the gospels. These "presentations" are not necessarily single-author compositions but do reflect embedded rhetorical strategies in earlier oral tradition. Bob Funk provocatively suggested that these scattered rhetorical forms include fragments of the voiceprint (rhetorical strategy) of the historical Jesus.

A Jesus Strategy

Even though rhetorical criticism is, properly speaking, a reference to the theological presentation of a gospel in which the whole gospel is seen as a strategy, a second level of rhetorical criticism affects the quest for the historical Jesus. This happens when, in the pre-gospel sources, it is noticed that there are identifiable and repetitive rhetorical forms that betray an early *gatung,* or genre, of oral tradition: in short, a rhetorical strategy. The strategy is called a voiceprint, and, like a fingerprint, a voiceprint leaves the trace of its style in mnemonic (memory) devices. As observed, these devices include such things as irony, hyperbole, parallelisms, delayed plot resolutions, and the like employed in aphorisms and parables. Jesus, of course, was not the only teacher in antiquity to use these techniques, but the style of the voiceprint found in the gospel sources does create for us a small window of observation on his persuasive intentions. The style suggests a Jesus rhetorical strategy.

To open this small window of observation, we need to return to the work of the source criticism by which the field of evidence is narrowed. Gathering from antiquity all the sayings attributed to Jesus is an enormous task but not automatically a needed one. Source criticism will eliminate a lot of material that is directly unhelpful. There are approximately sixty gospels that we know of from the first few centuries of Christianity. There are likely more gospels that once existed but are now lost forever.[6] Of those we do know, some are known only in name, and some only exist as a few sentences or paragraphs. Some are hypothetical gospels reconstructed from their supposed use by the authors of known gospels. The Signs Gospel presumably existed independently as a source for the Gospel of John, and modern scholars have tried to reconstruct it from John. The Q Gospel is a source for Matthew and Luke, and again has several modern reconstructed versions. Some gospels from antiquity are known fairly well, though not completely, since several pages have not survived; examples include the Gospel of Peter and the Gospel of Mary. The gospels in the Christian Bible, because they were so highly valued by the church, were consistently copied and survive in complete forms. However, even these gospels contain thousands of variations among the surviving texts and fragments. The variations are due both to centuries of copying and the fact that different text traditions existed in different parts of the ancient world. Finally, there are six known infancy gospels that propose to be accounts of Jesus' childhood.

When all this material, gospels and gospel fragments, is gathered together, it is quickly evident that many prove useless when it comes to the quest for the historical Jesus. The Infancy Gospel of Thomas is an easy example. In it, the boy Jesus performs strange and wonderful miracles that are obviously fantastic and imaginary. The writer of the Infancy Gospel wonders what "God" must have been like as a kid—we find out as we read that God does not do childhood very well—but the assumption that God was a kid in the first place assumes a theological belief about Jesus being divine. Interesting as the question may be, it's not history.

There are several other gospels that likewise prove interesting but not historically helpful. Gospels from the gnostic tradition

are similar in style to the canonical Gospel of John. In them,
Jesus stands as a single philosopher who speaks otherworldly
wisdom, often in the guise of the risen Christ. Like the infancy
gospels, these gospels can be very enlightening if the question is
the development of Christianity. However, when the question is
the historical Jesus, the gospels again assume a divine status for
Jesus that betrays established confessional beliefs. Occasionally,
like with the Gospel of Thomas, the gnostic tradition does rely
on earlier traditions and can help identify content from the oral
tradition. When it comes to the historical Jesus, the point is to
find the earliest sayings of the tradition, not later systems of
belief.

The narrowing process continues when source criticism helps
to highlight the many scattered sayings attributed to Jesus that
come from an earlier common tradition. For example, a saying in
one text, like Luke, is copied from another text like Mark. This
means the source text is Mark. But in some cases the source text
is neither obvious nor present. Sometimes sayings are found in
two sources and are similar, but there is no direct relationship
between the two. Instead, both rely on an earlier common tradition that may have been written (and lost) or may have been
orally transmitted only. If we describe these two phenomena
more succinctly, we can say that sometimes there is (1) a relationship of dependence between two sayings, and sometimes
there is (2) a relationship of tradition. When one text clearly copies from another, then there is a dependent relationship between
them. But sometimes the relationship is more distant. There can
be strong similarities between two texts but no direct copying
and no apparent knowledge of one writer by the other. In this
case the evidence suggests that some communities share a relationship of tradition to common material but no knowledge of
each other. Finally, there are sayings recorded in one text alone.
For example, the parable of the Workers in the Vineyard, which
we will look at below, occurs only in Matthew. When this hap-

pens, it is necessary to judge the quality of the saying in relation to other sayings for which there is more evidence.

The whole activity of source criticism can be tedious work. However, its results are manifestly significant. The task of comparing sayings with sayings in an attempt to narrow down the database to those lying closer to an originating voice is both invaluable to historical Jesus research and the point of departure for such research. After eliminating the imaginative infancy gospels, the philosophical discourse gospels, various dependent sayings, and obvious confessional material, there still remain approximately fifteen hundred sayings attributed to Jesus in the first two centuries of Christianity. Fortunately, source criticism is not finished yet. As previously noted, many sayings share the same basic expression though not exactly the same words. These are called duplicates and when eliminated the number of sayings becomes something like what the Jesus Seminar concluded: approximately ninety sayings attributed to Jesus belong to the authentic Jesus tradition.[7]

There is one caveat—there is always at least one—that needs to be raised lest we give too much credit to the results of source criticism. First, source criticism narrows down material but does not hit bedrock. No saying of Jesus exists for us without some element of redaction. The Jesus Seminar's claim that roughly ninety Jesus sayings belong to the authentic tradition may have attracted a lot of public attention and furor, but only after the popular furor died did the work actually begin. The database of sayings only gave scholars something to work with, but within the database it is still necessary to account for the hand of early church writers, be they scribes who copied material or authors who dictated material. Jesus never directly dictated any of the material. So, while it does sound impressive to say, "Here is the authentic tradition," authentic in this case is an approximating word (the consequence of narrowing the evidence) not a factual word (the consequence of eyewitness evidence).

Finally, having used source criticism as a model to narrow the historical material and redaction criticism to remain cautious of the early church's hand in shaping that material, it is time to introduce the value of rhetorical criticism. With rhetorical criticism, the point is to identify the voiceprint of a teacher in oral as opposed to written tradition. After all, the historical Jesus did not write anything. His use of parables and aphorisms was a mnemonic form of instruction designed to promote the persuasive rhetorical strategy of an ancient school, what today we might call a lifestyle. Somewhat like Socrates, the oral material—insofar as we can identify it—has a "market" value to it.[8] It belonged to the public sphere of discourse and gossip. It is packaged in such a way that it lends itself to word-of-mouth transmission. Despite all the modern devices of technical communication, marketing experts today still say that old-fashioned word of mouth is the best way to advertise. Ancient rhetoric can be looked at this way. The point of rhetorical criticism is to identify those forms of expression that would have played well as public oral strategies. It is on the foundation of such strategies that taking the historical Jesus to church becomes possible.

Rhetorical forms must be "reconstructed" on the basis of the saying's persuasive force. A more effective or sharper expression relatively free of interpretive material is most likely closer to the rhetorical intentions of the earlier form, whereas obvious elaborations, clarifications, duplicities, or obfuscations indicate editorial redaction from a later period. The parable of the Unjust Steward (Luke 16:1–8a) is a classic example. Scholars generally think that the parable ends half way through verse 8 with "and the master praised the unjust steward for his shrewdness." What follows after verse 8a are obvious elaborations attempting to interpret the parable; clearly "sons of light" in verse 8b, and "dishonest wealth" and "eternal homes" in verse 9, are commentary on the parable, but not part of it. Meanwhile, it has always been debated whether or not the "master" ("the Lord" in Greek) in verse 8a refers to the master in the parable or to Jesus. If it refers to Jesus, then the whole of verse 8 does not belong to the parable but is rather an early verse of commentary. Another example is Luke 10:7, "Eat whatever they provide." The saying is instruction to early missionaries presumably visiting households as part of the Jesus movement, and the saying is also found in the Gospel of Thomas (14:4), suggesting its early origins. These two sayings have a relationship of tradition. But Luke adds a concluding phrase, "for workers deserve their wages." Thus, we can place the advice to eat whatever is provided within a cluster of early material associated with the Jesus movement, and we can note its rhetorical force. Certainly, as the Jesus Seminar noted, accusations about Jesus eating with sinners (Mark 2:16) would follow from the practice of eating "whatever" without concern for the company or the content. The aphorism "eat whatever is provided" holds *persuasive* intention in relation to the lifestyle of itinerant teachers. The commentary about workers, however, adds nothing rhetorically to the saying and indeed is evidence that Luke the redactor, for some reason, needed to justify the act of feeding visiting missionaries. Luke's comment makes more sense in the context of later Christianity, when there was a question of why and how much hospitality should be extended to itinerant preachers. The point is if we are looking for aphoristic sayings that relay the rhetorical force of the earliest Jesus movement, we don't need to worry about obvious addendums that reflect a redactor's concern for commentary and further clarification.

Written sayings, then, can be from the earliest period of transmission, but since a third party wrote the sayings down there is no certainty that the saying is exactly what Jesus said. Every written record bears the theology of the writer. Nevertheless, when dealing with the written record the idea is not to determine the exact words of Jesus; in historical Jesus research, the idea is to focus on the rhetorical marks of an earlier oral form. This means that mnemonic characteristics are vital to analyzing the saying. Oral teachers in antiquity, and still today, used mnemonic devices to encapsulate teaching in striking images, turns of phrase, or ironic juxtapositions. These mnemonic characteristics survive in recorded sayings like traces of rhetorical strategies. It is the rhetorical strategy that is significant when it comes to taking the historical Jesus to church.

Parable Rules Supreme

It is not necessary to re-imagine antiquity to know the power of mnemonic devices as memory aids. We use them daily ourselves, and we know them very well. Some are not very fancy, like a child's nursery rhyme. Other forms are not as obvious as rhyme but equally effective. A good aphorism involves a turn of phrase and is usually memorable even at first hearing. Virtually everyone knows an aphorism or two from a figure like Oscar Wilde or Kurt Vonnegut. "Nothing worth knowing can be taught" is a Wilde aphorism often repeated as popular wisdom. It is easy to remember because of the sharp, ironic disjunction set between knowledge and education.[9] Learning the words to a song is easier than memorizing a paragraph of writing or a mathematical formula because the words are associated with vibration and rhythm. Stories are also easier to remember than philosophical arguments because stories have heroes and villains, tension and the release of tension, plots and the resolution of plots. Some ancient philosophers were extremely abstract, and their theories really needed to be in writing in order to be understood, but even great philosophers like Plato continued to use mnemonic devices such as short myths to make their theories easier to recall. Comedians normally employ forms of sarcasm in their descriptions of human behavior or political issues. Again, the sarcasm, when well done, is easier to recall because it is dramatic and involves more senses than just memory. Sarcasm mocks political figures or common situations and through humor makes an impression on listeners. Jesus stands in the tradition of Jewish wisdom, and like other great wisdom teachers he relied on mnemonic devices to relay his teaching and his wit.

The two forms of teaching that characterize the authentic Jesus tradition have been mentioned already—aphorism and parable. It is eminently important, when it comes to the historical Jesus, to understand these terms well. It is no exaggeration to say that breakthroughs in relation to the historical Jesus could not occur until breakthroughs in the understanding of parables occurred, which in turn brought focus on the aphorisms (for, in effect, a parable is an extended aphorism). The difficulty involved in understanding a parable raises the real possibility that even the closest followers of Jesus did not always grasp what he was talking about. The Gospel of Mark takes this likelihood as a matter of course (4:12, 33).

A parable is both a short story and an extended aphorism. Like a short story, it can have a few characters, truncated narrative, and memorable scenes. Like an aphorism, it turns on one surprising, if not poignant, point. Of course there are good parables and bad; some pull off surprise endings and hold unexpected scenes whereas others fall flat. Even Jesus could have a bad day.[10] Nevertheless, the one thing consistent about Jesus was his use of parable. He was among the earlier crafters of parable in the post-biblical Jewish tradition, and remains one of history's genius storytellers.

A parable regards the present world as pliable. Though the parable is cut from the fabric of everyday life, it is never really about everyday life. Common themes abound: an individual stands in a marketplace hoping to be hired as a day laborer; a woman is baking bread; a farmer sows a crop. It is all common life. Yet, as a story unfolds, the common reasoning we use to interpret the situation fails in the end to fit into the parable world. The parable turns or distorts the everyday world in an attempt to liberate the audience from a common to a new or unexpected vision of life. The parable, as Funk pointed out with reference to Kafka, is always "over there" and on the "other side" of life even though its content belongs to the everyday world. Understanding a parable as a vehicle used to cross over from a common to an altered view of the world—the world according to its vision—is a breakthrough originally made by Adolf Julicher, who wrote in the nineteenth century.[11] A parable is not an allegory or a moral. It's not referring to a heavenly world, and it's not making a point about ethics. It is re-casting the world according to a vision; it is story that carries vision and that makes the teller of parable a vision carrier. Jesus was a commentator on "over there": a place we can enter but can do so only by dropping our current habits of life. To be "over there" is not to be in a different world but to be in this world differently.

This basic introduction to a parable allows us to say a lot of things about what a parable is not. A parable is not a story about good manners versus bad manners. It is not advice. Neither does it counsel us to hold one political view or another. Most importantly—and this was Julicher's point—a parable is not a symbolic story in which the characters or actions represent some hidden spiritual truths. In the Parable of the Sower, the sower in the field is not God or Jesus, and the seeds being sown are not the Word of God or the Christian gospel. The hearer of a parable has to use Right View and figure out the meaning for him or herself. Unfortunately, the gospel writers did not always understand the distinctive nature of a parable. The gospel writers often want to interpret the parables definitively for us, and often they do so with the idea that the story has a mysterious, secret, and authoritative meaning.

The misunderstandings of the gospel writers suggest two things about them. One is that they were a few generations removed from Jesus and the setting of his story telling. They inhabited a different cultural reality. The second likelihood is that the gospel writers were somewhat wealthy, as opposed to the impoverished historical Jesus. To write things in antiquity required having material to write upon and, normally, having a scribe to write things down. Even though scribes were commonplace in antiquity, and employed by rich and poor alike, it was necessary to have money to pay them. It might be a tenuous point, yet it seems right to note that the gospel writers, by virtue of being engaged in the production of a manuscript, were of a different class from that of the historical Jesus. Likely they were not well versed in the Jewish parable tradition. Their concern was to state the theological conviction of their community about Jesus, which often meant they would employ apocalyptic (crisis) language to establish the divine authority of Jesus. Parables, unless they are presented as cryptic revelations, are difficult to use for authoritative conclusions about reality and God. Perhaps it is impossible to know exactly why the gospel writers misunderstood the parables of Jesus, but surely it is a tragedy of Christian history that they did.

The Workers in the Vineyard is an instructive example. It demonstrates the way the gospel writer Matthew believed the parable should be interpreted and, at the same time, when Matthew's comments are bracketed out, it demonstrates in a highly effective manner what a good parable is all about. Let's review the parable first. The scene is completely common: unemployed folks stand around the marketplace hoping to be hired for the day. We can well envision Roman policies that expanded agricultural lands for estate holders and displaced peasant farmers in ancient Galilee. Poverty and homelessness followed. Very much like today, the weakest members of society suffered the consequences of economic policies tailored to benefit aristocrats. The original audience of the vineyard parable would have known the scene all too well: a few workers get hired for the day before the break of dawn. About three hours later, a few more lucky ones are chosen. Still later, another few get a break and can work, though the hour is already late. Finally, the parable brings us down to the last hour of daylight. No one gets hired at such a time since virtually everyone has finished for the day. At this point the parable starts to warp reality. With only an hour of daylight left, yet another set of individuals gets hired. The fact they are hired so late is surprising, but so is the fact that they are still around waiting to be hired. The last group barely gets started when the day ends. Now, all the workers are called to receive their wages, from those hired last to first. When the ones hired last at the very end of the day receive one denarius—a full day's wage—it seems as if the landlord is in a very generous mood. Those hired earliest in the day can hardly wait to claim the bigger prize. Instead, one by one, each group of laborers discovers that the landlord's generosity is reserved only for the first group. Those who worked one hour get paid as much as those who worked all day long. It is patently unfair, yet in response to complaints the landlord is right: each worker agreed to work for a day's wage. It's the landlord's call.

This parable often irks readers; it seems remarkably wrong to pay a person who labored all day absolutely the same wage as one who barely even had time to start. Had there been a labor union in existence, there would have rightly been an arbitration hearing. On the other hand, the payment is the correct amount. The transaction was completed according to the agreement of one day's wage struck with each worker at the time of hiring. The workers see the situation as unfair only in retrospect when, at the time of payment, the landlord will not follow the formula of payment per hours worked. Even though the workers agreed to the same wage at the time of hiring, the workers' view shifts to the standard understanding that more work means more pay. The landlord does not shift the agreement. Rather, the landlord continues to hold the alternative standard of measurement. Payment is not for how long one labors but for the fact that one labors. Though couched in everyday reality, this story is not really about workers and landlords but about workers and land- lords "over there." It is about a location, a lifestyle, where value is not related to time and where human activity is not measured on scales of worthiness and privilege. To be comfortable with the parable requires a kind of breakthrough in life. It is a question of seeing equilibrium in all aspects of life and knowing that, in the parable world, waiting all day to be called to work is the same in value as working all day. The question is, can we cross over to the lifestyle of the parable world?

If we feel troubled about "going over" to the parable world, maybe there is some comfort in knowing that Matthew had trouble with the journey too. Matthew hones the parable down to two distinctive elements. Because there is payment involved from the landlord (the authority figure) to the workers (the dependants), Matthew's instinct is to interpret the landlord as God in heaven and the workers as disciples on earth who will receive an award when they die. Then, Matthew places the parable in his gospel into a scene where disciples argue about what reward they will receive for following Jesus. Well, according to Matthew, of course they are going to get an award when they inherit eternal life. Everyone who has left all to follow Jesus will receive a hundredfold in reward (19:29), but remember this warning, "The last shall be first" (19:30 and 20:16). Matthew successfully converts the parable into an allegory that illustrates the need to balance one's reward for following Jesus with the humility necessary to do it. The momentum and the persuasive force of the parable have been re-directed by Matthew from teaching about a different vision of life to teaching about rewards and humility for Christians. With this parable, the momentum, or rhetorical strategy, that Matthew has added needs to be identified and removed in order to hear the voice of Jesus. To hear the voice of Jesus means to hear, with Right View, the originating rather than secondary momentum of the parable.

Determining the authentic voice of Jesus, then, means identifying the style employed in mnemonic devices like a parable. The style reveals a momentum or rhetorical persuasion characteristic of the Jesus voiceprint. Identifying that voiceprint in greater detail helps us talk about a "lifestyle" associated with the teaching tradition. This is not at all untypical of antiquity. Virtually all schools in antiquity not only had identifiable teaching but also complementary lifestyles. Jesus and various schools in ancient Judaism were no different.

The only interruption in the task of taking Jesus to church involves the objection that it cannot be done. I call this objection the apocalyptic complaint, which insists Jesus was no wisdom teacher but an end-time prophet. I will address the apocalyptic complaint first, in the next chapter, before attempting to expand on the lifestyle of the historical Jesus.

Notes

1. Funk, Robert, *Jesus Reconsidered*, 5.

2. A lyric from the song, "Superstition" (Motown Records, 1972).

3. A saying of the Buddha from the Dhammapada.

4. Schweitzer said the historical Jesus was a stranger and an enigma (*Quest of the Historical Jesus*), but in this dramatic statement he failed to note how basically true this is of any ancient person. Jesus is just like anyone else we care to study from antiquity.

5. 1968 address to the Society of Biblical Literature, "Form Criticism and Beyond." See Thomas F. Best (ed.), *Hearing and Speaking the Word*.

6. The findings at Oxyrhyncus, for example, include fragments from unknown gospels and suggest the likelihood that there were more gospels in antiquity than we will ever know about.

7. Interested readers can refer to *The Five Gospels*, especially 34–38.

8. Market is one word we can take pretty literally because ancient popular philosophy was often conducted in town and city marketplaces.

9. The full aphorism is "Education is an admirable thing. But it is well to remember from time to time that nothing that is worth knowing can be taught." This originally appeared anonymously in *Saturday Review*, November 17, 1894.

10. The parable of the Shrewd Manager (Luke 16:1–8a), as Brandon Scott describes, is "one of the strangest and most difficult" to understand. It might be an example of the Torah being fulfilled despite the worst social practices. It may be brilliant; it might be too obscure: was it a good or a bad day? The history of scholarship seems to hold a reserved judgment. See *Re-imagine the World*, 85–95.

11. *Die Gleichnisreden Jesu.*

Unhearing
the Apocalypse

The historical Jesus is the rhetorical Jesus. What this means is
that the quest for the historical Jesus starts with the sayings
tradition and does not go any further than that. Yet, a perceptive
reader will ask, was it not just concluded that, in fact, no saying
attributed to Jesus can be assumed to be exactly what Jesus said?
Indeed is not every saying we have of Jesus necessarily and obviously a written saying, which means it has passed through the
hands of a redactor? Of course this is true. But the quest for the
historical Jesus is not a quest for exact words; it is a quest for a
rhetorical strategy, a quest for the force of word that impels the
writing words. It is impossible to know exactly what Jesus said,
but it is not impossible to hear Jesus.

The question now is, what sort of Jesus is heard? This question delivers us into the heart of a debate that demands pause
for reflection. Since the end of the nineteenth century, there has
been one overwhelming response to the question about Jesus'
identity. The response is that the historical Jesus was a prophet
of the end-times who announced the immanent return of a heavenly figure called the "Son of Man," a figure he either expected
or thought he himself was. "You will see the Son of Man," Jesus
says at Mark 14:62, "seated at the right hand of Power, and
coming with the clouds of heaven." This heavenly figure who
descends to earth is taken from Dan 7:13, and if Jesus said (or

quoted) this text, he was relaying his belief that a new age was about to dawn. From the close of the nineteenth century until about the 1970's, this Jesus, the apocalyptic Jesus, the Jesus who believed the end of the age was near, the eschatological or end-time prophet Jesus, was basically the only Jesus around. "Jesus thought that the history of the world would come to a screeching halt," Bart Ehrman confidently summarizes, "that God would intervene in the affairs of this planet, overthrow the forces of evil in a cosmic act of judgment, and establish his utopian kingdom here on earth."[1] Ehrman's blatant conclusion sounds more like a vision pulled from the books of Daniel or Revelation than from the parables of Jesus, which is already problematic, but nevertheless Ehrman voices what is often heard in the academy and accepted without question in the general public.

Defining Jesus as an "apocalyptic prophet" involves many and various problems, and Ehrman can be criticized for not sharing the subtleties involved. Care must be taken to note that in the biblical mind, the apocalypse is not about the end of history; it is not even about history coming to a screeching halt. It is, instead, about the transformation of history.[2] The apocalypse is about God re-arranging history—the sense and order of it—rather than opting out of history altogether. Apocalypse comes from the Greek word *apocalypsis*, meaning "revelation." Even if we should reach the conclusion that the historical Jesus is best understood as an apocalyptic prophet, it would still be wrong to think that in the act of announcing the end-time he imagined something beyond this world. In the apocalyptic view of things, the transformation of the world involves God ridding the world of evil and setting time back to square one, which was once the Garden of Eden. In ancient Judaism, the post-apocalyptic world order would have its capital in Jerusalem and a political existence like the time of King David. So, while not exactly the Garden of Eden, it is—following God's violent victory—an age of peace during which Gentiles stream to Zion to recognize, in worship, the God of Israel.[3] The Messiah in Judaism is not necessarily a kingly figure but is certainly involved in inaugurating the age of transformation. As in the book of Malachi (4:5), the messianic figure comes as Elijah to begin the age of judgment prior to establishing the new kingdom on earth. When Jesus is described primarily as an apocalyptic prophet, it means that he thought himself an Elijah figure, the Son of Man, whose appearance announced, and whose death was intimately wrapped up in, the transformation of the world.

The apocalyptic interpretation of Jesus has been, as mentioned, the standard interpretation of the historical Jesus since the end of the nineteenth century, but this is only partially true. In fact, the apocalyptic Jesus has been normative in Christianity since the end of the first century. The Jesus of Christian orthodoxy is the Resurrected One who is scheduled to return as some point in the future to inaugurate the new era. The Jesus of Christian orthodoxy is the one about whom the confession is written, "Christ has died; Christ is risen; Christ will come again." Jesus will come again, in traditional Christianity, to accomplish the great and long promised clean up of the world. When he returns, he will finally defeat evil, establish his kingdom on earth, and reign forever. The apocalyptic Jesus of many contemporary scholars and the Church's traditional Jesus are the same person. The only difference is that scholars who defend the apocalyptic Jesus admit that he was evidently wrong, at least in terms of timing; nevertheless, these scholars inadvertently offer a theological defense for traditional Christianity.[4] In effect, they conclude that the church is right: the apocalyptic Jesus is Lord. We don't need to take the apocalyptic Jesus to church. He is already there.

The apocalyptic interpretation of Jesus will always be an interpretive option when it comes to the historical Jesus, since in the long run no conclusion about Jesus or any other historical figure is absolutely secure. Nevertheless, by the same token, it is no longer the case that security can be found in the conclusion Jesus was apocalyptic. It might even be the case that more scholars interpret the historical Jesus non-apocalyptically than those who maintain the traditional interpretation. Certainly, many scholars now relate the historical Jesus primarily to the wisdom tradition of ancient Judaism rather than to the messianic tradition.[5] What has caused the change? Why is it now just as easy to conclude that Jesus was primarily a wisdom teacher as it once was to conclude that he was primarily an apocalyptic prophet?

The interpretation of Jesus as an apocalyptic prophet rests on the academic conventions associated with Albert Schweitzer and his epoch-making book, *The Quest of the Historical Jesus*.[6] Important though this book was, Schweitzer's main arguments for the apocalyptic interpretation of Jesus actually appear in another book, *The Kingdom of God and Primitive Christianity*.[7] In the latter book, Schweitzer addresses the kingdom of God in the teaching of Jesus and gives several arguments in favor of the apocalyptic interpretation. To Schweitzer, Jesus did not have a metaphorical, what he called a "spiritual," understanding of the kingdom of God. He accused "liberal" theology of holding this airy-fairy idea that the kingdom Jesus spoke of was utopian pie-in-the-sky. In place of this nonsense, Schweitzer believed that the Son of Man sayings preserved in the Christian gospels were historical Jesus sayings and historical Jesus beliefs. Schweitzer was convinced that Jesus believed his life and mission were tied directly to this promised Son of Man figure, whose return to earth would change the world. Schweitzer called these sayings the rocks of the gospel that stood out like ugly juts against the background of white snow.[8] With this conviction, Schweitzer relayed his belief that the apocalyptic predictions of Jesus never came to pass and that this fact jutted out as an embarrassment to the early church. The gospel writers needed to cover it up, which they did by pushing the anticipated apocalypse ahead to a remote and indistinct date. Schweitzer believed that he had uncovered this embarrassment of the early church about the messianic consciousness of Jesus, and to prove his point he presented what are now standard propositions. He stated that Jesus believed in a day of resurrection on which the righteous shall be seated at the table of a messianic feast (Matt 8:11); Jesus must have taken this vision, Schweitzer thought, from post-exilic prophets like Malachi and Zechariah. The resurrection and end-time beliefs of Jesus must have quickly spilled over, after the death of Jesus, into the theological development of the early church. Christianity first proclaimed the resurrection because that's what Jesus had believed. Then Schweitzer offered several other clues about Jesus to cinch his argument. He recognized a connection between John the Baptist and Jesus. Jesus was John's follower, but soon Jesus thought of John as playing the role of Elijah, the forerunner, to his role as the Messiah. Contemporary scholars are less likely to think Jesus consciously thought of John as his second fiddle, but the continuity between John and Jesus is often noted. If John had an apocalyptic vision, then Jesus must have had one, too. A third major point for Schweitzer is the crucifixion of Jesus. As in *The Quest of the Historical Jesus*, Schweitzer proposes in *The Kingdom of God* that Jesus purposely sought out crucifixion in order to jump-start the end-time scenario, with its apex reached when he would receive the messianic crown. Many scholars continue in Schweitzer's wake defending the apocalyptic Jesus interpretation while taking particular aim at the Jesus Seminar. For the present purposes, Schweitzer's arguments can be stated succinctly: Jesus was an apocalyptic prophet because (1) he was a post-exilic Jew, (2) baptized by John, who (3) believed in the heavenly Son of Man and (4) actively sought to kick-start the end time by means of his own crucifixion.

Many scholars today continue to defend the main points of Schweitzer argument but provide more historical background than was available to Schweitzer. Dale Allison adds to Schweitzer's arguments with discussions about the Q Gospel, including a broad analysis of first-century Judaism, and even admits the fact that he could be wrong.[10] Ehrman is among the most popular proponents of the apocalyptic Jesus who continues to hold Schweitzer's basic premises. According to Ehrman, Jesus believed in the immanent return of the Son of Man and held the same beliefs about the end of time as John the Baptist apparently did. Ehrman adds that the miracles and exorcisms associated with Jesus reveal something about his conviction that the messianic age would soon arrive to elevate the poor and turn the privileged hierarchies of the world upside down. Ehrman also associates the Jewishness of Jesus with the idea of apocalypticism. He holds, or at least implies, that a non-apocalyptic Jesus is a non-Jewish Jesus. This last point is not an argument so much as an *ad hominem* attack, since it suggests that people who disagree with him are anti-Jewish. To this it must be replied that not every Jewish person in antiquity was apocalyptic. Judaism then, like Judaism now, was represented by lots of different people who believed lots of different things.

There is much respectable scholarship that defends Schweitzer's picture of an apocalyptic Jesus, and no possibility or intention here to review all the material. Even so, the model of the apocalyptic Jesus is not as strong as it once was and, in a general sense, not as convincing. The historical Jesus could have been primarily a wisdom teacher; in fact, almost everyone agrees he was at least also this. The distinction between the two models, wisdom and apocalypticism, brings back into the picture questions that arise from source criticism, redaction criticism, and rhetorical criticism, and re-introduces the idea of a voiceprint. The apocalyptic Jesus model does very poorly when addressing the main thing to be said about Jesus: that he spoke in parable. Since a parable is not a proclamation but a metaphor, it is a very difficult form of language to hold to the one, reductive, interpretation that apocalypticism demands. It is impossible to claim that the end of the world is coming with the ambiguities implied in parables. It is a poor prophet who announces that "maybe" the end of the world is at hand, but maybe not. To say the least, parables make an ambivalent impression—that's their point—and ambivalence is exactly the ingredient of life that exceptional wisdom teachers exploit. Perhaps after two thousand years of the apocalyptic Jesus being in charge of Christianity, it is time to hear the other side. Perhaps it is time to encounter another aspect to his thinking and his life, one that deserves influence in the church.

Those scholars who say that Jesus was mainly a wisdom teacher point out several problems with the traditional apocalyptic arguments. It is not even, for example, a *fait accompli* that John the Baptist was an apocalyptic prophet. To be sure, it seems easier to make the case for John since the surviving statements about him in Christian sources seem explicit. John is the one who says, "You brood of vipers. Who warned you to flee from the wrath to come?" (Luke 3:7). That sounds straightforward enough. But Christianity is not the only tradition that holds a memory of John, and we shouldn't assume that Christianity is the most privileged or authoritative tradition when it comes to John. In the Mandaean tradition, which is the only surviving tradition related to John the Baptist, John is the "Good Man" (*Enosh-Uthra*) who taught the truth, performed miracles, and will return at the end of the age. According to the Mandaean tradition,[11] Jesus was a poor student who got things mixed up and failed to understand John. John, meanwhile, is revered not for announcing apocalyptic revenge but for providing ethical instruction. Neither does Josephus, the ancient Jewish historian, describe John as an apocalyptic prophet. Josephus, interestingly, also calls John a "good man" who encouraged virtue toward others and piety toward God. The John in Josephus sounds closer to the John found in the Mandaean faith than in the Christian faith. But even here, the supposition that John did proclaim mainly an apocalyptic message does not require us to conclude—any more than with Jesus—that John only did this and can only be seen in this way.

With ease, Schweitzer drew a line from an apocalyptic John to an apocalyptic Jesus, but since his justification was founded strictly on the Christian gospels, he saw both figures almost mechanically in the same light. Yet, not all apocalypticism is alike. The Apostle Paul also had an apocalyptic understanding of history. He also believed God would act in his lifetime. But Paul was a universalist in his vision (1 Cor 15:28) —he had to be because he was dedicated to including Gentiles—which is a form of apocalypticism far removed from the book of Revelation and not very near the baptism of John. Meanwhile, what we do see in a book like Revelation is explicit and full-scale violence that is at odds with the basic ethic of charity evident in the teaching of John.

The lack of discussion about different types of apocalypticism is one of several weaknesses in the apocalyptic Jesus argument. Other weaknesses are more striking. Schweitzer notoriously took *verbatim* quotations from the Gospel of Matthew and relayed them as what Jesus really said. He seemed not to care about source criticism, even though he lived and wrote at a time when the priority of Mark had been generally accepted. He drew the sayings concerning the Son of Man from Q (which he did not acknowledge) and Mark, the sources for Matthew. In fact, almost all the Son of Man sayings in Matthew are from Mark and relay the theme of persecution as a prelude to the coming Son of Man.[12] But the persecution theme in Mark comes from the post-70 CE era, when both Christianity and Judaism faced the fall out from the crisis of the First Jewish War (68–72 CE), so it is by no means obvious that the Son of Man material goes straight back to Jesus. It is more likely that Mark, not Jesus, relates the image from Daniel to the resurrection and return of Jesus in light of the persecution Mark and his community faced. Mark used Daniel as a lens to portray Jesus as the one who will return in judgment—presumably to get even with the church's persecutors—but the historical Jesus could not have had any such knowledge of late first-century issues. Some Son of Man sayings in Matthew are from Q, which demonstrates that some of the Son of Man sayings pre-date the Gospel of Mark. But how early do these sayings go? John Kloppenborg has demonstrated compellingly that the Q document needs to be understood as a layered text (see chapter XXX and appendix 1). He has numbered these layers Q1, Q2, and Q3. It is believed that the Q Gospel, as Matthew and Luke would have known it, was created over the course of a generation. It was first a collection of wise sayings and nothing more. This was Q1. Then a redactor put the sayings into shape and added apocalyptic material with "son of man" sayings. This redaction produced a revised version of Q called Q2. Then, a final hand of redaction added instructional sayings (sayings to the disciples) to the document to produce its final edition. The last layer of material is called Q3. The additions of each layer are distinguished for convenience as Q1, Q2, and Q3. The Q Gospel as a whole was available to Matthew and Luke in its final or Q3 redactional form. Kloppenborg does not mean to suggest that Q1 is the earliest material or that it consists of all the things that Jesus really said. What he proposes is that Q2 is the formative layer, the layer of theology, that interprets the Q1 wisdom material related to Jesus. Q3, meanwhile, is the final redaction. The formative layer, Q2, structures the document according to Deuteronomic theology, that is, a theology of blessing and curse. In Deuteronomy,[13] if Israel is faithful to God and follows justice, then God will bless the nation. But if Israel turns from God to pursue other gods or practice exploitation, then the wrath of God is kindled. In this way, the writers of Deuteronomy tried to understand theologically why Israel suffered at the hands of other nations. They explained that Israel suffered due to unfaithfulness to God in spite of warnings God sent through the prophets. Q2 is the main redaction, the organizing principle, in which the theology of blessing and curse shapes the intention of the whole Q Gospel. The Son of Man sayings in Q belong to the Q2 redaction, which compares the days of the Son of Man to the days of Noah, when people cared little about the crisis at hand. Though Jesus could have held features of a Deuteronomic theology, it is not the case that this is the only theology he employed. The aphorisms and parables associated with Jesus suggest that, against Deuteronomy, Jesus can be aligned with Ecclesiastes and Job, which stand in opposition to Deuteronomic theology. In Job, the problem is the unjust suffering of the most righteous person on earth. Such suffering is a mystery that has no link to good or bad actions on earth or to the level of one's faithfulness. The book of Job can be seen as a long parable: however impressive the blessing and curse theology of Deuteronomy may be, Job implies, it is a poor theology of history. This seems to me to be in the spirit of the Q1 saying, "the sun rises on the good and the bad; the rain falls on the just and the unjust" (Luke 6:35). This saying is the book of Job condensed to an aphorism.

These observations raise another problem with the model of the apocalyptic Jesus. Everywhere in the Jesus tradition there is evidence of wisdom as the fundamental memory of Jesus. In the canonical gospels, Jesus teaches mainly in parable. In gnostic gospels, Jesus is almost exclusively a figure of wisdom. And the Apostle Paul is acutely aware of the wisdom tradition that defines his opponents and that he claims to know equally well (1 Cor 2:6). It cannot be said that apocalyptic material holds the same omnipresent characteristic. Rather, apocalypticism is almost the exclusive property of the canonical tradition. Apocalypticism came to be the normative expression of Christianity *in its orthodox form*. Other Christian options that were eventually labeled heretical were originally as prolific as the orthodox tradition and shared with it the wisdom associated with Jesus. It makes more sense historically to conclude that the apocalyptic version of Jesus was developed later in the canonical line of Christianity and was grafted onto the wisdom of Jesus already present. In the earliest layer of the Q document, Jesus is seen as a prophet of wisdom, and this understanding of Jesus is everywhere in both orthodox and non-orthodox histories, but in Q2 the prophet of wisdom is converted to the prophet of warning who is persecuted and killed like all the other prophets before him (including John). Thus Jesus the wisdom teacher becomes also the announcer of the apocalypse and, even more than this, the Son of Man. Apocalypticism, then, is the theology of the early Christian movement but not the teaching of the historical Jesus.

The teaching of the historical Jesus was collected originally in what scholars believe was a *gnomologia* collection.[14] The Greek word *gnomos* is a noun that signifies one who knows. *Logoi* means words. A very flexible word, gnomologia can be used to label collected maxims, rules of thumb, and various instructions of one teacher or several, typically organized by themes. The collection of wise sayings into anthologies, then like now, was a widespread practice in antiquity. In the Jewish Talmud, the tractate *Aboth* (Sayings of the Fathers) is something like gnomologia in that it is an anthology of rabbinic wisdom containing the teachings, maxims, parables, and commentary of eminent rabbis. For example, Rabbi Eliezer teaches, "Repent the day before death." But a student asks him how such is possible since no one knows the day of his or her death. To this Rabbi Eliezer responds, "For that very reason one should make every day a day of repentance."[15] Here, wisdom instruction is offered in a very short story in which a fictional inquiry of a student creates an optimal setting for the impact of the maxim expressed, which is to make repentance a daily practice. In the Q document, gnomologia are the primary material of Q1, which is composed of sayings linked together in clusters either by way of catchwords or perceived themes. These linkages, however, are not just arbitrary.

Rather, the redactor—the students—likely put the sayings together as a rhetorical presentation, i.e., as teaching. Though we
cannot pursue the necessary delineation of what does or does not
constitute gnomologia in a strict sense, the teaching tradition
associated with Jesus presents two types of wisdom instruction
that can generally be called gnomologia. One is parable, and the
other is *chreiai,* which are aphoristic comebacks and one-liners
(as we shall see).

Neither parables nor chreiai are very adept for expressing
apocalyptic theology. Indeed, in the case of parables the gospel writers find them so inept for proclaiming the apocalypse
that they often forcibly turn the parable into an allegory. But
of course a parable is not an allegory, a conclusion that is one
of the seven pillars of modern biblical scholarship (see chapter
2). Unlike an allegory, a parable asks the reader or hearer to
imagine a differently organized world with differently set values.
The aim of the parable is to awaken the hearer in this present
world to an altered experience of reality. We can always enter
the parable world if we choose, but we have to drop our normal
sense of reason to do so. This is very much unlike an allegory.
An allegory is an illustration, and it relies on the normal use of
reason. An allegory simply uses an earthly story to point to the
heavenly world. The Parable of the Sower (Mark 4:3–8) is a case
in point. When the parable is taken as an allegory, as Mark does
in verses 13–20, then the seeds the sower throws stand for the
gospel being spread out in the world. There is no change needed
in our way of thinking about the world: in this allegorical interpretation, the seed is the gospel and the ground is the world.
Some people receive it, and some don't. It's easy. But when the
Parable of the Sower is actually taken as a parable, the picture
is quite different. Who, after all, sows seeds on rocks, pathways,
and thorns? The parable gives us a very strange, clumsy, sower
who, in a hit and miss way, manages some success.[16] As an image

for the kingdom of God, the parable contains nothing about the gospel and the world but, in their place, offers a satirical look at horticulture. The sower is a failure, and his failure is a prelude to an average harvest. It is with sympathy we must regard him, and that may be the point. But of course such humility is too far removed from the Gospel and the Great God, so it is with little wonder that Mark should turn to allegory.

In a short essay entitled "Is the Apocalyptic Jesus History?" Robert Miller makes a convincing case for interpreting Jesus primarily in the light of wisdom. He notes how parables like the Leaven Bread and the Mustard Seed fall flat when read apocalyptically. The Leaven Bread and Mustard Seed parables are growth stories and, if read with an apocalyptic mindset, must be moved into the category of allegory like other stories attributed to Jesus. As allegories they represent how little things one day can become big things. So, the kingdom of God may be unnoticeable now, but when the Son of Man arrives, look out! The kingdom of God will arrive with powerful vengeance. Miller states,

> In this respect the kingdom of God embodies the same values as the kingdom of Rome, which grew from a small town into a worldwide empire. . . . As growth stories go these parables reaffirm that God is on the side of the victor, exactly the lesson Rome wanted to teach its subjects.[17]

If the parables are forced into allegorical form, then the conclusion is that the apocalyptic kingdom of God Jesus proclaimed would arrive like the kingdom of Rome, except that in place of Caesar, his disciples and his religion would rule the day.

These two parables beg for a different interpretation, particularly given that both yeast and a mustard bush are ridiculous symbols of power. The two parables are linked together in Q and appear that way in both Matthew and Luke. Presumably, the compilers of Q saw the two as deliberate rhetorical strategy that the student was to interpret and apply, but both Matthew and Luke are one step further down the redactional line than the early compilers of Q. In relation to these two parables, Matthew is more proactive and attempts to influence or, he may have thought, clarify his audience's understanding. Matthew surrounds the two parables with interpretive material. Prior to the appearance of the parables, Matthew places another parable about wheat and weeds (called the Sabotage of Weeds) where, at harvest time, the weeds are bound together and burned and the wheat is collected into barns (Matt 13:24–30). Then follow the two growth parables. A sentence from Psalm 78 is added to explain that with these parables Jesus speaks of hidden things. Having crossed that bridge, Matthew returns to Sabotage of Weeds and begins an allegorical explanation. The growth of weeds among the wheat is symbolically the present time when good and evil co-exist, but when the Son of Man returns, evil people and their ilk will be thrown into fire like the weeds while righteous folks will shine like the sun. So it is that Matthew surrounds the Mustard Seed and the Leaven Bread parables with a third parable that easily suggests an apocalyptic allegory. The contrast Matthew expresses between the smallness of the mustard seed and the greatness of the mustard plant (if it can be called that) suggests that, for Matthew, these two growth parables should be interpreted as signs of the rising up of God's mighty kingdom. Luke seems less imaginative in comparison to Matthew and simply leaves the two parables alone.

Why is there a difficulty for Matthew and Luke such that Matthew surrounds the two growth parables with a suggestive interpretation while Luke keeps his distance? As wisdom-forms, parables defy normal modes of reasoning. An apocalyptic interpretation is an easier road to take and actually fits into our everyday thinking seamlessly. God, after all, is supposed to be powerful. Who on earth worships an impotent God? Yet, mustard is actually a wild plant that can easily take over a vegetable garden. In contrast to Matthew's allegorical Sabotage of Weeds, and despite Matthew's effort to influence the reading of the Mustard Seed parable as an allegory, the parable on its own remains the inverse of apocalypticism. In place of weeds being burned, the Mustard Seed parable masquerades a scrawny and troubling wild shrub[18] as the image of the kingdom of God. The Mustard Seed parable makes a mockery of a mighty God and a powerful state. It is the dignified Cedars of Lebanon that are supposed to stand for glorious Zion and the favor of God (Ezek 17:22–24), but the mustard plant places the kingdom as a nuisance growing at our feet. The Mustard Seed parable is a satire of apocalypticism, for a shrub spreading out at our feet is hardly a natural location for end-time vision. Similarly the parable of Leaven Bread is no image for God's presence at all, since leaven is unclean and is exactly the thing you get rid of to welcome God at Passover. Here, too, it is impossible to promote an apocalyptic vision with an image that excludes God. Inasmuch as Jesus could have been apocalyptic in some manner or other, it is nevertheless certain he could equally ridicule the whole idea. A major theme in the voiceprint of Jesus surfaces with parables. It is the theme of everydayness, which is bound to fall short on the scale of glory.

Parables are only one way to transmit the voiceprint of a teacher. A second way is to create chreiai. This form of recorded teaching, which is the form evident in Q1, can draw the wrath of various scholars. The problem is that chreiai are likely an invention of Greek Cynicism, perhaps beginning with Metrocles of Maroneia.[19] Some scholars categorically point out that Jesus was thoroughly Jewish, and seem to mean by this that he was not only necessarily ignorant of Greek philosophy and linguistic forms but also necessarily hostile in relation to them.[20] But this ignores another fact about Judaism, which is its rich history of inter-cultural awareness expressed as wisdom. The Torah (the first five books of the Bible), for example, is first instruction, and instruction is fundamentally the definition of wisdom. The Torah demands faithfulness to God, but it does not do so by asking for belief in God. It does so by asking for righteousness before God. To act righteously, regardless of belief, is to observe Torah. It is the case that in Judaism non-Jews who have never heard of the God of Israel or the Torah can still be righteous Gentiles. Since Judaism is emphatically instruction—wisdom—and not necessarily creedal beliefs, Judaism holds an international spirit such that anyone who does what is right in the sight of God can be honored. Cyrus of Persia is a prime example, for in the Bible he is called a messiah, or anointed one, because he liberated the Jewish people from exile. Cyrus respected the Jewish tradition even though he probably had little understanding of the Torah and, as a Gentile, had a different god. Despite these shortcomings, he was God's anointed (Isa 45:1).

It is the international spirit of Judaism that accounts for the ease with which, over the course of its history, the Jewish tradition collected many and varied teaching forms carved out from the crucible of cultures in which it lived and interacted. Teachers of Jewish wisdom have never been shy to adopt techniques characteristic of other nations or employ new philosophical styles in the setting of Jewish life. It has long been known and accepted that the book of Proverbs has many parallels to Assyrian and Egyptian wisdom forms. It compares so favorably to the Egyptian book, *The Instruction of Amenemopet*, that Proverbs was likely directly influenced by if not derived from it. Often in wisdom literature, two types of people are contrasted, and this is true for both *Amenemopet* and Proverbs. In *Amenemopet*, the contrast is between the silent person and the heated person; in Proverbs, it is the wise and the foolish. The flavor of wisdom is universal because its subject is a natural human question, which is how to live a fulfilling life. The answer is often given in practical advice about behavior, observations about the natural world, and various witticisms that provoke reflections. "Associate not with passionate people" is advice from *The Instruction of Amenemopet* (Chapter 10), and the parallel is found in Prov 22:24, "Make no friends with those given to anger." Such advice is humanistic; that is to say, it makes no appeal to divine sanction. In the book of Proverbs, God can be spoken of as just, and people who praise God can be called happy, but such acknowledgement is given in the context of advice about behavior. To be sure, in the Bible God always dances with wisdom, sometimes as an implied presence and sometimes as the source of wise teachings, but God as an object of veneration is not wisdom's aim. The point in wisdom is lifestyle. It is about a lifestyle consistent with a vision of the world. When the historical Jesus speaks of the kingdom of God, he is, ironically, not speaking about God; he speaks about what the world is like, and indeed what life is like, when it is viewed as the reality of God.

The chreia form of instruction exemplifies even more strongly the definition of wisdom as lifestyle. The Q document, in its earliest formation, is essentially a chreia collection. *Chreia* means "useful," which probably identifies its original instructional role. A chreia collection is an assortment of aphorisms, sayings, and short biographical situations relaying the characteristics of a teacher and the teacher's school of thought. In the chreia, an aphorism attributed to a teacher might stand alone as a simple statement. The teacher said this or said that. Sometimes the saying is given with a short biographical setting, such as, "When the teacher saw such and such, he said this," or "When the teacher was asked such-and-such, she said that." The expression of wisdom recorded in chreiai displays the wit and insight the teacher held over against common folk or another, competing school of thought. Chreia collections are a literary form specifically used for the transmission of wisdom. They are a brilliant, short-handed way to recall both what a teacher said and what the school is about, yet such collections are not simply about recording sayings. The point of chreiai is to promote in the student the rhetorical capacity of the school. The student is to learn and then exercise the rhetorical voiceprint of the school in the context of the student's life. Merely recalling what a teacher said falls far short of the goal. One also has to live what the teacher said in the new circumstances of one's own life. The chreiai do not record what a teacher said. They promote the rhetorical voiceprint of the teacher's lifestyle. The student's job is to make that voiceprint come alive. This is how the student becomes like the teacher (Luke 6:40).

A favorite chreia of mine is not drawn from Jesus sayings but from the lore of Diogenes. In the example to follow, note how the chreia is like a very short story where a situation is posed and then the teacher responds. We get, in the anecdote, an example of Diogenes' voiceprint—which is almost always one of sarcasm and double entendre. No doubt a redactor has created a situation in which to place one of Diogenes' famous anecdotes, so the question of the "historical" Diogenes is as difficult as the question of the historical Jesus. Nevertheless, for the student, the chreia serves a twofold function. One is to learn the teaching of Diogenes. The other is to integrate the teaching into one's own lifestyle. So, if I wished to be a good student in the school of Diogenes, I need to take this lesson and make it come alive in my own speech. The chreia goes as follows, "On being asked why people give to beggars but not to philosophers, Diogenes said, 'Because people suppose they might become lame and blind but they never suppose they might take up philosophy.'"[21] The first part of the chreia gives us a setting in which to hear Diogenes. The second part offers the aphorism that re-dresses the situation with irony and causes us to see the picture differently. Diogenes reveals through wit a different way of looking at the world and a different way to imagine what is important or of value. If we are outside the school listening in, we certainly get the point.

Philosophy is the subject of greatest value yet is for most people of least concern. That quick wit is the voiceprint of Diogenes, but it is also the lifestyle of his school.

Another example of chreia comes from the school of Thales:

Being asked what is difficult, he [Thales] replied, "To know oneself." "What is easy?" "To give advice to another." "What is most pleasant?" "Success." "What is the divine?" "That which has neither beginning nor end."[22]

This is part of several supposed questions and responses with Thales.

In this instance, the responses are not ironic; in contrast to Diogenes, the voiceprint is somber and even slightly boring. However, the responses lay out the framework for us to see four points in the wisdom teaching of Thales. Like crib notes, the chreia recalls some key advice: know yourself (a hard practice); do not judge others (for judging is an easy practice); watch out for the deception of success (it may be pleasant but it may not be you); and remember that "real" (or dependable) truth is eternal (divine). Like all chreia, this advice needs to be expanded in the lifestyle of the student. On its own, it only awakens the character of Thales but does not reveal how to be like Thales. That latter task is up to the student.

When it comes to the wisdom associated with the Jesus tradition, chreia proves to be a helpful way in which to understand why the aphorisms of Jesus remained a significant memory of his life and important for the first generations to record. If we can attempt to imagine how wisdom sayings were collected after the death of Jesus, we can suggest that, as with any great teacher, students would have regarded these saying as significant definitions of the school. Certainly, liberties were taken to compose short anecdotal situations in which a saying could be set, and it is always possible that the saying was made up. The saying may be something like what Jesus said, or it may be a student relaying what Jesus probably would have said given this question or that circumstance. Chreia was popular in antiquity not because it was exact but because it was rhetorical.

After the process of collecting the sayings of Jesus was complete, the nascent theological beliefs of the earliest Christian movement came to shape those sayings into apologetic forms. In place of the chreia, where the voiceprint is central, the gospel tradition turns the voiceprint into the confession. The process had already begun in Q2, where the Deuteronomic re-interpretation of the Jesus movement created an apocalyptic emphasis and a theological consistency. This new apologetic can be directly related to the first Christian confession, which is the confession that Jesus rose from the dead. The resurrection belief is the first overlay on the preceding wisdom tradition. Thus, though the first apocalyptic material is early, such as that found in Paul, it is still late in the sense that it is theology, not wisdom. Paul was far more concerned about the role Jesus plays as the Anointed One who includes Gentiles in God's universal plan. So, Paul will say that the earthly Jesus is of no significance (2 Cor 5:16) because the revelation of God begins with the resurrection (Rom 1:4). In the gospels, this results in submerging wisdom under apocalyptic interpretations. Sayings like "how blessed are the poor" (Luke 6:10) become understood to mean that the poor are blessed because in the end-time they will be rewarded by God. Here is the great irony of the historical Jesus. The birth of Christian theology is the silencing of Jesus.

Wisdom is the foundation of the historical Jesus, not as fact but as voiceprint. Unfortunately, wisdom also became his Achilles' heel. What began as a lifestyle became, with remarkable speed, the worshipping of the Lord of the apocalypse. What is necessary is to return to the school of Jesus, where Jesus is not confessed, not called Lord, and not even regarded as divine. To bring a silenced Jesus back to life—wisdom's version of the resurrection—means to initiate students in the lifestyle of the school. It means building a community that addresses and solves the problems of our times on our own terms. It means extending the momentum of the teacher and the contours of his wisdom into the context of today. This is the work of chreiai, not of doctrine. It is a work that needs students to become like the teacher.

Notes

1. Ehrman, *Jesus: Apocalyptic Prophet*, 3.

2. I do not critique Ehrman on this point, for he knows and states this conclusion. However, sometimes his flair for the dramatic hides the point he is making.

3. Zech 8:23.

4. It is important to understand the apocalyptic argument and consider its merits. In addition to Ehrman, readers might wish to pursue the question in the works of Geza Vermes, E. P. Sanders, John P. Meier, Paula Fredriksen, and Dale Allison.

5. Relating Jesus to the messianic (apocalyptic) tradition seems to me to be the theological act the Church committed after the life of Jesus, whereas the wisdom tradition is built on the sayings of Jesus that the Church has retained in its gospels but to which the gospel writers have added theological interpretation. For this reason, I see the wisdom material as prior to and closer to the teaching of the historical Jesus than later theological material expressed in allegories and apocalyptic warnings. Many scholars do not see it this way, but those same scholars seem to me to avoid interpreting the parables and aphorisms of Jesus in light of wisdom.

6. This is the English title given to the German book, *Von Reimarus zu Wrede*.

7. This book is a translation of *Reich Gottes und Christentum*. The English translation is by L. A. Garrard.

8. *The Kingdom of God*, 90.

9. See for example *Jesus of Nazareth*.

10. See *The Apocalyptic Jesus Debate*, esp. 109–44.

11. The word *Mandean* is from the Aramaic word for knowledge, and knowledge in Greek is *gnosis* (Gnostic). The Mandeans are founded on wisdom, with the basic idea being that human life is life separated from the light. It is interesting to note that the Q Gospel relates John (along with Jesus) to wisdom. Both John and Jesus are children of wisdom (Luke 7:35).

12. There are additional "Son of Man" sayings that I won't relay, where scholars agree that the expression simply means "I." For example, "The Son of Man has no place to rest his head" means, "I don't have any place to rest."

13. Deuteronomic history encompasses the books of Deuteronomy through 2 Kings.

14. See John Kloppenborg, *The Formation of Q* (1987) and Alan Kirk, *The Composition of the Sayings Source* (1998).

15. *Aboth*, chap. 1 (Soncino Babylonian Talmud).

16. Scott, *Hear Then the Parable*, 343–62.

17. "Is the Apocalyptic Jesus History?" *The Once and Future Faith*, 113.

18. Scott, *Re-imagine the World*, 35–39.

19. Kloppenborg, *Formation of Q*, 306.

20. Barrie Wilson's book, *How Jesus Became Christian*, impresses me this way.

21. From "Life of Diogenes" in Laertius Diogenes, *Lives of Eminent Philosophers*, chap. VI.

22. Vernon K. Robbins, *Ancient Quotes & Anecdotes*, 160.

5

Life Practices and Schools in Antiquity

Relating the lore and the instruction in various chreia collections to social movements and lifestyles in antiquity is an incredibly significant task. Very often scholars will explore ideas in philosophy or Christian thought without connecting the ideas to the practice of lifestyle. Gathered around great philosophers in antiquity were schools, and schools were all about *askesis* (training). *Askesis,* in turn, was about putting ideas into practice. Simple dialogue formulas and creative epigrams held the contours of a great teacher's personality, but most importantly they defined the manner in which the philosophy was a lifestyle. In antiquity, schools were not buildings but societies. They were social forces that defined the art of presence in the world. "When a woman from the crowd raised her voice and said to him, 'Blessed is the womb that bore you and the breasts that you sucked!' Jesus said, 'Blessed rather are those who listen to what God says and do what God says" (Luke 11:27–28). This incident recorded in the style of a chreia is not an event from the life of Jesus; it is a teaching of his school. The point of the school is not Jesus or his status, not his veneration or even his authority; the point is hearing and doing.

Many Christian scholars, progressive and conservative, assume that despite evidence to the contrary Jesus as the center of Christian faith must remain an object of veneration outside of history. It is as if scholarship must end where faith begins so that Jesus remains the divine power, who breaks into our world from above in a way no human being ever has or can. Even serious Christian scholars, who give Jesus his full humanity for a little while, will, upon completion of their studies, quickly take it back to return Jesus to the status of Christ, the Incarnation, and the Son of God, before whom we encounter and confess our human failings.[1] It seems that a Jesus who is human like anyone is too much of a disappointment. Invariably when occasion gives me the opportunity to speak publicly about the historical Jesus someone will ask why he or she should follow a human Jesus? "If Jesus is not substantially different from the Buddha," an interlocutor once stated to me, "then I should rather follow the Buddha." Yet, isn't this a strange comment to make, for in the end if minus his divinity Jesus counts for nothing, is not the questioner following Jesus for the wrong reasons? And, if this were the case, is it not better to follow the Buddha for the right reasons rather than to follow Jesus for the wrong ones? Is it not best to be attracted to Jesus because he had something to say and not on the chance that he might be divine? At the time of its birth, the emphasis of the Jesus movement fell on hearing and doing the right thing. Believing and confessing the right thing are afterthoughts that came to dominate the history of Christianity.

To look at the historical Jesus in a new way and to take the historical Jesus to church means understanding the ancient Jesus movement with what the French call *élan*, that is, the weight of momentum, a rhetorical trajectory, a school or lifestyle. Early in Christian history Jesus became primarily the one to confess in place of the one to hear.[2] Apocalyptic concerns overrode wisdom teaching within a few decades of his death, and on this rock Jesus became a religion. Returning humanity to Jesus and being in church with the élan of his teaching means to join a school. It means to enter a path of momentum and to enliven one's own life with the qualities and vision of the school's debate. The church as school, Jesus as teacher, and Christianity as lifestyle are all part of taking the historical Jesus to church.

Some Cynical Help

In an attempt to understand the historical Jesus as a movement, we can take some recourse to Burton Mack, who concentrates on the witness of chreiai to the earliest teaching of the Jesus movement. Mack pulls several examples from the Gospel of Mark to demonstrate how easily the sayings of Jesus can take the form of a simple question and instructional answer:[3]

> When asked why they ate with unclean hands, Jesus replied, "It is not what goes into a person but what comes out that makes unclean." (Mark 7:15)

> When asked who was the greatest, Jesus replied, "Whoever wants to be first must be last." (Mark 9:35)

> When asked if the rich could enter the kingdom, Jesus replied, "It is easier for a camel to go through the eye of a needle." (Mark 10:25)

In the Gospel of Mark, these sayings are now presented in the context of a full gospel narrative. But Mack upholds the long-standing conclusion that the sharp, aphoristic responses give a strong indication of an earlier chreia collection. "The Greek penchant for crisp formulation and clever rejoinder is obvious, as is the delight in quick wit and biting humor."[4] Mack concludes, "the chreiai were capable of creating the impression of a teacher's character (*ethos*), the way in which one lived in accord with one's teaching by virtue of one's wisdom and even in the most trying circumstances."[5]

It is possible that the school related to the historical Jesus held characteristics similar to Cynic philosophy, another school and lifestyle in antiquity.[6] It is instructive to note these characteristics even though doing so does not necessitate concluding either that

Jesus was a Cynic or that he deliberately copied a teaching style from Greek Cynicism. We need only imagine the common setting of the ancient imperial culture where exchanges in materials as much as ideas were part of the ordinary economic experience.

Both the Jesus movement and the Cynic movement share an interest in teaching about poverty. The Cynics "valued" poverty with ironic vigor; in their upside-down look at the world, poverty was wealth. An individual was fortunate to be poor. How is it possible to view the world in such an inverted way? Common experience tells us that wealth is wealth and poverty is poverty; there is nothing to admire about poverty or about the suffering that is a consequence of poverty. But the Cynics were not taking an everyday look at the world to see what is true. They were taking an ironic look to see what is false. Wealth is false in the sense that it is a cultural construct: wealth and money create a hierarchical value system where the top people are important and the bottom people are expendable. The value of people is measured with the same standards and language applied to money and commodities. If unaware, we easily get taken in and begin to assume this hierarchical value system is the normal way of the world or even how the world is supposed to be. Soon, money and status become equivalent to gods and blessings in the process of forgetting our common sense of humanity. In the Cynic understanding, the social structures effectively abuse us because they create a daily relationship to money and things that displaces a natural relationship to human beings. So, for example, I don't value the laborer or the creative artist involved in making a commodity. I don't actually care if the wage is fair or if the item, to use a twenty-first century example, comes from a Free Trade Zone. What I care about is the price of the item and the fact that I want it. The relationship I have to the item rests on my desire and on my ability to acquire money. But it also covers up and negates the human beings, human effort, and human suffering that lies behind the item and makes it possible.

To put this in short hand, in common social exchange, money is more important than people. The Cynics could mock wealth and live with little or no money, but claim in doing so that they were really the wealthy ones. They were the truly happy ones. Their values were set differently and they lived, or tried to live, outside the system of false needs and false humanity. There is, of course, an excellent chreia that goes with this very lesson. Once, the philosopher Aristippus, who lived comfortably on the king's favor, passed Diogenes on the roadside and said, "*If you would learn to praise the king you would not have to live on lentils.*" Said Diogenes, "*Learn to live on lentils and you will not have to praise the king.*"[7] The penetrating Cynic gaze through the contrived standards of money and value stands out here: to be poor is to be free of false piety. It is also to be truly involved in basic human struggle. It is a freedom wealthy folk will never know, never understand, and never accept. "How happy are the poor" (Luke 6:20). "How hard it will be for those who have wealth to enter the kingdom of God" (Mark 10:23).

Another characteristic shared between Jesus and the Cynic movement is an appeal to the natural world. Human society is literally a construction on top of nature. Cities in particular, even in the ancient world, mediate the human relationship to nature. In the Roman Empire, cities were significant centers of government that controlled surrounding agrarian lands for the enhancement of commodity trading and the enrichment of upper-class families. Cities were thus centers of administration and aristocracy, and in Roman times many rural people were impoverished when lands surrounding cities were purchased or confiscated and then leased in the context of expansionist programs. Small landholders either became landless or else had to place increasingly heavy taxes on the backs of even poorer stakeholders. This basic shift to large commercial farming enriched elites and impoverished the masses. It is no surprise that among the poor revolutionary sympathies ran high.

The Cynics seemed capable of cutting through social turmoil
with an appeal to basic truths for every human being. Everyone
depends on nature to survive; everyone is a child of nature subject to birth, aging, and death. No one really is any better than
anyone else. No one in reality has a status superior to another.
On the footing of nature, there is basic human equality. A chreia related to the Cynic Diogenes makes exactly this point. On
one occasion Diogenes was pleasantly sunning himself when
Alexander the Great stood before him. Said Alexander the Great,
"Ask me anything you desire," and Diogenes responded, "Stand
out of my light."[8] At the time, there was not a more powerful
person on earth than Alexander, and his offer to Diogenes recalls
the devil's temptation of Jesus with the kingdoms of the world
(Luke 4:5), but Diogenes is not even impressed. He is enthralled
with the joy of nature, and that is something Alexander cannot
possess and cannot give. Alexander can only get in the way of it
with his pomposity. A turn to nature in Cynicism is a turn away
from social constructs that hide the truth of nature behind human designs.

In Cynic philosophy, nature is the great equalizer among human beings. The appeal to nature reveals a third teaching of the
Cynic school, which is the teaching of simplicity. If one sincerely
tries to look at the world with a true or authentic natural attitude, the artificial constructs of social convention become obvious and even comical. It is as if on the ground of simplicity one
acquires an ironic third-person point of view. If the student successfully casts this ironic regard upon the self, then the student
recognizes there really is not a need for the praise of others, the
security of wealth, the customs of privilege, the zones of sacredness, or the powers of aristocracy. As the student, if I listen to
nature—assuming I know how—I can realize that, like all other
animals, I already have everything I need. Water, air, food, and
shelter, in Cynic understanding, are like natural gifts that human
societies misinterpret and reconstruct as possessions according

to the rationale of a humanly created economic system. Thus, Cynic philosophy is a bit like a back-to-nature movement in that the highest virtue is simplicity. To receive the praise of others does not indicate that the lesson of simplicity has been learned. It rather signifies failure because praise comes from the very value system the Cynic rejects. A successful Cynic is a contradiction in terms. "Many praise you," a disciple told Antisthenes, the founder of Cynicism. "Why, what wrong have I done?" Antisthenes answered.[9] To garner the well-prized reputation of an esteemed teacher is to fail to practice the essential lifestyle of the Cynic kingdom.

There are several typical Jesus sayings relayed in chreia form that express the themes of poverty, nature, and simplicity. One of the most striking is the instruction given to disciples sent out on a mission to "take nothing on your journey, no staff, nor bag, nor bread, nor money" (Luke 9:3). The instruction is almost exactly the same, but even more severe, as that normally issued to Cynic followers. Cynics typically took with them a purse, a staff, and no change of clothes.[10] In the purse, they would carry a small variety of articles like a few coins or some bread or even a scroll or codex of collected chreia. Some scholars dismiss this similarity because the instruction of Jesus is, in fact, opposite that of the Cynic: what the Cynic takes on the journey (purse, staff, bread), the students of Jesus are denied.[11] But of course in this critique the point is missed: it's the same articles. Why does the Q Gospel contain this list and not another? Where does the list come from? It comes from the Cynics. Even though one can argue if the Jesus school stresses a greater trust of human charity, familiarity with the Cynic ethic is assumed.

The instructions for travel given to students are certainly consistent with the teaching of simplicity that surfaces in other sayings outside of this striking parallel. Among the sayings of the Jesus school are several pronouncements about anxiety, each of which rests on an appeal to nature such that one should not fret about clothing or food or even death. The sayings do not deny anxiety exists—for otherwise there would be no reason for them—but stress the ways in which anxiety is a false construct that alienates human beings from their natural life.

> . . . Do not worry about your life, what you will eat, or about your body, what you will wear. For life is more than food, and the body more than clothing. Consider the ravens: they neither sow nor reap, they have neither storehouse nor barn, and yet God [nature] feeds them. (Luke 12:22–24)

> Consider the lilies, how they grow: they neither toil nor spin; yet I tell you, even Solomon in all his glory was not clothed like one of these. (Luke 12:27)

> . . . Can any of you by worrying add a single hour to your span of life? (Luke 12:25)

These sayings rely on common observations of the natural world that place an ironic if comical pale on human stress. It is again the economic exchange system that creates the value of clothing and casts as a virtue the need for acquiring wealth. But looking up from the ground level of nature, these constructs appear extreme, if not ridiculous. Anyone who has been a parent, or who has had occasion to play the role of a parent, knows how anxious a young person can be to have an article of clothing or the latest electronic gadget; being without these passing fads somehow makes life utterly unbearable. It is easy to see this in children, but sometimes adults cannot see it in themselves. It sounds like a naïve thing to say, "Consider the lilies." Yet here, too, if we have the ears to hear, if we look at the teaching from the ground up as the Cynics did and as the Jesus school demands, there is nothing innocent going on. At base, it is a call for a re-evaluation of all commoditization. It is an expression, a chreia, that punctures the pretense of the world order and uncovers the lost authenticity of human existence. Anyone who can puncture that pretense will no longer be anxious.

These minor themes in Cynicism could have influenced the Jesus school. In sayings related to poverty, such as "Congratulations, you hungry! (SV Luke 6:21), in sayings related to nature, such as "If God dresses up the grass in the field . . . it is surely more likely (that God cares) for you" (SV Luke 12:28), and in sayings related to simplicity, such as, ". . . What good does it do to acquire the whole world and pay for it with life?" (SV Mark 8:34), much insight is gained when Cynic philosophy throws light on the teaching of Jesus. Nevertheless, it is not necessary to turn to Cynicism to understand Jesus. The Cynic-like view of Jesus can be gained from Ecclesiastes alone. Cynic themes abound in Ecclesiastes. We might even suggest that Ecclesiastes is the *sine qua non* of Jewish Cynic philosophy. I once asked a scholar of Jewish history if it was possible to say there was Cynic philosophy in Judaism. "Of course," was his response, "the Jews invented Cynicism!" When I look at the book of Ecclesiastes, it seems this is indeed true. From the fourth century BCE onward, Judaism lived in the Hellenistic world and was well familiar with Greek literary forms. "Everything is empty," says the writer of Ecclesiastes, and with that basic claim he proceeds to show the misleading nature of human social constructs. The writer of Ecclesiastes knew well how to turn a phrase with an ironic twist, indulge in what we can only call chreia forms, and uphold themes that scholars often wrongly restrict to Greek philosophical schools. Many Jesus sayings are remarkably similar to Ecclesiastes. To say that the "heart of the wise is in the house of mourning" (Eccl 7:4) does not seem a far distance from, "Blessed are those who mourn" (Matt 5:4 // Luke 6:21). Both sayings reverse our common logic and require us, as Friedrich Nietzsche would say, to re-evaluate our values. In a Cynic-like way, the writer of Ecclesiastes conveys the deception of wealth, appeals to nature, and extols simplicity. Wealth leads to self-indulgence, and this, the writer tells us, is a "chasing after the wind" (2:11). The writer also explains in some of the greatest poetry recorded how nature teaches us the timing of things, "for everything there is a season and a time for every matter under heaven" (3:1), such that there is no need to be anxious. In Ecclesiastes the timing of nature is like God's gift to humanity where all human beings, not just the aristocracy, should "eat, and drink, and take pleasure in their toil" (3:13). If the Jesus school can be described as a momentum of wisdom teaching, then it seems plausible that the foundation of that momentum lies in the school of Ecclesiastes. Ecclesiastes is a witness to the brilliance of a movement in ancient Judaism whose nature consisted of paradoxical forms and the trans-evaluation of values. Before attempting to construct the themes of the historical Jesus school, it is worth considering how such movements existed on the ground in ancient Judaism.

Rabbis and Their Schools

The history of Judaism can be divided into seven eras corresponding to seven rabbinical periods, though for the first period the word rabbi was not commonly used (see below). The main concern here is the first century of the Common Era, but for review purposes the seven periods are the Zugot (200 BCE–70 CE), the Tannaim (70–250 CE), the Amoraim (250–500), the Savoraim (500–700), the Gaonim (550–1050), the Rishonim (1050–1550), and the Acharonim (1550 onward). Briefly, these eras are named after the general form of authoritative teaching within the Jewish world at the time. For example, *Tanna* is related to the word *Mishnah* ("repetition") and refers to those sages who first compiled the Mishnah. *Amora* means "one who says" and refers to that era where sages gathered oral tradition related to the Mishnah to form the supplement called the Gemara. The Mishnah plus the Gemara equals the Talmud, and thus the era of this gathering is called Amoraim. The Savoraim era (*savora* means "reasoner"), which is also called the Stammaim era, refers to the closing, or end, of the Babylonian Talmud compilation. The Gaonim (*gaon* means "splendor") refers to the era when two rabbinical colleges in Babylonia were the most authoritative centers in Judaism. Rishonim (*rishon* means "first one") refers to the leading rabbis of the eleventh to sixteenth century. And Acharonim (*acharon* means "last one") refers to the leading rabbis from the sixteenth century to our age.

The word rabbi (master) was not in use, at least not in the technical sense it acquired later, during the lifetime of the historical Jesus. At the time Jesus lived, the system in place was the Zugot system. *Zugot* means "pairs." It refers to the two leaders of the Sanhedrin or High Court (*Beit Din haGadol*) located on the Temple grounds. There was essentially a president of the High Court, called a *Nasi*, and something like a vice-president called the *Av Beit Din*, or Father of the Court. The two leaders presided over the court, which was like a Supreme Court, and met frequently to consider both legal and religious cases. In the Zugot system, the High Priest maintained authority over the Temple functions and ceremonies, but the intricacies of the law demanded an executive High Court composed of leading authorities. Even the High Priest was accountable to the High Court.

Since Jesus was alive in the Zugot era, it means he lived prior to the appearance of the Talmud and before a standard tradition of rabbinical teaching existed. Jesus lived when diversity within a very large empire defined the context of Judaism and when local renditions of the Torah, often only in oral recitation, proliferated. When Jesus was alive, there was no Mishnah and no Gemara. The title *rabbi* was not in use. But there were teachers and there were schools. Two of the greatest and most prominent schools were those of Hillel and Shammai. The two sages lived as contemporaries of Jesus—Hillel probably died when Jesus was a child and Shammai probably died about the same time as Jesus— and both sages formed schools called the House of Hillel and the House of Shammai. While both Hillel and Shammai greatly influenced the development of the Mishnah, in their lifetime they would have had no idea that a document like the Mishnah would one day be compiled. For both Hillel and Shammai, one of their followers would have been called a *talmid* (student) who would eagerly listen to the Hillel or Shammai *targum* (interpretation).[12] Had you lived in that era, how would you have learned of the Hillel targum and participated in the school? Were you to arrive on the scene after his death, you would likely begin by picking up on the chreiai, the collected stories related to him, which conveyed his voiceprint. A certain heathen once asked Hillel, so the Mishnah records, to teach him the Torah while Hillel stood on one foot. Hillel said, "What is hateful to you, do not to your neighbor: that is the whole Torah, while the rest is the commentary thereof; go and learn it."[13] That is a famous chreia related to Hillel. Even though historically it is an incident that probably never happened, it reveals Hillel's character or what Mack would call his *ethos*. That is the point of learning the Hillel targum. It is not just an interpretation of the Torah; the targum is a lifestyle that reflects the living of the Torah according to the wisdom of the sage.

A targum in Jesus' day need not have been anything written; rather, it consisted of oral tradition. The targum had its basis in the recitations of a particular Torah tradition (whether, for example, the Galilean or Judean tradition), but the teaching—that is, the school character—would come through the sage: the idioms, the parables, and the aphorisms. In the case of Jesus, he practically never quotes the Bible. His memory and his school are kept alive in repeated sayings. If John the Baptist was the teacher of Jesus, then John taught Jesus a targum. It would then have been up to Jesus to take the interpretive tradition of John and make it into his own. There is a hint of this in the saying associated with John, "whoever has two coats give to the one who has none" (Luke 3:11), and the saying of Jesus, "when someone asks for your coat, give your undershirt as well" (Matt 5:40). The theme of giving in an act of compassion seems the same, but on closer examination the Jesus saying might actually be a parody of the John saying. Since Jesus lived in a two-garment society, to follow his advice is to render oneself naked. If Walter Wink is right and the action proscribed is a social protest—where nakedness is used to embarrass the oppressor—then Jesus combines humor with deviancy in a form of non-violent resistance, which seems distinct from John.

It is impossible to know what relationship Jesus might have had to the Torah since we do not know how he heard it, what targum he was familiar with, and what chreiai he heard from his teacher. The only access we have to his way of understanding how to live the Torah in daily life is through the parables and aphorisms of his own school. At the time Jesus lived, teachers like Hillel employed parables more deliberately and with greater sophistication than ever before. This might explain why so many parables ended up in the Talmud while there are only a few in the written Torah. A parable would work to express a targum, an interpretive momentum that defined a school. What Jesus understood to be Torah is best given to us in his targum, that is, in his parables and aphorisms. What can these forms of rhetoric reveal to us about the school of Jesus?

Contours of the Jesus School

The authentic core of the Jesus sayings consists of wisdom material found in the Q Gospel, the Gospel of Thomas, the Gospel of Mark, and some teachings uniquely found in Matthew and Luke. The material that is unique to Matthew is creatively called the M-source, and material unique to Luke is with equal imagination called the L-source. We have already noted that the Q Gospel is composed of three strata: Q1, Q2, and Q3. The major redaction of Q occurs at the Q2 level. Parallels between Q1 material and the Gospel of Thomas give the strong impression that there are likewise stages in the development of Thomas and that the earliest layer of Thomas is consistent with the material of Q1. It is mainly in these sources—Thomas, Q1, Mark, L, and M—that the wisdom related to Jesus exists in aphorisms and parables.

In the wisdom material, several of the main building blocks for orthodox Christianity are noticeably absent. Foremost, there are no titles for Jesus, since the material is about the teaching of a school and not the confessing of a teacher. There is no Christ, no Son of God, and no apocalyptic Son of Man. Absent, too, is the crucifixion. Jesus makes no announcement about his impending death, and he says nothing about its meaning.[14] In the wisdom material, no one is saved because Jesus died. As a human being like anyone else, the historical Jesus did not know under what circumstances he would die and never made his death a subject of his teaching. What we have in the wisdom related to Jesus are not his words but a vision, the rhetoric of his targum, passed along by students. To be a follower of the historical Jesus does not require beliefs about him; it requires ears to hear him.

What is found in the parables and aphorisms of Jesus is a biting trinity of satire composed of paradox, hyperbole, and irony. Actually, these three rhetorical forms are only the tip of the iceberg. Robert Funk added several more: admonitions, parodies, global injunctions, proverbs, caricatures, and antithetical couplets.[15] But let us not get carried away. The trinity of satire mentioned above will elucidate many of the wisdom speeches attributed to Jesus and cherished by followers of his school. Typical among paradoxical sayings are the following:

Love your enemies. (Luke 6:27, from Q)

Leave the dead to bury the dead. (Luke 9:60, from Q)

Don't let your left hand know what your right hand is doing. (Matt 6:3, from M)

Since these sayings are part of the lengthy history of Christianity, today they sometimes fail to strike the target at which they originally aimed. For us, a second look and a third ear is required.

"Love your enemies" is a saying that negates its own meaning, for example. We cannot love our enemies. To do so means not to have enemies. This is typical of the voiceprint of Jesus: it has a certain attractive elusiveness, or perhaps an elusive attractiveness, that draws us into its grasp only to deliver an impact greater than first imagined. It seems attractive and innocent to extol love; it sounds like, to the modern ear, something from the sixties. But it is not what it seems. The advice actually requires giving up enemies, not loving them. One is not invited to hold enemies just so that we can have some of them to love. There is no "them" in this lesson. To be in the school means to transcend the natural divisions of social prejudice in order to identify with the other. In the Jesus school you can learn anything from anybody because in the end you, too, are an "anybody" in the world.

Loving one's enemies, and therefore not having enemies, is only one example of the kind of paradoxes—self-negating wisdom—found in the teaching of Jesus. The same style is evident with the saying about leaving the dead to bury the dead. The dead, of course, cannot bury anything, let alone a body. It's impossible to take the saying literally. So the question turns back upon us with a haunting, metaphorical reverberation: how is a living person dead, or in what way might there be the living dead? The great existentialists like Søren Kierkegaard, Friedrich Nietzsche, and Martin Heidegger spoke of the masses. They meant that we all live among innumerable people with a set of common social customs, following what is supposed to be the recipe of life, without awareness of that fact. The philosopher Michel Foucault would rather call the "masses" the bureaucrats: those among us who need to keep the papers in order. The point is that life can paradoxically become the opposite of life. It is possible in life to forget we are alive. While still breathing, it is possible to already be dead. The call of the school of Jesus is a call away from loyalties to repetition and habit. It is a move from what we are supposed to be or supposed to do toward who and how we are honestly. In the case of the historical Jesus, the saying advises a break from family obligations through the difficult admission that built-in expectations alienate one from the liberty of the kingdom of God. What is that liberty? It is not carelessness about obligations; it is resoluteness about choosing one's authentic path.

"Don't let your left hand know what your right hand is doing" is a riddle difficult to understand. It is, in the first place, impossible advice to follow, if it is even advice. Though we have two hands, we only have one brain. It sounds like Jesus is offering a Zen koan, something like, "What's the sound of one hand clapping." Some think the saying means to hide your piety or generosity from public view so as to do good on the one hand but not receive credit on the other.[17] This certainly is Matthew's interpretation (6:2), but Matthew is not very good at humor and seems to prefer fulfilling scripture to upholding paradoxes. My tendency is to take the saying as one that interrupts the normal course of habit. I am not literally able to operate my right hand without any knowledge of my left, but I can imagine how separating the two in effect causes me to do things differently. I have to break the everyday coordination involved in my regular life and be quite deliberate in thinking and doing. I must practically force myself to be present. Of course, that might not be what Jesus means at all. The "left" hand in antiquity does hold the status of being unclean, and there could be something to this. Yet the very fact that the saying is a paradox, for the sense of the words are contradicted by the impossibility of the action, suggests that the meaning is created out of the way the student tries to figure it out. Creating that effort in the student is the essence of teaching wisdom.

Paradox is only one aspect of the Jesus voiceprint. As a satirist, Jesus also mastered hyperbole. Oscar Wilde, one of the greatest coiners of aphorism, once stated that a little sincerity is a dangerous thing, and a great deal of it is absolutely fatal.[16] We get the point. To be honest with others sometimes leads to hurt feelings that in turn create difficulties in common relationships. But Wilde takes things a step further by exaggerating the idea that honesty is the best policy. He offers, through hyperbole, a comical twist that demonstrates we don't really need to, nor should we, seek to tell everyone, everything.

Jesus also plays with hyperbole in ways that drew the hearer into self-examination or more significantly issued critical social commentary. The aphorism concerning a speck of sawdust in your friend's eye when there is a plank of wood in your own is a classic example. Found at Luke 6:41, which is from the Q1 material, the saying attacks the hypocrisy of assumption. It is a long-standing truth that what we criticize most frequently in others is what is true about ourselves. For this very reason Buddhism teaches that people who bother us the most are most likely those from whom we need to learn since, in them, we are recognizing a truth about ourselves. In the Jesus aphorism, the point is made with grossly exaggerated humor. The Greek word used in the saying denotes a tiny flake of wood that no doubt came from the log or plank over which a worker toiled. To not notice the log that needs to be cut or honed for use but only the consequential sawdust from the labor is unbelievable narrow vision. The speck and log contrast is a sharp and unforgettable image of hypocrisy by way of superb hyperbole.

Hyperbole is nowhere better expressed in the Jesus tradition than with the parable of the Dinner Party—another Q1 story found in the Gospel of Luke (14:16–23), Gospel of Matthew (22:1–14), and Gospel of Thomas (64:1–12). As with familiar sayings heard over and over again, sheer repetition also hides the original comedy and social poignancy of parables, so it is work to recapture their sense. In the parable of the Dinner Party, an anonymous householder of some means invites a number of folk from his social class to a banquet. The point of such gatherings in antiquity—and even today—was not only social but also commercial. It was necessary to reinforce one's community standing among class peers and reinforce economic ties. So, this is a gathering of like-minded folks of comparable wealth. The parable assumes the invitations have already been sent out and accepted, and the day of the gathering has arrived. According to custom, the householder sends out his servant to accompany his guests to the dinner. Shockingly, at the very last moment when all the plans are completed, the banquet ready, and the servant is standing at the door, the guests start handing in their excuses. They are all lame excuses packaged in comic exaggeration: the first guest indicates that he just bought a farm even though he has never laid eyes on it; another has bought some oxen without ever having inspected them; the third guest indicates that he had forgotten he was getting married. So there is a great feast prepared, but not a single person is coming to dinner. We can still laugh at the excuses. It is easy to see the humor. What is more difficult in the modern context is to see the depth of insult that has happened here. Since the excuses are so ridiculous, we know that they are not true. What is true is that the household master has been shunned by members of his class. He has effectively been demoted; he is probably on the verge of financial ruin. Yet, remarkably, the householder does not wish a plague on his peers or some other act of vengeance. Instead he discards the norms of his class-based society and begins to invite anyone off the street to pack his house in celebration. What began as economics ends as social defiance. The householder gets even, if you like, by creating an open society. The story seems to be the parabolic version of the saying, "How happy are the poor."

In the Christian gospels, each writer interprets this parable with the motivation of revenge and the biases of special interests. In the Gospel of Thomas, merchants are particularly highlighted as those excluded from the banquet (64:12). Luke holds special interest for the underclass. Thus, the banquet concludes with invitations sent out to the poor, the crippled, the blind, and the lame (14:21–24). Matthew turns the whole parable into an apocalyptic allegory illustrating end-time salvation. The householder is a king, the banquet is a wedding feast for his son, and the rejected invitations are effectively the rejection of the son. Matthew concludes the scene with the casting out of the unworthy (22:11–14). Yet, the traces of the original parable remain evident despite the redactional efforts of the gospel writers. The parable does not ask us to leave this world but to change it: it is a parable about altering, if not eliminating, the privileges and identities of social class. Indeed, the parable corrupts privilege by turning the gathering into a party of nobodies. The revolution reveals a vision, a vision of life with a different texture, and it does so through the creative use of humor transforming social stigma. It is truly a brilliant parable, but it is also the evidence of a rhetorical strategy, a Jesus school.

Irony is the last expressive form I wish to emphasize in the rhetorical strategies of Jesus. Though there are several other classifications that could be explored, such as caricature, which is a type of hyperbole,[18] irony is a central feature. Jesus is a master of irony. He is capable of holding in parable and aphorism images simultaneously empty and full. Irony is precisely that double meaning. Loving your enemies, as we saw, is both paradoxical and ironic. It has "fullness" in the sense that it demands a genuine act of love to go outside the comfortable borders of family and friends. To try to understand my enemy is to accept that the force of love demands both my personal growth and the annihilation of my prejudices. That is the fullness of the lesson. Yet, ironically, in carrying out the lesson, the emptiness is concurrent. If I really love my enemy, than my enemy is no longer my enemy. Ironically, you can't love your enemies if you love your enemies.

There are many sayings associated with Jesus that hold such double entendre. "To save your life is to lose it" is another example. No one can reach greatness in life without the realization that greatness is not the point. Even though it is easy to criticize

the wealthy and most powerful among us for their arrogance
and presumption of importance, successful people will say that
pleasure is not in success but in its pursuit. The goal is achieved
by letting it go to focus on one's true happiness.[19] Jesus was not
a CEO, and his aphorism is not about modern business practices.
Still, a parallel remains. Only those who understand life beyond
the desires of the ego have life. Since in the end all life is composed of relationships, fullness of identity comes with the fullness
of relationships, and the latter is only possible when concern for
identity is let go. Ironically, only the empty are full.

Another gripping example of irony comes in the parable of the
Prodigal Son. Usually this parable is interpreted as an illustration
of God's forgiveness, and the story certainly holds that force.
The profligate life of the younger son stands for the temptations of the world, the father stands for a forgiving God, and the
banquet stands for heaven. This is the allegorical interpretation
of the parable, but we now know a parable is not an allegory. A
second look is in order.

A son asks his father for his inheritance. He is a younger son,
so his inheritance is a smaller portion, but he has asked for it
while his father is still alive. In effect, he has told his father to
be as good as dead to him and to let him leave the household.
The father should be angry and probably deny the inheritance,
if not write the son out of the will; remarkably, the younger son
gets his money. The son is Jewish and spends his inheritance
among gentiles, pursuing all the attractions of the Greek life:
we can imagine theatres, banquets, athletics, and brothels. Of
course, he ends up with nothing and in need of a job. There is
a play going on with the job he gets since, as Jewish, one cannot get much lower on the scale than working for a gentile,
feeding pigs. The son decides to quit and head home on the
chance that he would be better off working for his father. On
arrival home, the miraculous seems to happen. His father runs
to greet him, which already is strange behavior for the dignified

patriarchal dad. Then, everything that follows suggests that this lucky young man is going to get the full inheritance of the farm. A meal is prepared for him. His father gives him the patriarchal ring. He is seated at the head of the table. He is given the patriarchal robe. It looks like the father is not only welcoming back his younger son but is also handing everything over to him. As the reader or listener, we are almost forced to ask, what about the older son? To say the least, the older son is less than pleased. He respectfully sends a servant into the feast to question the father. The older son wants to know what is going on. Has he in fact lost his inheritance, not to say his authority by right of birth, to this negligent younger son? The father comes out to the older brother to deliver the answer in person. It is noteworthy that the father changes the language of relationship. This is not about, as the older brother had said, "this son of yours." Rather it is about, as the father says, this "brother of yours." That line sets us up for what follows. The father repeats, "Everything I have is yours." The younger son arrived home with nothing and is given a great banquet, but he still has nothing. The older brother has the full inheritance, while the younger brother is inside celebrating nothing. After the party ends, the younger brother will work for his older brother. The older brother has to choose between entering the party and celebrating the homecoming or waiting to get even when he assumes the position of household master. The parable leaves us standing outside with the older brother and wondering what he will do. It is hard to avoid, while standing there, the irony of this situation: the loser is celebrated and the winner feels jealous. The one with all the power is insecure and cannot let it go to enjoy the moment. The one with nothing is having the time of his life. The first one is last, and the last one is first. How happy are the poor. The empty jar is full because it is empty (Thom 97:1–4).

A cursory view of the wisdom associated with Jesus through the themes of paradox, hyperbole, and irony serve notice that this style of wisdom is neither a common nor religious one. Jesus seems committed to the everyday. His stories and aphorisms, as we can see, are related to such mundane things as a dinner party or sibling rivalry. Yet despite the common images, he does not offer common advice. His is not conventional.[20] He does not advise the ancient equivalent of a penny saved is a penny earned. The voiceprint of Jesus is the trajectory of a satirical wisdom honed and matured in paradox, hyperbole, and irony. But to what end? The end for Jesus is not the climax of God's great plan for the universe; rather, it is the descriptive contours of the world he calls the kingdom of God. It's not a place but a way of being. It is his targum. It is his school.

How does one live by the precepts of this school?

Notes

1. N. T. Wright is an example of good scholarship that constantly returns itself to confessional Christianity in spite of contrary historical evidence.

2. As has been often pointed out, the Nicene Creed tells us what to believe about Jesus but says nothing about what Jesus taught. We confess, ". . . born of the virgin Mary," but we don't say, ". . . taught us to love our enemies."

3. To refer to this style of rhetoric I have been using the word *chreia,* which was first employed in nineteenth-century biblical studies (Martin Debelius); Rudolf Bultmann spoke of "pronouncement stories" to identify these short incidences that ended with a wisdom saying. The study of the Q Gospel has brought the word chreia back into contemporary discussion. See chapter 4.

4. Burton Mack, *Who Wrote the New Testament?*, 54.

5. Mack, 54–55.

6. There were, generally speaking, six schools/lifestyles in ancient Greece following the time of Socrates: the Platonists, the Aristotelians, the Stoics, the Cynics, the Epicureans, and the Skeptics. There were also earlier schools like the Milesians and Pythagoreans, and later schools like the Neo-Platonists.

7. This popular anecdote is found in many sources. Though I have cited it from memory, I first heard it in a sermon in my youth and then later read it in Anthony de Mello's *Song of the Bird*.

8. *Ancient Quotes and Anecdotes*, saying 902b.

9. Mack, 55. For more sayings and anecdotes of the Cynics, see Diogenes Laertius, *Lives of the Philosophers.*

10. M. W. Meyer, *From Quest to Q,* 146.

11. Craig A. Evans, *Fabricating Jesus,* 105.

12. Bruce Chilton, *Rabbi Jesus,* 2–3, 41–43.

13. Seder Mo'ed, Shabbat, 31a: 12–13.

14. For commentary about the Q Gospel and the death of Jesus, see Bernard Brandon Scott, *The Trouble with Resurrection* (Polebridge Press, 2010).

15. See the appendix in *Honest to Jesus.* Note also chapter 8, "The Search for the Rhetorical Jesus" (San Francisco: HarperSanFrancisco, 1996).

16. Oscar Wilde, *The Critic as Artist,* 125.

17. Geza Vermes, for example, follows this typical Matthean interpretation. *The Authentic Gospel of Jesus* (2009), 420.

18. The Good Samaritan parable, for example, relies on the caricatures of Priests and Acolytes as those who avoid compassion in the name of religion. Then along comes the Samaritan, who is the enemy of ancient Israelites, who belies the prejudices set against him in portraying deep loving kindness and faithful observance of the Torah.

19. For example, Steve Jobs, CEO of Apple, Inc., reportedly said, "I think we're having fun. I think our customers really like our products. And we're always trying to do better." The aim for Jobs was less important than the environment and the process.

20. See *Honest to Jesus,* 159.

6

Life Philosophy in the World of Parable

I n the course of daily life, if we discover that a conclusion is
wrong, then it is necessary to change the premise on which the
conclusion is based. If I was to enter a room with the idea that
everyone there speaks English and then embarrassingly discover
that no one can understand me, obviously my assumption was
wrong. Sometimes in life our assumptions (premises) have to
change and our reasoning has to start over again. The assumptions that we live by can be called our "default" reasoning or our
default reality. These are ideas that are difficult to question and
to change because they seem normal and right. Prior to the classical Greek era (approximately 500 BCE), many cultures accepted
the idea that the earth was flat and that it floated on the great
waters held within a spherical dish. This image was "default reality" when it came to interpreting the world. It is a picture that
we can read in the Genesis creation narrative (Gen 1:6–9). This
default reality, which was a premise held in many traditions internationally, has long since become untenable as reliable knowledge. It is, in other words, an ancient assumption that proved,
even as early as classical Greece, to lead to false conclusions.

In the history of Christianity, and indeed of religion generally, the usual recourse to changing the default reality is blocked.
To question the premise is to attract accusations of heresy or,
at best, infidelity, especially when a religion, like Christianity,

starts with the belief in a revelation from God—and, thus, other-worldly truth—as its point of origin. Default reality, when it is assumed to be a revelation from God, is assumed to be perfect and outside the realm of questioning. In Christianity, this default reality includes the authority of the Bible, the perfect union of God and humanity in Jesus Christ, and the authority of the Church in its doctrinal confessions and ecclesiastical offices. In Christianity, it is often the case, if you end up having trouble with the default reality—with, that is, the unquestionable premises—rather than Christian beliefs being at fault, the problem is assumed to be you.

When I was about sixteen or seventeen years old, I discovered these unquestionable Christian premises, or default Christian reality, in dramatic fashion. Even though my family roots are in a liberal tradition of Christianity, as a youth I explored what is commonly called evangelical and fundamentalist Christianity. My searching led me to a Bible camp and into the audience of a resounding and convincing camp leader. Somehow, despite myself, I could never fully accept the authority of the leader or the study material I was offered. I raised the question about evolution as science and creation as myth only to discover that one was not permitted to use the "m" word ("myth") when speaking of the Bible. The Bible, the leader promulgated, says that God created the world. That was default reality. Human beings might think that evolution makes more sense, but human beings are sinners and sin—among other things—is deception. So it was impressed upon me that I had a problem, which turned out to be sin, that needed to be expunged from my heart and mind. Being stubborn as I am, I further pointed out that there are two creation narratives in the Bible. One is Gen 1:1–2:4a, the six days of creation, and the other is Gen 2:4b–2:25. I asked which one was right. Of course in my youth I was being somewhat arrogant, but much to my chagrin, no longer to my surprise, I discovered for a second time that the problem lay not in the Bible but in myself. The Bible is the Word of God; that was the premise of the argument set against me. So, the Bible cannot be wrong. The fault lay in my interpretation. In short, I was the problem, and every effort was made to alter my perception by way of conversion.

The point of my story is that when Christianity starts with the belief that the Bible (or Jesus or God) cannot be wrong, then the Bible (and Jesus and God) become separated from honest human thinking because they occupy a default position that cannot be questioned. It is impossible to reach good conclusions if a premise is unquestionable. Under these circumstances the questioner is converted into the problem and can be made to feel isolation or guilt. Under these circumstances the remaining choice becomes a tragic one: either to feel shame for raising questions or take leave of a community that does not permit questions.

There is a better way to deal with the history of Christianity than to create an impasse based on certain unquestionable premises, and that way is to change the premises. The historical Jesus is an entirely different premise from Jesus Christ. He was not God incarnate, not revelation, and not a savior. Human like us, he was just an exceptional wisdom teacher. Re-capturing the historical Jesus creates a certain liberty for Christianity and brings in some fresh air. Admitting that Jesus was human like anyone means he could be wrong. That is what makes the historical Jesus attractive: not the holiness but the realism. It is the very humanity we share with Jesus that makes it possible to imagine, without guilt or shame, ways of extending his ancient wisdom teaching into our time and our form of default reality. In his context, Jesus traded in the market of wisdom with the images of his world to created a vision for his times; the challenge of following the historical Jesus is the challenge of grasping hold of that momentum and extending it into our time.

Unfortunately, it seems that in its history Christianity has not been tolerant of those who delve into the realm of wisdom for fear of what they might come up with. The wisdom path, after all, can lead to such things as the Gospel of Thomas, which is a non-canonical gospel, and therefore a non-default gospel, rooted in the wisdom tradition. Wisdom can also lead to mysticism, where the intention is to unify the soul with the divine (indeed, even to understand the human soul as divine). Neither is this "default" in Christianity. Meister Eckhart (1260–1327 CE) might be the most famous non-default Christian mystic who sought spiritual unification with God. Nevertheless, the historical Jesus does not necessarily inspire specific forms of mysticism or claim specific authority for certain gospels. Rather, since the very task of hearing the historical Jesus demands historical research, the historical Jesus invokes, above all, honesty about our knowledge, more so than any specific way to participate in the momentum of his wisdom. It is not a question of finding the truth. It is a question of extending ancient metaphors of life into the default realities of our time to challenge the premises of our thinking.

Jesus was a first-century Galilean Jew; his life, context, and voice belong to that era. There is no point or profit in asking what Jesus would do were he alive today. A response is not only impossible to offer, because Jesus is not alive today, but the question is also silly. If Jesus were alive today, like back then, he would do the same thing everyone else does. Like all of us, what he might do in the midst of any particular circumstance would depend entirely on where he was born, what he learned, what economic status he held, what religious tradition, if any, he inherited, and what he might judge important or insignificant at a given moment. The question that is raised in relation to the historical Jesus does not concern what he might have done; the question is, who shall the student of the historical Jesus become? To follow the historical Jesus consists not of the task of becoming like him or doing what he might have done but rather the task of genuinely becoming who *we* are and doing what *we* do. The point, like with students in antiquity, is not to be a student forever, though we must start here, but to be someone who is the presence of wisdom in our own way.

Giving Jesus a demotion from God incarnate to regular person is, to be sure, a long journey down, but down here as a human being we can see him appropriately, not desperately. A desperate relationship to Jesus is one that wants from him the fulfillment of *eros*. Let me carefully state what I mean. Eros was—among other things—the Greek god of sexual love, but this is not the only aspect of *eros* and probably not this god's primordial function. *Eros* is also love for the missing self (for *psyche*). It is love for that part of us that is achieved in union with another. Beyond sexual attraction, *eros* is the desire for the elusive other, even out of simple curiosity, which drives the search for wholeness of the self. To love Jesus out of *eros* is to love him out of the desire for self-completion, but such a love is desperate. It is to want from another human being what cannot be given: a final answer in the trouble of life. The Jesus of *eros* is the Jesus of the final victory, the Christ who hides from us the identity markers of our genuine human experience: our ignorance, our prejudices, and our responsibility for ourselves. It is possible to be serious about Jesus and seek the path of wisdom that he inspired without being desperate about Jesus and demand from him our own salvation. It is possible to stand in the momentum of Jesus, troubled but hopeful, not in search of final answers but in the spirit of awakened wisdom. That wisdom, to my mind, can be expressed in five gospels of the historical Jesus.

The Five Gospels of Jesus

The Gospel of the Anonymous Self

Is there any woman with ten silver coins, who if she loses one, wouldn't light a lamp and sweep the house and search carefully until she finds it? When she finds it, she invites her friends and neighbors over and says, "Celebrate with me, because if have found the silver coin I had lost."

—Luke 15:8–10, from Q

Whoever clutches and grabs after life will lose it.

—Luke 17:33, from Q

When Robert Funk spoke about the default world, he spoke not of unquestionable Christian premises, as I did above, but of our common world experiences in contrast to the parable world of Jesus. Funk demonstrated his point by appealing to the normal course of everyday life. Usually we operate in the default world almost unconsciously, according to what he labeled *procedure knowledge.*

> The knowledge most of us have and use daily consists of formulas for performing routine tasks. We know where to go to buy a loaf of bread; we know how to do our job at our place of employment; we can start the car and drive to Aunt Nan's; we know a doctor to consult when we get sick; we routinely prepare and eat meals; we can go to bed without the advice of experts. Knowing how to do all these things and countless other tasks like them is called *recipe* or *procedure knowledge.*[1]

The default world is the world of procedure knowledge. It is composed of what we commonly accept, see, and operate in as the world at hand. We can easily add to Funk's list above. Every weekday morning, my family gets up, has breakfast together, and we all go our various ways to work or to school. If we wished, we could go through the routine without a spoken word. It is a classic case of procedure knowledge; millions of families around the world can do the same thing. But procedure knowledge involves more than just customary routines. It also identifies how individuals within a society expect the world to work. Procedure knowledge includes the broad assumptions of social life, the unquestioned premises, that form our political outlook as much as our daily activities. We may be conservative or liberal, we may believe primarily in the rights of individuals or place more stress on collective rights in a just society, but these differences reflect variations in political persuasion, not political worldview. Living in the West, virtually all of us expect the world to turn according to the consumerist economy in which we live. I expect, for example, there to be rich and poor;[2] I expect and depend upon a functioning infrastructure composed of roads, motor vehicles, sanitation systems, public buildings, various private and public services; I expect the right to vote when there is an election; I do not expect politicians or lawyers to be honest, I might joke, but in fact I do expect them to uphold the integrity of our system of government and law. Procedure knowledge is not just about knowing how to perform routine tasks; it is also about expectations related to the normal experience of the society in which one lives. If someone were to call me liberal or conservative, the sense of that judgment can only rest on the foundation of a default social system in which both my interlocutor and I live.

Procedure knowledge is the assumed knowledge used daily in the default world, the world at hand. The parable world, however, is the world in contrast to the default world, and the knowledge needed to understand a parable is counter-intuitive to procedure knowledge. Franz Kafka, one of the great twentieth-century existentialist authors, was a master of parable, and the figures in his parables constantly employed procedure knowledge only to be stung by the counter-intuitive situations in a parable. Indeed, Kafka's novel *The Castle* can be looked at as an extended parable. On the surface, this is a novel that is an endless story of a protagonist's sorry attempts to gain access to distant and hidden bureaucrats in an effort to clarify his work order. The main character, simply called K., is a land surveyor and a quintessential figure of procedure knowledge. K. is caught in a world that he simply cannot measure according to the standards his training assumes. He arrives in town with the intention of taking up his employment, for which he eminently qualified, and he needs to see the Count at the castle. With his hardened procedure knowledge in head and hand, he assumes he knows exactly what he needs to do and where he needs to go (he even thinks he can see the castle) without ever recognizing that the world he has entered works according to a different set of norms. His land-surveying mind will find no home here. Instead K. is forever lost in an odyssey of failures to meet with the Count in the castle. If we have sympathy for K. and his endless journey, Kafka's novel is most frustrating to read (and it has no definitive ending, for Kafka never finished it); but if we understand the novel is not set in the procedural world of making an appointment and attending a meeting but rather is set in a parable world, it is joyful reading. The reader who understands the novel as parable knows that there is no literal castle. Rather, K. has always been in the castle, before the novel ever began and ever finished.

When reading a parable, we must necessarily free ourselves of procedure knowledge, but the most difficult part of this insight involves recognizing that procedure knowledge includes the habitual way we think about the self. To enter the parable world, I must overcome assumptions I hold about myself—assumptions such as my self-importance, my fixed identity, and my preoccupations with self-satisfaction. The act of getting into the parable world begins with seeing my self as a social construct. The self is my identity. It is constructed from my status in society: the amount of money I have, the class I belong to, the influence my status gives to my decisions, the reasons people know or want to know me (or avoid me), the level of self-esteem gained in relation to my colleagues, and many other factors constructed out of relationships to others or within social systems that become vital to the self because they signify to the self the importance (place, position, power) of the self. In the world of procedure knowledge, the self can win or lose, can hold status or shame, can achieve the goal or miss the mark, can be recognized or ignored, can be satisfied or disappointed. The default world consists of the interactivity of the desires and the social positions of human selves. Yet, in the parable world, there is no self. Or, another way to imagine it, in relation to itself the self in parable is an anonymous self, a self without a name. The self in parable is not self-important or self-centered; it is not a self in need of a system of meaning to signify importance to itself. The no-name self of the parable, the self that is anonymous to itself, is one that accepts itself merely and miraculously as a location of awareness, as a "happenstance" as Don Cupitt says, born out of the history of coincidental human relationships on our planet. The anonymous self sees the fabrication of relationships that create default reality and can pierce through the fabric with a liberty of consciousness that accepts the self as a host of the coincidental history of relationships that have produced this one location of awareness. The anonymous self is a self that accepts itself anonymously as a location of awareness.

Clutching and grabbing, so essential to winning in the default world, are a loss in the parable world of the anonymous self. In the parable world, I celebrate winning by losing, gaining by letting go. In the default world, winning and losing create or harm my self-esteem, but in the parable world winning and losing are exactly what need to be pierced in order to be free. In the parable world, there is no such thing as the power of God or the blessing of God or the favor of God for a worldly, historical figure. These things in the parable are seen as the way the default world hides its emptiness from itself. They are the lights and the sounds of importance that, in parable, distract from the joyfulness of authentic life. Indeed, in parable, ironically, the sounds of importance are the least important thing. When the values of success in the default world become that for which I clutch and grab, the "I" of myself has lost the parable's gift of anonymity; default reality has become who I am and how I think. In the world I may have won, but in parable I have lost.

To be in the "counter-intuitive" world of the parable is to be an "anonymous self," a self who is not the consequent result of clutching and grabbing after life. In parable, everything in the world that is and that can be is already part of the whole world story. Everything that is in the world is already the consequence of the total relationship of things that compose the world. Nothing exists in isolation; nothing is self-created; everything in this sense is anonymous, that is, without singular identity or without an absolute name. Like in a Kafka novel or a Jesus parable, the quest to find a stable identity is not the point. One's name or occupation is no privilege. Of course, we need names and identities in order to build societies and to advance learning, but in parable the emptiness of these default necessities is exposed in the larger vision of anonymity. Every "thing" in parable breaks across the line of singular identity to the other side of anonymity, where it can play host to a world liberated from the *status quo*. A vineyard worker who strains all day crosses over to anonymity when his co-worker who strains less than an hour is paid the same wage. The older brother of the prodigal son crosses over to anonymity when he cares less about his inheritance and joins the celebration of his younger brother's return. In parable, the promise is that the world can be differently arranged and differently reasoned because its current default form is only one set of possibilities within an infinite set of possibilities. Parable is liberation for the possible.

A woman searches in her hut for a lost coin. She is diligent and finds it. Her wealth is restored, and in the default world the story is over. But she is an anonymous self; she is not in it for gain. She spends the lost coin she has found, and several others, to celebrate the act of finding. The divine reality is not present in the world because she is successful. It is not there because she has money. In place, she uses her presence in the world to awaken joy: the divine reality was already there, but she celebrates its awakening. The default person will say, "You silly woman! It was a great party, but you were only down one coin and now you are down four!" But the woman will respond, "You silly man! You were at a party but never experienced it."

The default self is driven by the ego, by the procedures of calculation that compile the statistics of personal loss and gain. For the default self, status is important because it defines one's place and meaning in the world. It is not so for the anonymous self. The anonymous self lives without the strain of meaning—that is, without attachment to meaning. The anonymous self accepts its self as one manifestation of human awareness in a strange and mysterious universe. The anonymous self knows that in the end the question is the trust of the universe and the acceptance of one's presence in the world as gift. There is no insult for the anonymous self and no threat. There is no need for the apocalyptic. There is, rather, the astonishment of mystery, which is everywhere to be seen, and which is with or without the self. The anonymous self holds the liberty of meaninglessness, which is the art of losing in the winning of parable.

The Gospel of Equilibrium

You won't be able to observe the coming of God's imperial rule. People are not going to be able to say, "Look, here it is!" or "Over there!" On the contrary, God's imperial rule is right there in your presence.

—Luke 17:20–21, from Q

The Father's imperial rule is spread out on the earth, and people do not see it.

—Thomas 113, from the Q-Thomas common tradition

In the anonymous world of the parable, everything is equal. Every moment in life is as valuable as every other: that is the equilibrium of life. To view all things on par—to understand that every event is of equal importance or, if you like, of no importance—is possible only when one stands before all things anonymously. The anonymous self is the person who is the host of the divine party, who accepts the self as the product of evolutionary wonder, and whose perspective understands the self as both an occasion and location of awareness in the midst of endless relations. With the attitude of equilibrium, the world and what happens to me in it is not taken personally; life can be sad, tragic, and unjust. All of that is true. Sometimes terrible things happen to us, which leave an indelible mark on our personalities and form our outlook. Still, such things were not part of God's plan; they did not happen to us particularly at the exclusion of all others; they are not the hidden will of the universe, and not something after which there is no tomorrow. Whatever happens to us—even the most tragic events to be faced, challenged, and overcome—does not negate the basic fact that life starts first as a gift. Behind every event is the miraculous presupposition that life is possible at all. This perspective is the perspective of equilibrium; it is the quiet recognition that the world is fully capable of functioning without us.

In existential philosophy, this recognition of equilibrium marks the tragedy of human life because life is bound to time and as such only to momentary significance. In the parable world, however, the recognition is joyful. The moments of life can be given to the world without attachment to ultimate significance or apocalyptic frenzy. Life is free, and this radical liberty is the heart of equilibrium.

To put this insight in the language of the historical Jesus, one can say that, in the parable world, the reality of God is equally everywhere even though, in the default world, we do not see it. To see the reality of God everywhere is to move from default notions of religion with its sectioned-off times for worship, its privileged customs, and its sacred spaces, to the ground of equilibrium where all places and times hold abundant life. The reality of God does not belong to any one religion, not even to avid atheists or fundamentalist theists, but rather is what the world is. God as mystery and as life is not one place in preference to another, not one national will set against another, and not one social history privileged over another. God does not have a flag. God does not have a religion. God does not have a God. In the end, by God we simply mean life.

Equilibrium consists of admitting that I am merely among and with all things in the world for the moments that I am. While I am alive, things in the world compose my setting in life, my time, and my circumstances, but nothing is here especially for me or because of me or set against me. People and circumstances are with me because, collectively, we compose and share the moment of being present. If I can manage this understanding, then I can participate in equilibrium. The meaning of winning and losing passes away, for now the rules of the game have changed. I know now that winning is the same as losing. Losing holds unexpected victories, and winning unexpected losses. In equilibrium, losses and victories are emptied of meaning. Equilibrium is the peace that passes understanding.

My experience in the Christian church has well acquainted me with how unacceptable the conclusion of equilibrium is to most Christian leaders. It is difficult to imagine worship without sacred space, and even worse is the trouble of addressing social or political issues without relying on "God's will" and "God's plan." Then, for many, it is unacceptable that Jesus could ever have proposed that God and reality are basically the same thing. What are Christianity and the Church without special locations, special histories, and a scheduled end-time? In response to such criticism, remember that equilibrium is not a doctrine, which perhaps is a point difficult to make in a religion like Christianity. It is rather a way of being present in the world. It is the parabolic presence that can be lived in the default world. In response to the critic, equilibrium as lifestyle actually addresses more effectively than Christianity as beliefs the social issues of the world, for the world only changes through the energies of those who hold vision, and equilibrium is the liberty of vision.

Equilibrium belongs to the momentum of the historical Jesus school, which teaches that the reality of God is spread out on the earth. "Reality" can never be something that comes at some point in the future; it is always the already here. And as that which is everywhere across the earth, it belongs to no one because it is not a thing. It is life. To the critic who charges that no social system can be built without principles, the parabolic response is that equilibrium does not exclude compassion but systems and principles do. Equilibrium is essential to justice because it can have no owner. As the Tao of Lao Tzu says that "superior human beings take action but have no ulterior motive in doing so,"[3] so on the basis of equilibrium the school of the historical Jesus takes action without attachment to the contrived prejudices of the default world.

The Gospel of Comedy

Is there any one of you who owns a hundred sheep and has one stray off, who wouldn't leave the ninety-nine in the wilderness, and go after the one that got lost until he finds it? And when he finds it, he lifts it up on his shoulders, happy. Once he gets home, he invites his friends and his neighbors over, and says to them, "Celebrate with me, because I have found my lost sheep."
—Luke 15:4–6, from Q

It is not what goes into a person from the outside that can defile; rather it's what comes out of the person that defiles.
—Mark 7:15; cf. Thom 14:5

The practice of the anonymous self rests on the liberty of vision that comes with equilibrium, but these two modes of being only arise with departures from the default world. These departures are often momentary. Often, they are experiences of enlightenment that defy description and lack permanency. We live, after all, in the default world. It is where we have life; it is our condition of being. We may take our leave and enter the parable world, but eventually there are dishes to be done. As the Zen saying goes, "after enlightenment, the laundry." What path can be taken to experience, in the default setting, the flash of parabolic liberty? In the school of Jesus, invariably comedy forms the signpost of the parabolic doorway. Comedy does not mean laughter, though it can include this, so much as disarming wit. The purpose of comedy is to disarm the student of the normal habits of reason and expectation in the default world and to create the novel atmosphere of the parable. When comedy reveals the contrived nature of social life, with all its various relationships of status and importance, then the parabolic life has a chance to surface.

One sheep among a hundred goes astray, and the shepherd takes off to find that one sheep. It is already a strange scene, for why leave unguarded a flock of ninety-nine sheep to the wiles of the world for the chance of finding one stray? The odds are more than favorable that something will happen to the ninety-nine. They will scatter, or a wolf will come upon the open flock. Or, most likely, both scenarios will occur. A wolf will come upon the open flock and the flock will scatter. To some degree, we must ask if this shepherd is crazy. Some commentators suggest the parable is really about Israel and God.[4] After all, the "Lord is my shepherd" in Psalm 23, and in Ezekiel 34 God says, "I will search for my sheep" (verse 11), but Israel as God's sheep are a group, like the ninety-nine, and not a single (stupid) sheep. The writers of the Christian Bible apparently noticed this, so for Matthew the story is about early Christian leaders caring for one of the "little ones" (plural) whom Jesus has left them (18:10), and in Luke this is a story about a lost sinner (all such) whose repentance returns her or him to the fold of God. Despite the questionable strategy of leaving a flock to its own devices, the shepherd takes off in search of the stray. In the default world of religion, this makes some sense. Religion is supposed to be about finding lost souls. And God is supposed to be happy at this occurrence. However, we must remind ourselves that this is a parable. The last thing we should expect is the confirmation of default religion in a default world.

In the parable we never do find out whether or not the flock of sheep left on its own stays together or is lost. It is as if our thoughts are momentarily sidetracked by this concern, and then suddenly the parable springs its trap. The stray is found and now it's all about a party. The flock suddenly doesn't matter, and neither does the found stray. Our attention is shifted to the celebration. So, if you are a shepherd and you decide to throw

a party, what shall you serve? Given the economic status of a
shepherd in first-century Israel, you will absolutely have mutton
served for dinner. The parable never lets us know what happened
to the flock, but it does let us know that a banquet, not a sheep,
was found.

This is the comedy of the historical Jesus. It is disarming. It is
so disarming that even the gospel writers stayed the course of default religious pretense in order to avoid the peculiar irony of this
story. It is safer and more popular to believe in religious imagery
where God is like a guardian angel who does not let anyone out
of sight; it is quite another matter to hear a sleight-of-hand story
where what was lost was found only to be lost again in a banquet
to celebrate the finding. It is the comic turnaround of this story,
pivoting on an ironic twist, which should shake the hearer out of
default thinking. As ancient as the story may be, it can still make
us laugh, but will that laughter still hit its mark? Does the hearer
have the ears to understand how the story draws us away from
a concern for livelihood and into the celebration of life? From
behind our backs the default world raises this criticism, "That's a
great interpretation if you are from the middle class and have the
luxury of time for such reflections, but what about the poor?"
However, that might be the point. The celebration is initiated
by a poor shepherd who has little to begin with, and perhaps has
just lost everything he had if the flock he left to its own is now
gone. Once again we meet the celebration of the poor and the
grumbling of the wealthy, who cannot enter through the eye of
this needle.

It is curious that the gospel writers take the parable to be
about losing and finding, whereas in the parable world it is about
finding and losing. Finding the "lost" sheep is about releasing it
or letting it go into the banquet. And this is the comedy. With
the historical Jesus, and within the momentum related to his
memory, comedy is no joke. It concerns the release of self-pres-
ervation to universal celebration. It is the happy consequence of
anonymity and equilibrium.

If comedy is present in turning around lost-and-found logic, it is also present in reversing the sense of inside and outside. It is a simple saying, and at first blush perhaps one we readily agree with: "it is not what comes into a person that defiles but what comes out." As usual, there is more to the saying than what first appears. The church's habit has been to take the saying in two ways. Either it is a critique of Jewish dietary restrictions or it is a moral about virtues and vices. Most people follow the church's lead. What we eat does not matter; purity lies in what we say or do not say. The Gospel of Thomas is explicit about this since, as Funk points out, in Thomas the saying is revised to focus on the mouth: "what goes into your mouth will not defile you; rather, it's what comes out of your mouth that will defile you" (14). In Matthew, the mouth is also assumed to be the right reference, but a familiar moral interpretation is added: "for out of the heart comes evil thoughts, murder, adultery, fornication, theft, false witness, slander" (15:19). Both these readings, the one that assumes dietary restriction laws and the one that assumes moral injunctions, add a default layer to a saying that is in essence a riddle. But in Mark's edition, recorded above, the comedy still stands out. The aphorism offers no specific critique of dietary laws—indeed, not even food is necessarily involved—for what comes into us from the outside also includes sights, sounds, smells, and various social happenings. It is impossible to be in life without being someone who receives things from the outside. It is only what comes out of us that defiles, but here is where the joke begins. What comes out of us is as ambiguous and as varied as what comes in. It is not clear what an individual is to associate with in and out, and, as Funk once explained, it is particularly unclear what orifice Jesus has in mind.

In some ways, this is a saying about nothing in that it literally takes away what it gives. We are asked initially to focus on what comes into the body but then we can't do so because the point is what goes out; however, what goes out is deliberately skewed in ambiguity. Are we being mocked with an oblique reference to private parts? Or, are we being humbled because, among other things, what comes out includes our language, our expressions, and even the acts of our prejudiced assumptions. In the creation of this ambiguity, the comic savant has accomplished his task. In the end, it is never a question of what we take in from the world, for who can control that? Rather, it is always a question of what we add to the world. For those with ears to hear, it is possible to stop worrying about judging the world and start paying attention to one's presence within it.

In the world of the parable, comedy is grace. It is the gift of lightness to the self, the lightness of being, but it comes at a price. The price is the loss of the self, which in Western society is sometimes an impossible amount. Still, that is the comic doorway, and when the threshold has been crossed the question shifts from who must I be in the world to what can I add to the world?

The Gospel of
Non-Violent Resistance

> If anyone strikes you on the right cheek, turn and offer your left.
>   —Matt 5:39, from Q

> If anyone would sue you for your coat, let him have your shirt as well.
>   —Matt 5:40, from Q

Facts about the historical Jesus are flimsy and uncertain, so much so that some argue there never was a Jesus of Nazareth; the whole story is fiction.[5] But there are a few things that seem absolutely certain, that is, as certain as one can be about events that happened two thousand years ago. One is that Jesus died, and so—as one of my professors once pointed out—we know for certain that he was born. There are probably a few other things that we know: he came from Galilee; he was once a student of John the Baptist; and he was a teller of parables. No doubt, though, among the most secure if not spectacular things known about Jesus is the way he died. Crucifixion in ancient Rome was the sentence of capital punishment, but this severe penalty was carried out as an act of public shaming. Visibility was important, which is why crosses were on hills or along roadways. But what crime is so heinous that the perpetrator should be publicly shamed by forced exposure and then buried in a common, unmarked grave? For Rome, this manner of execution was reserved for non-citizens, that is, the common poor, who were perceived as thieves, disturbers of the peace, and, above all, traitors. Jesus could have been crucified for any number of reasons, including mistaken identity, but most likely he was crucified for sedition. To whatever degree Roman authorities knew about his movement, it was perceived as a popular threat to Roman social order. The idea, as Dominic Crossan has persuasively argued, was to take out the leader and scatter the following. To some degree this must have worked since the gospels do suggest the absence of followers at the time of the crucifixion and immediately afterward. In Roman eyes, Jesus was not a teller of parables but a disturber of the peace.

The problem for the historian is to determine why Jesus was crucified. The problem for the theologian is to determine the meaning of the crucifixion. Neither of these problems, however, is of concern to the student of Jesus. To the student of Jesus, it is a question of the integrity of his life. What in the teaching of Jesus made his voice to Roman ears one with a radical political edge? How can an anonymous self, a comic self of equilibrium, also be a social deviant?

Social deviancy in the teaching of Jesus is found in case parodies. A case parody is a specific life example where an exaggerated action can bring critical focus to the situation. In the Tianammen Square protests in Beijing in 1989, famous news footage shows a student refusing to move from in front of a military tank. The student is willing to give his life for the cause of human rights. To stand in front of a tank and to be willing to be run over is absolutely not a funny situation, but it is a case parody. It is so because the student tries through non-violent resistance to publicly humiliate the army in an exaggerated and literal demonstration of its callous oppression. Openly shaming the army in this particular case could bring changes to the government regime by means of sheer international embarrassment.

The advice that when someone slaps you on the right cheek, you should turn and offer the other is case parody *par excellence*. Since the listening audience consists of those who do get slapped, we know the audience is not made up of household elites or government officials but socially impoverished people subject to such discipline. To be slapped on the right cheek is to receive the backhanded blow of your oppressor's right hand. It is symbolically a "downward" blow meant to put you in your place; it is the blow a master inflicts on a slave, a parent on a child, and a Roman soldier on a Jewish peasant. To turn the other cheek is to ask to be hit again, but this time it is to be hit as an equal. It is an exaggeration to offer a second chance to strike a blow, but this time the right hand must be used either as an open slap or as a fist to strike a blow that assumes equality. It is likely the oppressor will not strike the second blow that would declare equality, either because once equality is established the other party might answer back or because there is too much humility required from the oppressor to acknowledge the other as an equal. Regardless, the point is made. The exaggeration operates as an act of critical resistance to power. It demands the recognition that all human beings stand on the same ground.

The same critical resistance to power is present in the aphorism concerning the cloak and shirt. Since we are dealing with a two-garment society, here the exaggeration is expressed when giving your shirt (undergarment) means to stand naked before your accuser.[6] Public nakedness is humiliating, but being the one who has caused it is even worse. The shame falls on the accuser's heartless act, a transgression of common decency. Using the exaggerated gesture of being stripped of one's dignity reverses the direction of shame. The accuser is in the spotlight. The hubris of power is scorned upon, and perhaps the re-evaluation of such exploitation is in order.

When a political or social system enacts violence on its weakest members through the disrespectful attitudes elites cast upon the poor, through powers that advantage the wealthy and moral proprieties that sully the destitute, then the systemic violence inherent in society brands each of its members. Violence becomes an element of the soul, a way in which we learn to speak about ourselves and our relationship to others; violence becomes a norm, a default, that circulates in the repetitions of language. As George Lakoff points out, we learn to "attack" another's position, to "wipe out" the opposition, and to "target" our criticism. We learn to condemn desperate acts that result from hunger and homelessness rather than address the problem of hunger and homelessness. As Sarah Palin, or perhaps her advisors, failed to realize, the provocative act of placing people or states in the "crosshairs" is more than just sharp political discourse. It is an act of condoning, in language, the norm of violent relationships.

What is surprising about the historical Jesus is the consistent presence of non-violent social resistance. Violence is a violation of human dignity, and this needs to be acknowledged prior to conceiving paths of resistance. If the answer to violence is greater violence in return, then the cycle is never broken. In place, the circulation of violence becomes the habit of life, and everybody makes a contribution. Only the conscious recognition of the cycle offers the freedom to break it. The power of the historical Jesus, and the momentum of those who choose to participate, is non-violent resistance to social exploitation. The use of case parody in this respect is genius, but the historical Jesus is not alone. Everybody knows, or should know, that Mahatma Gandhi brought down the British Raj without firing a single shot. It is likely the most remarkable example of the transforming power of non-violent resistance in human history. In case after case Gandhi was able to shame the British regime by demonstrating to them the indignity of their own actions.

In the school of the historical Jesus, non-violence is the practice of wisdom. Wisdom uses non-violence to interrupt the circulation of injury in the normal violence of society. This makes sense because, in the parable world that Jesus advocates, there is no such thing as enmity.

The Gospel of Joy

A full measure of grain, pressed down, shaken together, and running over will be poured into your lap.
   —Luke 6:38, from Q

Just look at him, a glutton and a drunkard, a friend of tax collectors and outcasts!
   —Luke 7:34, from Q

The practice of the Jesus movement is the practice of the banquet. The banquet is the activity of joy. Deeply embedded in Jewish history, the banquet is perhaps the most significant way to celebrate the culture of Judaism. The banquet is the promise of equality: a plenitude that welcomes the messiah in the fullness of time, an economic state that means the end to exile. "Listen everyone who thirsts, come to the waters; and you that have no money, come, buy and eat! Come, buy wine and milk without money and without price" (Isa 55:10). Israel celebrates the joy of heaven with the act of sharing abundance. But of course, it is not just Israel. All around the world, the banquet is the consistent image of human celebration. It is the time and the place where news is shared, where consolation is offered in the face of sorrow, and the great ideas are debated in the company of one's peers. The banquet historically defines the relationship between nations, when treaties are concluded or longstanding agreements are ritually acknowledged. The Greek symposium meal and the aboriginal potlatch work to express the fullness of time in human experience. *Kairos*, the Greek word for the fullness of time, is the time of the banquet.

Nevertheless, the banquet as the image of joy cannot be conceived naively. A banquet is paradoxical in nature, as George Bataille, following Marcel Maus, noted in *The Accursed Share*.[7] To hold a banquet is to create debt (indebtedness) in those who receive it. This is the basis of the symposium meal of ancient Greek and Roman culture. One holds a banquet among those of the same class, creating debts of exchange among colleagues. Fellow class members receive the invitation and attend the banquet, but in so doing they become indebted to the one who throws the banquet. The debt might be used for the purpose of gaining or consolidating trade deals, for re-enforcing one's position in a class or expressing one's superiority, or it might be in response to a debt incurred for having participated in a banquet thrown by another member of one's class. The banquet is a vehicle of exchange, and when, as in the parable of the Dinner Party, invited guests refuse the invitation, the individual is effectively disgraced because participation in the debt economy is vanquished. The shamed individual becomes a nobody. The Dinner Party parable, as we saw, ends with a banquet for nobodies (see chapter 5).

The historical Jesus seems to have been known as the ancient equivalent of a party animal. Yet, his banquet persistently is a banquet for nobodies—"tax collectors and outcasts." Among nobodies, that is, among those whose class status counts for naught, a banquet cannot have the effect of creating indebtedness. There is no gain in holding the banquet because the consequence is not indebtedness. No deals are made and no deals are lost. The contrast should not be overlooked. In a Roman symposium, aristocratic news was shared and deals were made, and as this business unfolded bones and various other inedible remains were tossed upon the mosaic floor to be cleaned up by slaves. The banquet expressed the fullness of time only at one level; at another level, it defined the fullness of oppression. Since the Jesus movement was among the poor, banquets were not feasts and did not need to be. In the Jesus movement, a symposium meal was converted from privilege to common sharing. It expressed solidarity and a trust that, with collective goods and basic compassion, indebtedness will be replaced by inclusion. Crossan calls this form of banqueting open commensality. It is closer to the ancient sense of fullness—"a full measure of grain, pressed down, shaken together, and running over." Such is not to be confused with wealth; rather, since it is solidarity and radical inclusion—since it is debt-free—it is joy.

Thus, the banquet as an expression of solidarity and radical inclusion defines the theme of joy in the Jesus school. In Latin, *gaudium* is the word for joy and means peaceful satisfaction or completeness. The English word "gaudy" comes from the Latin. In Greek, joy is *chara*, which is a derivative of *charis*, or grace. In Greek, joy is not a feeling but a state of being. Like in Latin, it denotes completion. The only avenue to these states of fullness in human experience is self-acceptance, but self-acceptance is not possible in isolation. Self-acceptance is the peculiar experience of being equal with all things. Ironically, accepting myself only happens when I accept myself as one experience among many. With this, I can laugh at myself: here I am an interesting coincidence of history, wrapped up in a moment, amidst all that is. I am a beautiful, if strange, happenstance. In Kierkegaard's philosophy, one who can stand here and say yes to life with such light-hearted joy is a knight of faith; in Nietzsche's philosophy, the same person is a cosmic dancer. In the Jesus movement, such is the one who stands in the banquet.

The quotations given in Luke 6:38 and 7:34, both drawn from Q, are not sayings of Jesus. They are, however, considered to be in the momentum of Jesus. The first one is an accusation that might have been cast against Jesus. His association with outcasts meant, by default, his character was morally questionable.

Using a banquet to be in solidarity with outcasts brought guilt by association. But we must insist that Jesus, in any case, held this status because he was poor. He was not someone of great wealth who offered charity; he was someone of great poverty who sought solidarity. Such a person is often judged someone out of place who should be put back in place, and the vehicle for doing so is usually the application of *ad hominem* labels. The second saying is difficult to place on the lips of the historical Jesus because the images of fullness (a full lap of grain) suggest a reward is the result of following Jesus. By contrast, it is rather clear that the historical Jesus claimed no favorites. To Jesus, the banquet was an activity in life—a way to practice the parable. The banquet is the definition of the Jesus movement realized not as reward but as solidarity, not a privilege but an unexpected joy.

What Does It Mean for Church?

By identifying five streams in the momentum of the historical Jesus, we can define features a church of the historical Jesus can emphasize. However, before moving forward, there are a few clarifications to make.

It is not the case that the historical Jesus walked around Galilee teaching these five "features." It would be a misinterpretation to think Jesus can be known with such calculation. That's not the point. The point is to extend ancient wisdom of the Jesus school into our time and language. Such acts of extension are the same acts historic Christianity accomplished with its doctrinal development of theology; the difference is that while the historical Jesus can be extended into wisdom, the Church's Christ was extended into dogma.

The Christian Church has had 2000 years to develop and articulate the momentum of dogma associated with Christ. Dogmatic Christianity is the default expression of the Christian religion. For those who quickly conclude that the development of good theology in the momentum of the historical Jesus is not possible, remember that we have barely scratched the surface of thinking about the church and its future with the wisdom of the historical Jesus. The challenge, the hope, and the vision of creating a new sense of community from the momentum of the historical Jesus is far from realized. The point at this juncture is to find creative ways to center community life in the teaching of the historical Jesus.

I have tried above to name five teaching streams in what I have called momentum. Now the challenge is to take them to church and to allow these streams to influence the sense and meaning of a Christian community. I must leave aside, for now, the question of whether or not such a community is still Christian. In place, I wish to explore how a community can be a historical Jesus community while remaining in a Christian setting. Certainly, the language in such a community must change from transcendent to immanent. The language of God must be replaced with the language of life. The reason for such community gatherings must change, also. To gather is no longer to worship a divine something or somebody but to participate in an atmosphere of learning, dialogue, and growth. Positively, the theme of gathering is honesty. The act of gathering is a banquet. And even though the historical Jesus is the inspiration of such a community, he is not the only one from whom we can learn. Open commensality demands openness of mind.

Notes

1. *Honest to Jesus*, 159.

2. I do not like the fact that there is debilitating poverty in the wealthy societies of the West, but I still know such debilitating poverty exists. Such awareness is so ingrained in my social experience that it is impossible not to "expect" to see poverty in everyday social reality. So, even though I don't accept poverty as inevitable, I still have to live with poverty in society as part of the normal course of reality.

3. Tao Te Ching, chap. 38

4. Scott, *Hear Then the Parable*, 405ff.

5. Likely the most prominent book on this subject is Tom Harpur's *The Pagan Christ*. Freke and Gandy's *The Jesus Mysteries* is also popular, but see the critical review by Susan Elliott, "Pseudo-Scholarship Illustrated" (*Fourth R,* May–June 2011).

6. For a comparison of the teachings of John the Baptist and Jesus on this subject, see chapter 5.

7. Bataille, *The Accursed Share,* vol. 1, 70.

7

The Church of the Historical Jesus

I seek, in this chapter, to speak frankly about Christianity and its perceived shortcomings from a historical Jesus perspective. I will suggest that from its earliest phases to the present, Christianity has been mainly an apocalyptic religion in its theology and worship forms. By this I mean that its historic reasoning has rested predominately on a model of crisis and crisis resolution. The crisis consists of being in "sin"—that is, human beings being in a condition of separation from God—and the resolution consists of a final reconciliation with God at the end of history.

Christianity historically aims to define existence as crisis: humanity has turned away from the initial plan of God for the world. The world was meant to be paradise, but human sin has marred that possibility with social violence, social injustice, and personal ingratitude for life. The situation is hopeless; human beings cannot save themselves and cannot reconstitute, on their own, the original intention of God or the original relationship to God. What is needed is an end-time scenario where God acts to restore the world through divine intervention. Christianity shares this basic structure of present crisis and future divine resolution with its monotheistic cousins Zoroastrianism, Judaism, and Islam. Each religion holds the belief that the world is stained with sin and that, at the end of time, a divinely commissioned messianic figure will arrive to inaugurate the clean up of the world. The Zoroastrian messiah is Saoshyant; the Jewish messiah is the Son of David; and Christianity and Islam share the expectation that Jesus is the messianic figure who will return. In contrast to this apocalyptic model stand the five gospels of the historical Jesus, discussed in chapter 6. When the historical Jesus is taken seriously, it is very difficult to use his wisdom teaching to formulate an apocalyptic model of history. In contrast, wisdom is about presence in life and about a vision of an alternative way of being in the world. Wisdom expresses itself through riddles like parables that are never entirely solved. Wisdom is instruction about the path of life, not the end of life. It is about coming into being, not about ending or concluding being. Wisdom is about the presence of the eternal in the now.

It is not enough, though, merely to contrast the historical Jesus as a wisdom figure with Christianity as an apocalyptic religion. If a return to the historical Jesus is to take hold as a movement, there needs to be a practicing community. While the historical Jesus inspires ideas like the anonymous self, equilibrium, and other wisdom practices, only a community gives life to those practices through liturgy, language, and solidarity. In this regard, I will refer to my own community and the liturgy that is used there, the Quest Learning Centre for Religious Literacy.[1] People gather there and hold a service. To the outside, it looks like regular Christian worship, but inside, the content of the gathering is different. The language and metaphors are different. The attitude and atmosphere are different. The purpose of the gathering and its subject matter are different. The difference is this: it is a wisdom-based gathering.

Moving to the historical Jesus foundation as a model for community gathering does not necessitate dismissing Christianity or thinking somehow that one is outside or beyond it. It is not an arrogant move. Christianity, despite its bleak history of violence and support of oppressive regimes, is still a faith tradition filled with incredible art, philosophy, and literature. A move to the historical Jesus foundation is not about rejecting Christianity; it is simply a question of moving Christianity onto a different and more credible path for our time. Perhaps someday a church model based on the historical Jesus will be the main expression of Christianity, and what we have known as Christianity until now will be understood as the precursor to its historical Jesus form. The early church, for example, can be seen in the same way when compared to the medieval church. Medieval Christianity is a different animal when set against the earliest forms of Christianity. Yet, despite the differences, if the long view of history is taken, medieval Christianity is what became of the early period. Using the same perspective, maybe one day the church of the historical Jesus will be what Christianity has become.

Of course, no one can know the future, but it does seem as if the time has come for the human family to start understanding religion honestly as its own creation and to move forward on a path that positively affirms the role religion can play in the development of human experience and imagination. My effort below is to describe a possible shift from the apocalyptically centered Christian church to the wisdom-centered church of the historical Jesus.

The Christian Apocalyptic Form

Christianity as a world religion was born out of and formed within the structures of apocalyptic thinking. Apocalypse derives from a Greek word that means "to uncover or reveal." Since in Christianity it is related to writings like Mark 13 and the book of Revelation, apocalypticism generally refers to the cycle of crisis and redemption and, specifically, to warnings about the end of world history. When I speak of Christianity as an apocalyptic religion, I mean that the model informing its orthodox form of worship and expression is that of crisis and redemption. In other words, the underlying drama of public Christian worship is a movement from crisis to redemption.

Here, we can briefly note that in the spectrum of Christian apocalyptic theology there are moderate and extreme expressions. The moderate expression defines the Christian emphasis on social criticism. Moderate apocalypticism is the prophetic voice that warns society of the direction it is travelling and calls power centers into account. The book of Amos is an example of a prophetic voice that issues a warning to ancient Israel about an impending crisis. The warning is supposed to have the effect of shocking the hearer or, in this case, the ancient nation, into changing its actions and its politics before it is too late. "For thus says the Lord," Amos proclaims, "the city that marched out a thousand shall have a hundred left, and that which marched out a hundred shall have ten left" (5:3). In its history, Christianity has often expressed social criticism in the style of moderate apocalypticism comparable to Israel's ancient prophets. The voice of social criticism warns society about the path it is engaging. That voice today is especially focused on the dangers of depleting the environment, the call for economic equality, and the conviction of many Christians that the exploitation of the poor is unfaithful to the God of justice. These moderate forms of apocalypticism are to be applauded; nevertheless, they rest upon the model of crisis and redemption. When it comes to the historical Jesus, one question to address will be the following: Can the historic emphasis of Christianity on social justice be better expressed through wisdom?

Meanwhile, extreme apocalytpicism, unfortunately, is not about the call for justice and equality but rather strictly about indulging in end-time scenarios whether they happen or not. This form of apocalypticism is troubling in two respects. First, it restricts the purpose of Christianity as a religion to saving X number of individuals before the final bell of judgment is sounded. Second, and perhaps most regrettable, extreme apocalypticism assumes that, aside from being a platform for a few personal conversions, human history is irrelevant. There is no need in this form of apocalypticism to link human well-being to the well-being of the planet earth, and there is little to study let alone learn from other cultures, languages, and histories. The aim is restricted to getting the inside track on God's plan.

Whether it takes the moderate or extreme form, Christianity historically depends on a crisis/resolution or sin/redemption model of apocalypticism. Human beings are in crisis, and God's final act of reconciliation to end history expresses divine grace. The language and liturgy of the Christian tradition are built on this apocalyptic model, where human beings approach God as unworthy individuals due to their condition of sin. The form of grace is Jesus Christ, God incarnate, who was born of the Virgin Mary and who suffered "for our salvation."[2] The Christian vision is that the world has its origin and ending in God, and that in the death of Jesus, human sin will one day be overcome.

Even though it is true that the structure of crisis and redemption can be taken in moderate or extreme forms, the Christian proclamation of salvation is difficult to make without an apocalyptic structure. Without the apocalyptic ending set as the purpose of history, the need for and aim of God incarnate in Jesus Christ evaporates. Why should anyone worship a savior if salvation is unnecessary? The heart of Christian theology is the apocalyptic cycle, and it is in this setting that the Christ both enters the picture and makes sense. But since the historical Jesus is not the Christ his life can do no better than any other human life when it comes to saving humanity or inaugurating the cosmic clean up. In fact, as a historical being he does not really offer a foundation for an apocalyptic model at all.

To set a community's foundation on the historical Jesus rather than on Christ the Savior is no easy matter. There are virtually no models to follow.[3] Even if we turn to the alternative gnostic Christianity, the apocalyptic vision remains paramount. Though the human crisis in Gnosticism is the result of human ignorance and not sin, the solution remains an end-time, supernatural, reunification with God mediated through Christ. In Gnosticism, too, there is no need for Christ if there is not first the crisis of separation from God that explains the state of human ignorance. Stephen A. Hoeller talks about the gnostic savior as the "maker of wholeness," but such a term presupposes the default state of the human condition as one of sickness.[4] What if that default state, whether sin or sickness, did not exist? What if it was simply a human creation?

When Christianity is doggedly approached on the basis of the historical Jesus, the apocalyptic emphasis is displaced. History is no longer a sickness; it is simply the condition of human existence. Every human being is necessarily in history and limited by place and time; the frank ability to see one another in our humanity as creatures of this earth is fundamental to holding a heart of compassion and a desire for wisdom. Apocalypticism can harm the human sense of presence in the world because it can deny this honest reality in the rush to interpret the course of history. Apocalypticism can overlook the struggle of individuals with their lives and in their particular circumstances because the emphasis falls on the vision of the end rather than the quality of the now.

If the apocalyptic model is rejected in the practice of religion and especially as the operating model of Christianity, then a certain freedom in relation to history and the Christian tradition emerges. It is not necessary anymore to see Jesus in absolute terms. He does not have to be a savior; he need not supersede all other great teachers in value, and he need no longer be the only answer. The Jesus movement or school can be seen as one expression among many in the wisdom traditions of human history. A historical Jesus community can take advantage of this new situation to center itself on learning wisdom rather than endlessly performing the apocalypse. Historical Jesus communities can be understood as learning centers; the point of gathering together is not to gain or express salvation, whether in the liberal sense of arriving at wholeness or the conservative sense of ensuring one's place in heaven. The point is to experience the parabolic life. Still, in the absence of an end-time vision, why would one want to be in a parabolic community at all? That is the question of the elder son in the parable of the Prodigal, who stands outside watching the party. There is unfortunately no answer in the parable world. There is only the invitation.

In the parable, nothing is necessarily as it is. And the world can be differently created if human beings sincerely want to be in the world differently. This new energy is what is celebrated in a historical Jesus community. It is celebrated in learning and it is celebrated in banquet.

For a community to hold the historical Jesus as its centerpiece and to put into practice themes of life such as the five gospels of the historical Jesus (see chapter 6), that community requires a ritual form of gathering, that is, a liturgy by which community is created and sustained. Whether we are religious or not, whether we are academics who gather at a conference or business folk who sit at a board meeting, rituals shape the gathering of human communities. Christianity has a longstanding form of gathering in its liturgical history. A historical Jesus community does not have to re-invent the wheel in this regard. However, a historical Jesus community does employ a different language and a different rationale when it gathers. To approach the new language and rationale, we must first understand the tune of Christian liturgy in apocalypticism and then re-set it in the key of Q.

Table of Comparison
Historical Jesus Community

Act	Movement	Linguistic Center
Liturgy of Gathering	1. Issue of Peace 2. Solidarity Meditation	Common Humanity
Liturgy of Learning	1. Content 2. Discussion	Education
Liturgy of the Banquet	1. Living 2. Celebrating	Compassion
Liturgy of Parting	1. Thankfulness 2. Good Tidings	Honesty

The Apocalyptic Form
of Christian Liturgy

Liturgy is the poetry of Christianity that enacts the beliefs of the church in the context of community. Traditional Christian liturgy is based on the apocalyptic *movement* from crisis to resolution (sin to redemption). Liturgy structures the functions of proclaiming the Word and receiving the Grace. The Word is proclaimed as the consequence of crisis (indeed, it names the crisis), and the Grace is received as thanksgiving for the resolution (indeed, it is the resolution).

There are four movements from crisis to resolution (see the table of comparison above). In each movement there are two acts, and the two acts can always be elaborated further with added rituals. The first movement of Christian liturgy is the gathering or calling of the people together, which is the introductory rite in the Roman tradition. The first act of the liturgical movement of gathering is the Greeting, issued in the name of God or Jesus or the Trinity, and the second act is the Penitential Act (the confession of sin). When approaching the

Traditional Christianity		
Act	*Movement*	*Linguistic Center*
Introductory Rite	1. Grace of Our Lord	Guilt
	2. Penetential Act	
Liturgy of the Word	1. Reading	Judgment
	2. Proclaiming	
Liturgy of the Table	1. Thanksgiving	Forgiveness
(Eucharist)	2. Receiving	
Concluding Rite	1. Blessing	Proclaiming
	2. Commisioning	

holy, and when assuming an apocalyptic framework, the human condition must first express its separation or alienation from God. Humanity as the creature is unworthy of the majesty of the creator. We come before God as sinners, and we seek to hear the Word. But we cannot hear the Word proclaimed until we have confessed the separation that necessitates the proclamation and opens us to hearing it. Without the penitential act, we remain too proud to hear or even believe we need to hear the Word. The first movement in traditional Christianity, then, is the Gathering, composed of the Greeting and the Penitential Act.

The second movement is the proclamation of the Word, and its two elements are the Reading and Proclaiming of the Gospel. There can be, as in the first movement, many rituals accompanying these two elements: prayers, music, hymns, antiphonal responses, etc. The Word is first heard in the reading of scripture, and then the Word is proclaimed in the exposition of scripture. In response, the community might recite the Apostles Creed to express its collective faith as a response to hearing the Word. The collective faith is important, it might be noted, because symbolically it resides outside of or in transcendental relation to the variation of beliefs and doubts held by individuals. The Creed as a collective expression makes up for the variations experienced at the individual level. The whole of the second movement is usually called the Liturgy of the Word.

The third movement involves the Eucharist, or communion. Its two acts are the Recitation of Thanksgiving and the Receiving of the Bread (and wine). In some traditions, except for special occasions, the laity receives the bread alone. In many Protestant traditions, the Eucharist is held infrequently, and this is due mainly to the historical context of Protestantism, which arose at a time when the laity practically never received the Eucharist (sometimes once in a year; sometimes once in a lifetime). The Protestant worship service technically is always open to the celebration of the Eucharist—for there is almost always a prayer of thanksgiving—even though practically the bread and wine are infrequently blessed and served. This third movement in the traditional order is called the Table or, more formally, the Liturgy of the Table (or Eucharist). Again, its two acts are Thanksgiving, in which in the blessing occurs, and Receiving, in which the elements are taken.

The fourth and final movement is the dismissal. In the Roman tradition, this is usually called the Concluding Rite. The first act here is the Blessing of the People, and the second is the Sending Out, or Commissioning, of the People. The blessing underlines, in gesture and word, that the community has received the grace of God. Often a leader (minister, pastor, or priest) will hold arms out in the cross position, symbolically laying his or her hands on the head of all the gathered to bless them. Having received the grace, the gathered body is then commissioned to go out in the world to proclaim the gospel.

The four movements of Christian liturgy are apocalyptic in form because the whole act of Christian worship rests on acknowledging human separation from God. From here, the poetics of the liturgy unfold to culminate in radical inclusion in the body of Christ. In Christianity, the Eucharist is the supreme act of reconciliation with God. Even if the historical Jesus community seeks a new path beyond ancient Christian belief, the deep beauty of art and philosophy associated with the Eucharist can still move us.

The historical Jesus community exists, though, because the metaphysical ideas inherent in traditional Christianity are no longer tenable. The state of separation from the divine (sin) and that act of the divine breaking into history (the Christ) assumes the ancient universe where gods live upstairs to oversee the woeful history of human affairs. A historical Jesus community exists after the age of the gods or God, but, to be sure, it still extends from the Christian tradition. Despite any shortcomings or criticisms directed against the Christian faith as a whole, it is still the ground on which to build a historical Jesus movement. A historical Jesus community can still employ the four basic movements of Christian worship, but these movements demand a new liturgy based on a wisdom understanding. We can now look at what can be called the four linguistic centers of apocalyptic Christianity and contrast them to the four linguistic centers of a historical Jesus community.

Four Linguistic Centers

The first linguistic center of traditional Christianity is the presupposition of human guilt. Christianity holds humanity guilty of sin, which means that the primary human-God relationship is one of contrition. Christian liturgy begins, almost universally, with the approach to God in awe and with a contrite heart. A lot of churches today work to minimize the emphasis on guilt and, it must be said, a lot of others continue to exploit it for all its worth. Either way, guilt remains structurally part of Christian liturgy in the first movement of worship. The Word is not heard until guilt of separation is acknowledged. Openness to the Word depends on recognizing the need for the Word.

Guilt in popular Christian theology is often limited to specific acts, like robbing a bank. This is incidental of guilt in the sense that it is guilt determined in a specific incident. But in Christianity there is not only incidental guilt; there is also structural guilt, or what we can call the condition of guilt. Structural guilt is based on the fact that finite humans fail to grasp the perfection of the infinite God. The separation between the finite and infinite is permanent, and guilt expresses the permanent or structural alienation of human existence from the divine. The rational foundation for Christian worship rests on the need to offer thanksgiving to God for the solution (salvation) to the problem of guilt (sin). Without this foundation, there is no reason for Christian worship.

Yet the historical Jesus community is not founded upon the infinite difference between God and human beings. God, in a certain sense, is irrelevant to such a community since the vision is focused on the parabolic teaching of Jesus and the cultivation of the parabolic style of life for community members. Guilt does not really play a role except for expressing common human responsibility for harmful acts. Guilt is not structurally part of the reason for gathering. It does not work to create the need for hearing and doing the Word of God. There is no hidden reality behind life that speaks the purposes of God; there is only the phenomenal fact of life that is open to creativity and becoming.

The second linguistic center of traditional Christian liturgy is judgment. Here we have to be subtle since although the word judgment can carry a negative connotation, in Christianity judgment is grace. Karl Barth famously indicated that the Word of God strikes the hearer as the hammer that breaks the rock to pieces (Jer 23:29). The power of Christianity as a prophetic social voice lays here. Though the Word of God comes upon us as an act of judgment, it is nevertheless grace since ultimately the Word bridges the gulf of human separation from the divine. This is the paradox of the Word of God. It shakes us to the foundation, to use a Paul Tillich expression,[5] but it does so to draw us nearer to God and to the reality of God. Nevertheless, the logic of the paradox is completely circular. There is no way to know that one should even be in need of the Word, let alone be awakened to hear it, except that it has first judged us in the statement of sin. At the same time, sin must already be in operation in order for the Word to be relevant. This circle creates a logic wherein it is necessary to assume what is given. There must first be the Word to awaken humanity, but there cannot be the Word without the prior need to be awakened; but there cannot be such a prior need without the Word acting first, but it cannot act at all without first the need to act, etc. The conclusion assumes the premise. The proof of the Word of God is based on the Word of God. In philosophical logic this circularity violates what is called the Law of Excluded Middle: two propositions cannot occupy the same space at the same time.[6]

To think Christianity anew with the historical Jesus does not require invoking or employing the classic paradox of Christian faith wherein the premise is its own proof. The problem disappears because there is no need to give an absolute standing to the Word of God. The Word of God takes that authority only insofar as the apocalyptic model remains a given, for in that model God is the both the creator and final judge. God must necessarily stand outside of history as its initiation and its culmination, its first and its last breath. In apocalypticism, God is the authority of God, or God is the foundation of God. In the historical Jesus community, the circle of judgment is broken because the question is about presence in history and responsibility for history without a hidden divine agenda. Presence in history and responsibility for history require discernment in the world of action, and discernment is the consequence of comparison. The historical Jesus

expressed his wisdom through comparison, which is evident in
the parables and aphorisms. Comparison means that things do
not stand alone as absolutes but rather are present as relationships. So, for the historical Jesus, God's reality is in the relationship of things. Wisdom speaks of reality as composite relations:
everything that is exists in dependent relationship to everything
else. In chapter 6, this was described as equilibrium. The reason a
historical Jesus community gathers is not to negotiate the tricky
paradox of absolute being but to cultivate the discerning power
of comparison in wisdom.

The Eucharist, which involves the taking of the body and
blood of the Son of God given for humanity, defines a third
linguistic center to traditional Christianity: that of sacrifice. The
Eucharistic act *per se* is not the sacrifice, since the sacrifice has
already occurred and can only occur once, in the crucifixion of
Jesus Christ. The Eucharist stands in place of the original sacrifice
and celebrates the gift that this sacrifice issues, which is the gift
of forgiveness gained through the reception of and belonging to
the body of Christ.[7] Thus the Eucharist is the holy mystery in
which Christian believers are united as one redeemed body. Even
so, the Eucharist centers itself on the cross of Jesus and upon
his death and resurrection. It enacts this sacrifice both as the
memory and presence of Jesus. In the long course of history, the
centering of the meaning of Jesus on his sacrifice has had more
of a psychological than theological effect on many Christians. It
seems to express the idea that God likes sacrifice and that we are
faithful to God when we suffer. Even though—were I to defend
orthodox Christianity—I would say that suffering is the "red
herring" of the cross, for it distracts from God's self-sacrificial
love, it is nevertheless the case that if the focus on Jesus is restricted principally to his death, then his death encourages the
identification of true faith with suffering. Such identification can
be significant insofar as the reality of God is in solidarity with
suffering, but it can be and more often is culturally the justifica-

tion of suffering as part of the necessary plan of God.[8] Suffering as the necessary plan of God is, in fact, key to the apocalyptic model of Christianity.

In a historical Jesus community, the suffering of Jesus on the cross is not a necessity but the tragedy of his life. It has nothing to do with his message. The central image of the historical Jesus is the banquet, and, unlike the Eucharist, the banquet relates to the life of Jesus, not his death. To be sure, the crucifixion expresses human violence, and the suffering of Jesus in relation to violence no doubt involved his personal fear. The crucifixion can be looked upon with compassion for Jesus as a historical being caught in the machinations of empire and power. No one then and no one now should endure such suffering under the hands of the state, but of course such suffering defines the functions of empire.[9] In a historical Jesus community, the crucifixion is related to the integrity of Jesus as a human being who died because of his vision, but his death is not the message of his life. That message instead is found and celebrated in the banquet.

The fourth linguistic center of Christian liturgy comes out of the proclamation of the Christian gospel in the world. It is the linguistic center of confession. The Christian gospel would be pointless if it did not inspire people to go out in the world to confess its message of salvation. The word salvation means healing, or wholeness, so the proclamation of the gospel does not have to mean converting people to Christianity. It can indicate the social imperative of the gospel to go out and change the world through the activity of making justice and sharing compassion. Acting out justice in the world can equally be an act of confessing Christ in the world. However it is conceived, the confession of the gospel is the outward movement of proclamation to the world.

A historical Jesus community need not be critical here except that the foundation on which the Christian confession rests presupposes a hierarchical (*hieros*, or sacred) relationship to truth.

What is proclaimed to the world is what has been received in revelation, but the reception travels through a line of authority understood to be authentic. In orthodox forms of Christianity, authority lies in an office such as a bishop or presbytery, and in puritan forms of Christianity the authority lies in the authentic experience of an individual tested by other individuals who have had the same experience. In the historical Jesus community, by contrast, the act is not a matter of confessing the faith but of engaging in the momentum of the Jesus movement. Such engagement is accomplished primarily in a lifestyle grounded in wisdom. We have seen already that wisdom is necessarily "unbrokered"; true, it has teachers, but it does not benefit from confessional lines of authority. Of course it cannot so benefit because, in wisdom, one can only move forward on the back of one's own experiences in life. In wisdom a student must recreate his or her life to become a master. This is a personal work of will and lifestyle.

Liturgy in a Historical Jesus Community

I have presented the four basic movements of the Christian liturgical drama, and I have tried to show how, in relation to a historical Jesus community, the linguistic centers of traditional Christian fall short in terms of theology, language, and practice. The traditional linguistic centers assume the default reality of apocalypticism, where human beings are in sin and in need of redemption. It is indeed a powerful theology and can be seen culturally in the ways we understand history and human psychology. We often conceive of human history as a set of challenges that must be overcome, and psychologically, we often assume that until sins are fully confessed there is no healing. Default reality is like that: it becomes a set of operating assumptions without anyone being particularly aware of how or why it is necessary to think like that.

A historical Jesus community, like the Quest Learning Centre, is not a confessional community designed to gather people around a set of default beliefs. In practical terms, this means that while the Christian structure of the gathering can be employed, the linguistic centers of the liturgy hold fundamentally different orientations. The four movements in the liturgical drama can be recast to hold a different substance. This is what the Quest Learning Centre has done, and I hope here to indicate how this can happen (see appendix 3 for sample liturgies based on this chapter).

Traditional Christianity opens with the act of gathering that leads to the penitential rite. The historical Jesus community of which I am a part also opens with an act of gathering, but the act leads to a solidarity rite. Solidarity moves outward toward the other, which is opposite to the inward movement of penance toward confession. The language has shifted from petitioning words directed upward and toward a deity to words directed outward and into a common humanity. Historical Jesus language participates in the language of solidarity, which is immanent humanism, not transcendental theism. Wisdom, even in its ancient forms, is primarily humanist in nature. It concerns giving practical advice, as in Proverbs, or philosophical insight about life, as in Ecclesiastes. In the Jesus tradition, the humanism of wisdom is expressed in parable. Aside from the added introductory words, "The Kingdom of God is like . . . ," the content of the parables hold virtually no references to God at all. Wisdom shifts the language to humanism, and, practically speaking, this shift means two things. The first element of the Gathering is an expression of peace. It is not peace issued in the name of God; it is peace expressed on the foundation of human relationships of hospitality. The signal opening is taken from Q (Luke 10:5) with the greeting, "Peace be upon all who enter this house." The second element of the Gathering is a solidarity meditation. The meditation can be words or silence, but the point is to express an open trust of one another and a connection of solidarity to all forms of life. The word meditation is used in place of prayer because to pray means to petition for something, from God or another superior. It comes from the Latin word *precari*, which means "to beg." The Hebrew word *tefilah* holds the sense of judging oneself or the community in light of God's presence. This too, like the act of begging for mercy, implies the apocalyptic understanding that confessing sin before the divine is prior to and necessary for human actuality. The historical Jesus community does not petition for things since it holds no priority for sin; its focus is placed on inspiring the community to live responsible and thoughtful lives. Neither does the community use "God" as a starting point for self-evaluation. Since God is a human creation, such a starting point is self-referential. It is an affirmation about abstract beliefs human communities have created for themselves. In place of this circularity, a solidarity meditation (from the Latin *meditatus,* or consideration) expresses deliberate thinking about the relationship of the community with the human family and the taking up of relationships within the dynamics of history, in which all life is embedded. Thus, the Introductory Rite composed of the Call and Penance is, in the historical Jesus community, transformed into a Gathering Liturgy composed of Peace and Solidarity.

The second movement in traditional Christianity consists of the Hearing and Proclaiming of the Word, the Liturgy of the Word. In a historical Jesus community, the second movement can be called the Liturgy of Learning. This linguistic center emphasizes a practice of openness, where the concern is content and discussion rather than hearing and repenting. Since the historical Jesus community is not tied to canonical Christianity, it has greater liberty in terms of what content in learning is employed. On many occasions in my own community, invited guests have come from the traditions of Islam, Judaism, Hinduism, Buddhism, and humanism. The point is to learn and to interact with different traditions and to address social or personal issues today. In my community, readings from gnostic and other non-canonical texts are also the subject of learning. Since Christians know the Bible but commonly know very little about biblical criticism, the history of Christian thought, and Church history generally, these subjects can be spoken of openly and with questions in ways that are excluded from traditional Christian worship. In a certain way, strangely, the historical Jesus community that I belong to is more "Christian" than the Christian churches that condemn it: the community, centered on the historical Jesus, is often far more biblically and religiously literate than its apocalyptic Christian neighbors. Indeed, the linguistic center in the Liturgy of Learning is religious literacy.

I have sometimes wondered how much the criticism directed at the historical Jesus community to which I belong is due to the customary dichotomy placed between Christian worship and learning. Learning is supposed to happen in church parlors or basements, where it can seldom make a tangible difference to worship. I would venture to guess that few if any traditional Christian communities openly read from and debate Thomas Aquinas in the context of their public gathering, yet this is what happens at the Quest Learning Centre. To see someone like Aquinas as a creative thinker whose ideas are in need of debate is to express both a respect for him and a recognition that his effort needs to be seen in the context of change and creativity in his own age. I use this example not because it expresses a unique experience possible in a historical Jesus community but because it shows that when Jesus is given back his humanity, so, too, is the whole of the Christian tradition and those of the past who defined it for their time. The practice in the Liturgy of Learning, then, is to encounter a subject and engage it critically for the purpose of making mature decisions about life and religion in the world. Religious literacy is about creating an atmosphere of openness to this essential possibility.

Traditional Christianity has as its third movement in worship the Liturgy of the Table, with sacrifice as its linguistic center. A historical Jesus community can refocus its center in the Liturgy of the Banquet. In traditional Christianity, the acts of the table are Thanksgiving and Receiving; in a church of the historical Jesus, the acts are Living and Celebrating. These words are not taken lightly, for they relate expressly to acknowledging the "Kingdom of God" as a present reality. For the historical Jesus, a banquet undermined a system of social privilege that excluded a vast number of people from the symposium of life. Arising from the poor and destitute, the Jesus banquet was an activity of solidarity among outcasts. It was the banquet of nobodies. It awakened joy by means of inclusion and expressed through common sharing human acts of loving kindness. The linguistic center here is not sacrifice; it is compassion.

In contrast to these simple joys, the Christian church's concern is overwhelmingly focused on qualifications and formalities. To celebrate the Eucharist, a priest or minister must be ordained, must say the words of institution ("this is my body"), and must state the *epiclesis* ("send down your holy spirit"). Without these, the Eucharist is merely a disappointing lunch. The banquet liturgy does not have formal words and is not "real" or "empty" based on an individual's merit or status. The banquet can be served with the same elements of bread and wine found in traditional Christianity, but again the content is quite different. In my community, the banquet often starts with words like "We gather to honor life," or a defining statement like "We are a community of openness and solidarity." These words set a tone for the character of the community. Then, the bread and wine are distributed as "bread for your journey" and "wine for your life." These are not the elements of Jesus' body but elements of community solidarity. Sometimes, in my community, a full banquet meal is held in place of bread and wine. The banquet is held at every gathering because it is so central to the community and the historical Jesus. Though it can look like the Eucharist, it has shifted in language and in practice from ecclesiastical propriety to a platform of open commensality.[10]

The final movement in traditional Christian liturgy is the Blessing and Dismissal of the Concluding Rite. In a historical Jesus community, this rite can be is transformed into Thankfulness and Good Tidings. The liturgical movement is called the Liturgy of Parting.

There need not be a detailed discussion here, because the Liturgy of Parting is a minor element of contrast with the traditional Church. The final blessing in Christianity is normally issued at the beginning of this movement, but it implies a certain condescension. A leader in front of the congregation transmits, as it were, energy from on high cast down upon the people at large. The words (such as, "and now may the grace of our Lord Jesus Christ . . .") do not come from the heart of a human being but are passed on in formula from God to the audience through a leader. It is difficult not to see a certain built-in pretense. An otherwise mighty God has paused here to pass on some good cheer to the human subject. Then, with the blessing received, the commission to go out into the world is issued to the people. The Greek word for blessing that is implied here is *eulogein,* which means "to speak well of." A more literal translation of the Greek to English is "good tidings" rather than "blessing" (in English, *blessing* is related to *blood*). Here is one place where the historical Jesus community is, in English expression, more literal than an English-speaking Christian church. A historical Jesus community can employ the expression "Good tidings" in place of "Blessing." This is not a moot point. Good tidings do not consist of passing along divine encouragements; to offer good tidings is to speak on the platform of compassion. Good tidings express a basic thankfulness for being alive, and then issues genuine good wishes to the community without using God-language. From the historical Jesus perspective, traditional God-language offers compassion vicariously on the basis of divine permission. Traditionally it might be said, "May God bless you," implying that one might care for another only if God thinks it's a good idea. A historical Jesus community moves to a foundation of humanism not out of an attempt to spurn God but in an attempt to create in individuals the honest heart of compassion. Human beings do not need divine permission to care for one another. Rather, such compassion is something everyone must learn to accept as part of his or her own being. That is the lesson of wisdom. Therefore, the parting expression of good tidings supports the sharing of peace by which the whole historical Jesus liturgy opened.

As indicated above, a sample outline of the Liturgy for a church of the historical Jesus is given in appendix 3, including examples of a banquet liturgy.

Four Linguistic
Centers Revisited

Like traditional Christianity, the liturgy of a historical Jesus community can hold four linguistic centers. In the tradition, I have named the four centers guilt, judgment, sacrifice, and proclamation; in the historical Jesus context these can be recast, I believe, as humanity, education, compassion, and honesty. I will try to indicate how these new centers can be expressed in a historical Jesus community.

The first linguistic center in a historical Jesus community displaces guilt with humanity. The language of the community is the language of humanity, that is, of the human connection to all that is. Such a connection assumes no condition of guilt; really, it is the opposite of guilt insofar as guilt in traditional Christianity is related to the separation of humanity from the divine. In historical Jesus thinking, no separation exists; instead, being human (being historical) already assumes a deeply connected relationship to the earth. Humanity is emergent with the earth. We are because the earth is. Like any other animal, we were born out of the history of this planet. In traditional Christianity, guilt denies the priority of this fundamental union because it moves attention from the earth to the sky. Overcoming guilt through a sacrifice offering forgiveness in traditional Christianity requires an act of divine intervention in history. Forgiveness comes as something extra added to human life from the outside. To affirm the historical Jesus is to affirm that there is no outside. Every human experience is of history; every human experience emerges from the fact of being in history. Every human experience is evidence of our connection not to what is transcendent but to what is immanent; every human experience is now and right here, not up and over there. The linguistic center of a historical Jesus community displaces the transcendental relationship that justifies guilt with an immanent relationship to others that justifies compassion. The linguistic expression of a historical Jesus liturgy is necessarily humanist because is it necessarily about relationships.

The second movement in traditional Christianity consists of the Liturgy of the Word centered on judgment, which is here displaced with the Liturgy of Learning centered on education. It was noted above how education can, in the Christian church, be relegated to special occasions or meeting rooms outside of the worshipping context. This hurts Christianity in two ways and, equally, contradicts the wisdom of a historical Jesus community in two ways. It hurts the traditional church first because when education is segregated from worship, it becomes the property of only a select section of the community. This means a community does not develop as a whole but in parts. Invariably one part is against another, and the community may eventually collapse. It hurts in a second way because the community experience is not about integrating education with spirituality but practically the exact opposite: leaving education outside the door of worship to create for many worship experiences that are incommensurable with the modern world. Wisdom, on the other hand, is certainly about integrating education and spirituality, so much so that the learning experience is a centerpiece of gathering in the historical Jesus way. Hearing the voice of the historical Jesus entails the use of biblical criticism, which means teaching biblical criticism openly, that is, publicly, in the gathering such that the journey of the community is collective rather than segregated. The rejection of education at the heart of human spirituality contradicts a historical Jesus community first by denying that human spirituality has intellectual content and, second, by failing in this regard to admit that the parabolic vision of Jesus was given through teaching. In our time it is right to say that never has humanity simultaneously held so much ability either to destroy or cooperate with the earth. The difference between the two options will be determined by how well we learn to think. A historical Jesus community, to my mind, will hold a linguistic center in the union of spirituality and thinking through education.

In traditional Christianity, the linguistic center that follows from judgment is sacrifice. It is through sacrifice that a link is made between guilt and reconciliation, and this relationship constitutes the metaphysics of Christian salvation. God in Jesus sacrifices human blood to create a crossing point between the human and divine worlds. In the historical Jesus community, the emphasis falls not on sacrifice but on inter-connection and inter-relation. These define the linguistic center of compassion in place of sacrifice. Approaching life with a historical understanding, "truth" is seen as a phenomenon or product of relationships. Truth is not an abstract principle but what happens between and among people, within economies, and on the basis of ecological limits. Truth is the activity of living: it is what defines the relation between myself and another. This understanding of truth as that which is created within relationships is consistent with the momentum of the historical Jesus. For Jesus, truth is situational; it arises in parables that constantly reference everyday life. It is a major oversight in Christian history and theology to fail to notice that, for the historical Jesus, compassion is the same as God. Both come to life in the situational choices of the everyday world.

The emphasis on compassion counteracts the long history of Christian language of prayers, praises, songs, blessings, and love directed upward beyond the earth to the sky. Compassion is the movement downward into history and toward people. It is the sharing of passion, of *pati,* that is, the sharing of common feeling. Compassion marks the end of religious battles between the mighty gods of human creation who set their truths one against the other; compassion is the turn to complementarity, which is the understanding that human beings create truths and live them only in relation to others. A truth remains in existence only so long as the relationships that created the truth remain to sustain it in existence. Ancient Samaria consisted of a mixed population that practiced a form of Judaism not acceptable to the Jews of ancient Judea and Galilee. The relation between the two peoples was one of rivalry and hatred. That was the truth of the world they created together and would remain so as long as the two nations allowed those truths to stand. Compassion is the parable of the Good Samaritan who offers loving kindness to his Jewish enemy and, in this, changes the truth of the world; compassion is the complement to that parable given as the instruction to love your enemies. Loving enemies means not having enemies: that means a changed world.

The final act of traditional Christian worship is proclamation, which consists of leaving a church building with the admonition to confess out in the world what was received inside the community. Thus, the linguistic center here was named confession. It is not a matter of questioning anymore what was received, for questions become the substance of a doubt that undermines the act of confessing. In traditional Christianity, confessing the truth of Christ in the world is the positive act of witnessing to the story. Though questions about the story can be raised and doubts can be held, these are overcome collectively in the confession of faith that secures the tradition outside the boundaries of reason.

Honesty is a linguistic center in a historical Jesus community that both displaces confession and tears down the security wall called faith. When history is affirmed as the platform of relationships on which human truth is created, it is not difficult to recognize and admit that religious convictions are often the consequential result of embedded cultural norms formed out of human imagination and fear. The act of honesty is the act of admitting that our knowledge is limited and always subject to revision, and that gaining wisdom is a lifetime's work that requires both patience and courage in the act of breaking down the defaults of our cultural norms.

The momentum of the historical Jesus movement rests on honesty. It cannot be otherwise if the intention is to walk in the path of one who taught in parable and who confounded in symbol and parody the majesty of his cultural God. It was the courage of his honesty that confronted the political and social limits of his time. There is no going beyond the limits if there is not first the honesty to state what the limits are and then to know, in the spirit of parable, that they are not really there after all. I was born and grew up in Canada. When I was born there was "no such thing" as homosexuality: that is what the culture of the time imagined. That was a created truth to satisfy a cultural need, but brave homosexual people stood outside that truth and re-imagined the world. Today, same-sex marriage is an accepted norm and constitutional right in Canada that not even a Conservative government will question. It was an act of national honesty to admit that human sexuality has always been pluralistic and that the cultural confession, which here and there is still voiced, that there is "no such thing" as homosexuality was only the default of fear but not the integrity of honesty. A historical

Jesus community stands in the momentum of overcoming fear with the integrity of honesty.

This chapter challenges the Christian tradition to change its language and concepts on the basis of the historical Jesus. To do so in practice means to do so in liturgy. It means to change linguistic centers such that a community can gather in ritual to uphold humanity, education, compassion, and honesty. Then, beyond liturgy, there lies theology. Developing theology with the historical Jesus against the background of centuries of theology with Jesus as Christ is no easy task, but to this we must now turn.

Notes

1. The Quest Centre, of which I am the director, meets regularly in Hamilton, Ontario.

2. Nicene Creed

3. There are, to be sure, hints of a non-apocalyptic, non-Savior, Jesus in the Gospel of Thomas and some of the Q material. The problem is the Christian Church historically never developed on the basis of these hints, which is why in our day there is much work and experimentation going on based on these long neglected hints.

4. Stephen A. Hoeller, *Gnosticism*, 116.

5. Paul Tillich, *Shaking the Foundations.*

6. Tertullian (160–240 ce) loved this built-in contradiction of Christian faith. He claimed to believe Christianity because it was absurd. That was fine for his age, when God was a sufficient answer to many questions about the universe. In our age, the argument is not satisfactory. Naturally, the universe is still a mystery, but neither God nor faith is a necessary response. Awe about the universe today is often better expressed in science than in religion.

7. It is not necessary for my point to discuss here the traditional Roman Catholic and Protestant difference of whether or not this "standing in place of" is best reasoned as transubstantiation (the whole body and blood become the whole bread and wine) or consubstantiation (the whole body and blood exists together with the whole bread and wine).

8. This is the theology of so-called "cultural Calvinism" which, of course, does not belong to Calvin but is rather pervasive as an experience in Christianity.

9. See Dominic Crossan, *God and Empire*.

10. See chapter 6. Open commensality is a key term from Dominic Crossan's *Jesus: A Revolutionary Biography*.

8

Theological Challenges
after the Historical Jesus

aking the historical Jesus seriously requires us to change
Christian liturgical language, practice, and rationality. Though
the fourfold[1] action of classical Christian liturgy can remain, the
reasoning and the words—the content—are set on a different
platform. The historical Jesus community does not worship; it
gathers. It gathers not as a church but as a learning center; it
gathers not in praise but in solidarity. Gathering happens in the
name of and for the reason of our common humanity. The shift
to humanitarian language in a historical Jesus community arises
precisely because Jesus was "historical": a human being like
anyone. In place of a supernatural reality, in the wisdom of the
historical Jesus there is compassion for reality.

The task of re-thinking Christian theology with the historical
Jesus awakens a different problem. In contrast to re-imagining
Christian liturgy, the task of reconstituting Christian theol-
ogy demands more than retaining form but changing content.
Something more fundamental is afoot that calls for changes in
thinking about history, human religious experience, and a new
set of theological questions now placed on a new foundation.
These types of changes require taking a new direction from the
heritage of the past. They require, what philosopher Martin
Heidegger called, wandering off the beaten track.[2]

Traditional Christianity has had two thousand years to contemplate theology and to create theological systems. By contrast, the historical Jesus community is only beginning to propose some basic ideas. Certain contours are clear. Doing theology after the historical Jesus means altering and maybe dismissing the idea of God. At the very least, the momentum of the historical Jesus does not support the literalism about God that has come to define our age. If the idea of God is to hold meaning in light of the historical Jesus, then "God" has to change. God, like Jesus, needs a demotion.

Another problem is, what becomes of all the profound theology Western history has produced in the name of God? What of hope? What of the idea of sacredness? What about morality and the sense of purpose to the world order? In traditional Christianity, hope has been built on apocalyptic expectation, but with the historical Jesus this door has been closed. How is there hope without the sanctioning of the divine?

Then there is the problem of the title of Jesus, the Christ, which is the earliest confession of the Christian movement. Yet the historical Jesus lived and taught wisdom before this title was cast upon him. Is it even desirable to keep this burden fixed on his head? God, hope, and Christ: these are three critical questions, and the trouble begins with God.

God

The idea of God in traditional Christianity is a complex yet simple notion. This paradox has always marked Christian theology. The contradiction arises because Christianity is a combination of biblical stories and Greek philosophy. The images related to God in the Bible are distinct from the systematic working out of the idea of God in philosophy. The reader might think that the systematic philosophical God is surely the complex part of the equation and the biblical God is the simple part. Yet this is wrong. Even though philosophy can be a very complicated subject, the systematic idea of God in philosophy is absolute simplicity. Meanwhile, in the Bible, God is anything but simplicity. In the Bible, God is often like a person who, though big and powerful, is spoiled. God has immature emotions, feeds on prejudice, demands immoral acts, puts up an amazing and dangerous fuss when ignored, threatens those of a different opinion or nations of a different God, and generally delights in recognition and praise. It is hard not to see the biblical God as a complex of emotions not often guided by compassion. Yet, the biblical God is also filled with compassion, abounds in forgiveness, has a non-negotiable standard of justice particularly to the advantage of the poor, and is the foundation of moral order. God in the Bible is complex because somehow, if the picture is to be coherent, the drastic emotional swings must be reconciled within the identity of God as the voice of justice and compassion. Sometimes this reconciliation is completely impossible. A being who stands outside history as the creator of the world simply should not be so petty as to express jealousy. Yet, the biblical God does exactly this. A being who is the principle of universal justice simply should not also be the one who issues commands for vengeance. But this, too, characterizes the God of the Bible. It is a natural paradox, as the theologian Kierkegaard understood, to combine images of God as an overseer of history with images of God as one personally involved in history. From the perspective of the Bible, God stands in this paradox and is defined by it.

In the Greek philosophical world, which is also the heritage of Christianity, the idea of God is based not on the Bible but on the concept of absolute simplicity. By definition, God is not a person, that is, an individual, and does not have emotions. The distinction is drawn between existing things, like people, or existing qualities, like anger or peacefulness, and God, who is the principle of things. In classical philosophy, God does not exist but is existence. God does not have emotions but is the foundation of being. God is not in history—because God cannot be a "something" among other things—but is the whole of the historical order of things. Neither can God have a past or a future, because God is not in time, like "things" are in time, but rather is all time (or time-less). In classical philosophy, which defined Christianity from the time of Justin Martyr (approximately 250 CE) to the Protestant Reformation (approximately 1525 CE), God is virtually *nothing*, but is nothing in a very special sense. The sense is that God cannot be a *something*, since this would turn God into history and make God part of time. God is beyond time and history, which means that what happens in the world and how things happen are not specifically intended by God. Nothing that happens to individual things or individual people is to be taken personally. In place, one has to have the whole of the cosmic order in mind. God is the simplicity of this order: the basis of its functioning and the aim of its motion. Life and death in this sense are simply part of the order of things, which is God.[3]

Historically, Christianity creatively combined its biblical heritage with its Greek philosophical heritage. Christianity combined complexity and simplicity in the idea of God. It is a very difficult marriage, but for centuries it managed to work. It worked because theologians understood a difference between the *personal historical* and the *universal transcendental*. The personal historical is the human experience of time. Human beings cannot imagine what is not in time and what is not in history. Our imaginations fail us in this regard because time and history are, so to speak, the presuppositions or the state of the human *modus operandi*. We cannot grasp what is not experienced. To put this in practical terms, we must first be human beings before we can raise questions about our humanity and our beliefs. So, to us, God is always thought about within the experience of time and history. God seems to be emotionally involved in life because we interpret historical events on this level. We use images of justice to think about God, and this leads us to speak of God in relation to justice issues, but we so think and speak on the basis of what justice means to us. Unable to hold the cosmic vision, it may seem in our experience of history that God has chosen one side against another or has favored one person or nation against others. These feelings exist on the level of our personal historical experience, but they do not exist in the perspective of the transcendental universal. Christianity in its classical expression explained the distinction between the biblical complexity of God and the philosophical simplicity of God as a consequence of human finite being trying to comprehend divine infinite being. The Bible expresses itself through finite imagery that reaches into and affects human experience. On the other hand, human reason is still capable of understanding the essence of God in the idea of perfect simplicity.

Even though the God question still occupies a lot of attention, in truth the problem we face today is not really the question of God's existence or lack of existence. When properly understood, the classical notion of God in philosophy is not that far away from modern atheism. To say that God is absolute simplicity is the same as saying that God cannot be thought (since God is the foundation of thinking but not the object of thinking). But to say that God cannot be thought is basically the same as saying God's existence cannot be thought. This is close to modern atheism, since the conclusion of both the classical idea of God as absolute simplicity and the modern atheistic denial of God's existence agree that God does not exist. Atheism tries to prove God does not exist by demonstrating that there is no evidence for God as an existing thing. The classical theistic position is actually more sophisticated because it concludes that, as absolute simplicity, God is beyond the question of existence and non-existence and, even further, is misunderstood as an existing thing. The classical position holds that God is so simple human beings can only grasp the idea in a negative way by saying what God is not. So, for example, God is not existence or essence but beyond the question of existence and essence. Or, God is not good or evil but beyond the question of good and evil. God is not space or time but inaccessible to the categories of space and time. In other words, the simplicity of God can only be expressed, finally, by saying what God is not, which is, in effect, a statement of "atheism." It is a peculiar but important insight to recognize that properly thought out theism and properly thought out atheism are different routes to the same practical conclusion.

The problem about God today does not lie in the sophistication of classical philosophy but in the almost total conversion of modern theism to literalism. On a popular level, the question concerning God is no longer metaphorical. The enormous popularity and use of technical science has progressively created a culture of literalism where religious questions are imagined within the same framework as evidence-based science. We are used to thinking that when we talk about something, the "thing" we talk about is necessarily an object in the world to be experienced, and this technical form of thinking slides over from science to rest also on metaphorical religious language. For the past two hundred years or so, when speaking about God the assumption is almost exclusively that such talk is about an object who either exists or does not exist. The metaphorical vision of the historical Jesus about an alternative lifestyle called the "kingdom of God" has been forced to take a leave of absence.

In light of the historical Jesus, neither classical theism nor modern atheism manages the shift from God to history. On the one hand, the trouble with the classical position is that, in its highly metaphysical expression, it does not bring God meaningfully to earth and into the mix of existential reality. On the other hand, the literalistic debate about whether or not there is a thing called God seems like the modern equivalent of debating how many angels can dance on the head of a pin. In its context, the latter question was really a debate about whether or not angels occupied space, but the question has come to symbolize completely irrelevant issues. We can easily understand why: for the answer to the question is, who cares? Though the modern question about God's existence seems important, it is a red herring from a historical Jesus point of view. If God-talk is metaphoric language for vision and lifestyle, then it does not make sense to debate if a metaphor is literally true. Metaphors are artistic expressions, not theorems. And in this sense, who really cares if God exists or not, or, for that matter, how many gods can rest on the head of a pin? On the platform of the historical Jesus, we can say that the world is as it is whether or not God exists, and the world can be imagined differently in parable whether or not God exists. God does not need to exist to be metaphorically available to parable.[4]

When one seeks to understand God within the momentum of the historical Jesus, there are a few options to consider. But modern literalism is not one of them. The historical Jesus presumably thought that God existed, and the God who existed was the God of Israel, but even so, the God of the historical Jesus is only available in metaphor. God in the sayings of Jesus is always "like" something, but the thing that God is like is a situation in life. To the historical Jesus, God's existence seems not to matter all that much because, in the end, the question is about how one practices life.

God for the historical Jesus is an activity rather than a transcendental principle. In light of this, it is possible to say that with the historical Jesus, we have reached the place where God is too problematic for use. To speak about God today inevitably turns God into a "thing" that one either believes in or rejects. God is no longer about the very mystery and absolute beauty of life, and no longer functions to take us beyond literalism into parable. If the main point of a historical Jesus community is to shift the experience of the world from the default reality, which is our literalism, to the parabolic reality, then God is not a necessary part of the journey. Indeed, God can often be a kind of tempting distraction who will convert the lifestyle question to language about belief. In place of God, life-language is the better choice for vocabulary in the parabolic world. Life language takes us "into" life and how we live it, and that is the momentum of the historical Jesus. In the words of Don Cupitt, who more than any other has advocated for the transformation of religious language from God to life, "Life is that in which 'we live and move and have our being' (Acts 17:28), within which we are formed, and of whose past we will remain a part. Both our ultimate Origin and our Last End are within life. Life is now as God to us."[5]

Admittedly, some people who attend the historical Jesus community of which I am a part grieve the loss of the word God. They insist that God is a word we need to keep because the concept of God adds stability to culture, a foundation to ethics, and a sense of purpose to life. While it is true that literalism has been detrimental to religion, they say, not everyone who believes in God is a literalist. There can be belief in God that is free from literalism. I have sympathy for this objection, and with sympathy I will address it.

Contemporary religious literalism, which constantly turns God into an individual who lives somewhere in the sky, is only one problem with the idea of God. There are several other problems, like the alienation of the self from the self and from the world that is introduced with the idea of God.[6] There is also the problem that God language does not convey the sense of the historical Jesus momentum in the way life language does. Added to these objections is the larger problem that stressing one's belief or lack of belief in "God" does not say anything anymore. God may be a statement about what one believes, but the statement does not add any information to our understanding of the world or inform us about how we should live. To answer questions about the world, we turn to science; and to answer questions about how one should live, we turn to authoritative things that human beings have written, even if those things are sacred things like the Torah or the Bible. Wherever we turn for information, the source of the information is human imagination. God is not an explanation of anything, anymore. It is wrong, in my mind, to hold on to God purely for psychological reasons and, in this, to face neither history as humanity's creation nor the authenticity of one's own life.

Yet, if one were to insist on the need for God, then it remains possible to use the word somewhat in the classical sense of simplicity mixed with the modern sense of the personal. Doing so, however, requires a lengthy explanation. First, one would have to understand the classical notion of God as absolute simplicity and the post-Reformation notion of God as a literal person. To combine these two means to recognize that by God we are signifying mystery as a definitive experience of human life. So, mystery is the classical sense of God as ineffable reality, yet we could say that reality as such is still "personal" because it is what we live in. To live in the parabolic world means to live with the conscious awareness of mystery that can liberate us to be in the world differently. This very act of living in the awareness of mystery is certainly spiritual and can be defined as the awareness of God. This sense of God is entirely possible to uphold beyond literalism and without alienation from the self.

Still, it is troubling and difficult to make such explanations whenever God comes up in conversation. Secondly, the explanation still involves a lot of troubling talk about metaphysical notions without ever addressing the question of vision, lifestyle, and social justice. It still holds the God-problem of abstract effort directed away from historical living. God's demotion with the historical Jesus involves the movement out of abstraction and into the address of life directly. With Nietzsche in mind, it seems best to declare that the word God is dead. We can never mean it in the same way ancient people did because we are not ancient people. And we can spend a lot of time with God without really saying anything significant about life. We need to create a whole new language of life in place of the language of God. This is a genuine challenge in theology with the historical Jesus.

Hoping Without Praying

In the latter half of the 1960's, the German theologian Jürgen Moltmann wrote what quickly became a classic text, *The Theology of Hope*.[7] It was the first book of what became a trilogy, and by the time I was in seminary in the early eighties, the three books together were a must-read. Moltmann struck a chord because his book, and the sequels, addressed what then seemed to be the heart of the gospel for our time. He managed to articulate the suffering of the world, which consisted, as it still does today, of the overwhelming exploitation by wealthy nations of poor nations and, as a parallel, the overwhelming depression experienced among progressives in wealthy nations who sought and failed to change the priorities of their governments. In the midst of this experience, a *theology* of hope offered not only a way to cope but also a word to proclaim.

Moltmann's theology was not a new but re-newed expression of Christianity in a new and challenging time. It was an apologetic work, and it is this word, briefly, that I want to concentrate on before addressing the problem of hope and prayer in relation to the historical Jesus.

In its originating Greek form (*apologia*), apology means "defense." The *Apology* of Plato, for example, presents the defense of Socrates before the elders of Athens. Socrates explains himself and his actions against the accusations brought upon him, even though, in the end, he is sentenced to death. An apologetic work in theology is an explanation of theological concepts in a new situation or before new issues. Paul Tillich (1886–1964), the greatest of Christian apologists in the twentieth century, recognized the difficulty modern folk have with understanding theological concepts like "sin" due to the restriction of its meaning to bad or evil acts. Tillich spoke about sin as "estrangement"[8] and indicated that sin is more than an act. It is a state of being that lies behind immoral acts and defines the human condition. In talking about estrangement, then, Tillich was offering a Christian apology. He was explaining what sin means in depth and trying to find a way the Church could talk about it in the modern world.

The problem with apologetic theology is that it places before Christianity the temptation to avoid thinking that Christianity needs to change. Instead, apology suggests that the only thing we really need to do is explain Christianity better. Sometimes this is true. Sometimes Christian theologians unearth profound insights into human psychology that our modern ears cannot hear very well without a good explanation of an ancient concept. So, sometimes an apology or explanation is both appropriate and enlightening. However, there is another side to the coin. Sometimes, despite apologetic attempts, the original notions are nevertheless wrong. A word like *sin* may not be just outdated; it might be a fundamentally flawed way to think about life. It might be better to disband the notion of estrangement and substitute, as in historical Jesus liturgy, the linguistic center of solidarity as a better way to think about human life. Sometimes ancient problems, even when explained with modern sensibility, remain ancient problems. Sometimes the more significant task of changing things and thinking things anew is lost to apology. Apologetic theology can seem like "new" thinking, but insofar as it remains the task of explaining ancient assumptions, is it really thinking?

Both the concept of hope and the practice of Christian prayer may fall victim to the apologetic problem. They are no longer the words that need to be explained; in their place is the challenge to think with new language. Apologetically, hope, as Moltmann wrote some decades back, is rooted in Christianity's eschatological nature: that is, it is rooted in the *aim toward the end*. Moltmann understood that the Greek concept of order (*logos*) in the universe was poorly combined, in Christianity, with the biblical understanding of a promised aim (end) to history. He explains how real Christianity is about engaging God's eschatological promise for the end of history.[9] Christian hope is the living out existentially of the promise of God for creation. Moltmann's thinking is instructive because it shows how Christian apology can inspire the modern world with ancient Christian faith, but it also shows how the apology must still assume there is a God, a creation, and an intention to the creation. Though a critical thinker might find it difficult to talk about God and about creation, the greatest difficulty lies in the idea of intention to the universal order. Is it not presumptuous, and even an act of hubris, to hold the idea that the universe has an intentional promise for humanity? Intention in the universe is most likely a projection of the human ego onto the horizon. In other words, that God intentionally aims the universe to a great fulfillment is a human story. It is a fiction that arises from our ancestors and from our general need to survive. The trouble is that in our time it is no longer a tenable picture of the universe, and on a psychological level such a belief does not allow a realistic confrontation with our human responsibility for the course of history.

The historical Jesus lived in and was formed by the ancient worldview. It is admittedly an apologetic task to enliven his wisdom in our time by focusing on what I have called the momentum of his movement. The effort to define the five gospels of the historical Jesus was precisely an apologetic effort (see chapter 6). These gospels are not lessons that Jesus explicitly taught, but they are ways of thinking about how the direction the theology of the historical Jesus moves in our time.

When it comes to hope and to prayer, however, there is no obvious apologetic way to recover their use, since here, more than elsewhere, we stand in great contrast to the ancient worldview. Jesus lived when the world was a three-storied universe. It was not very difficult in his world to think that "up there" in the heavens was a divine, that down here on earth dwelt fragile human beings, and that below us all dwells the underworld of the dead and the demons. Nor was it regarded strange to link human suffering to the activity of malicious spirits. When dealing with antiquity, we are dealing with a setting where the course of one's life and the sorrows of one's time (and even the political decisions of one's empire) unfolded in a three-storied universe with gods readily available upstairs. One would beg (pray) for deliverance and offer a pleasing sacrifice to win a god's favor. The structure of Christian prayer and the content of Christian hope are more or less derived from this ancient three-storied universe. Christian prayer takes two basic forms. It is either petitioning prayer or it is thanksgiving prayer. Both forms assume that not far beyond the clouds lies a divine figure who can intervene in human affairs, or at least be persuaded to consider them differently. So, in Christian churches, petitions to God are typically offered for the sick or the dying, for those who suffer tragedy, for the well-being of governments, for the success of athletes, for the curriculum in schools, and victory in war. All these forms of petitioning assume a limited universe where just beyond the clouds a divine figure sits and listens and contemplates whether or not to respond. Christians, with the same assumptions, "send up" prayers of thanksgiving to the god for good things like a harvest, safe journeys, gifts received through friendships or businesses, and honors from academic institutions. Sending things up and hoping for things to come down reflect the ancient understanding of a much smaller and divinely inhabited cosmos.

It is possible, apologetically, to indicate that prayer can be a form of concentration that helps us psychologically even though, realistically, an individual is not even thinking of a three-storied universe and may not even particularly believe in God. However, my critique is not the private life of individuals but the public language of church. Prayers in church normally employ expressions like God's "will" or God's "vision" or God's "plan" or

God's "way." All of these expressions deflate the community experience by directing the collective will away from history and from authentic language about life. Instead, a transcendental reality, the cosmic upstairs, is addressed as if that very signification will change events or convince an audience to act differently in the world. An imperative of a historical Jesus community must surely be that the language of the community needs to be directed to history, raised from within the solidarity of people, and hold inspiration to act now. This form of spiritual language is not that of petitioning and thanksgiving. The move is towards the "humanism" of the historical Jesus. It is language directly related to human beings that can sincerely invoke change. To pray for someone might create a fantasy of hope, but it can never match the sincere comfort of genuine care for another.

Inasmuch as traditional prayer implies an upstairs to the universe where a divine figure holds the power to arbitrate events, Christian hope historically rests on the apocalyptic worldview that defines traditional Christianity as a religion about the end. It might be the case here, too, that an apologetic theology can save the Christian understanding of hope, but equally the question is, how far can apology take us before we start to deny our modern understanding? We can speak of "destiny" as that which is influenced by human acts and distinguish this from "fate" as that which cannot be so influenced. Paul Tillich spoke of this distinction. Christian hope then can be understood as the final reconciliation of destiny and fate where the two become one and where our efforts and our suffering in life find meaning in God. Hope in this way is the act of trusting in a meaning that cannot be seen. It is as the author of Hebrews poetically states, ". . . the conviction of things unseen" (11:1).

Eventually, though, the same problem encountered with prayer exists for the idea of hope. Since traditional Christianity rests hope on an apocalyptic worldview, it, too, implies the ancient three-storied universe. Like prayer, hope relies on the assurance of a cosmic designer who, from outside history, will, despite all, guide it to the end. Christianity can pray in hope for God's will to be done on the assumption that "up there" and "out there" the divine will is busy working out a scheme. History moves to its appointed end; Christian hope consists of believing one day this end will arrive. The wisdom of the historical Jesus, however, is non-apocalyptic. It throws a wrench into the divine scheme of things. Now, there needs to be a way to speak of hope in a non-apocalyptic universe.

In the wisdom tradition associated with Jesus, cosmic images of a powerful and directing God get disrupted in parables that comically collapse the divine reality into mundane activity. At first, a parable lures us in with a glimpse of the world as we expect to see it—the normal, or default, world—and then the parable corrupts this reading through startling reversals. God is supposed to be too holy to be associated with unclean leaven, but in the parable of Jesus where a woman conceals leaven in three large piles of flour, the reality of God *does*, in fact, come alive in the unclean. In apocalyptic theology, hope is supposed to lie at the end when the whole world will be purified (through fire) in reconciliation with God; in wisdom theology hope exists not in the anticipated cleansing but in the present dirt. Another way to think of this is to imagine that the work of the parable is to dislodge hope from a future reality and then to place the future in the present as reality. This is perhaps a strange twist of phrase, but if we imagine the parable as the practice of bringing an alternative reality to life, then hope becomes the practice, not the future. Recall the Good Samaritan: the Samaritan, the first-century enemy of the Jewish people, offered loving kindness to an individual who would normally recoil from a Samaritan's touch. But this is the parable. It is not about the present world but about the present world of a different reality. It is not about a world where someday there will be no enemies; it is, rather, the practice of compassion that shatters the present world of enmity.

In the audience you can hear a voice say, "That's crazy; I'll never treat an enemy like a brother or a sister." But in the parable you can hear the practice of hope. It is possible to be in the world differently. It is possible to bring to life an alternative future in the present activity. The world is not directed to the future; the future is converted into the present. That is the character of non-apocalyptic hope with the historical Jesus. Like with the idea of God, it is indeed a sincere challenge of the historical Jesus for the church to convert its theology of hope accordingly.

A Christless Jesus

Christ is a Greek word ancient Jewish scholars used in the Septuagint to translate "Messiah" (the Septuagint is the Greek translation of the Jewish Bible). New Testament writers used this word, too, so *Jesus Christ* means *Jesus the Anointed*. When the writers of the Christian New Testament say that Jesus is Christ, they mean God chose Jesus for a special task. However, depending on the author, both the title Christ and the task of the Anointed can be differently understood. The Christian New Testament offers different ways to think about the task of the anointed Jesus. The Apostle Paul is relatively clear that the task for Jesus the Anointed was to bring the gentiles into the house of Israel as worshippers of the true God. To Paul, this was part of God's faithful action toward the gentiles, rooted in the promises given to Israel, for Israel was to be the witness to God among the nations as a light to the world. Jesus is the Anointed for Paul because he is that light, the one who, through death and resurrection, has brought the gentiles under the promises of God. Paul speaks of gentiles and their former life under the law[10] and contrasts this with their new life in the body of Christ. This is why Paul does not appeal to Moses concerning the Torah but to Abraham, who came before the Torah and through whom the promises of God were given to the nations.[11] To Paul, en-lightening the gentiles, the nations, in Christ completes both

Israel's mission and God's intentions. This is why, apparently, Paul thinks the world will shortly come to an end, that is, to its completion.

The Gospel of Mark most specifically relates the suffering of Jesus to the confession of him as the Christ. But for what purpose is Jesus anointed? Mark provides no clear answer, even for himself. Certainly for Mark to relate the mission of Jesus to the eventual glorification of Jesus is a mistake. Mark insists that any disciple who thinks the life of Jesus is about triumph is wrong, and more than just wrong, he or she is working on the side of Satan (Mark 8:33)! In place of glory, Jesus must suffer, and that is both his task and the constant refrain impressed upon the reader or hearer of this gospel. It could be that the audience to which the Gospel of Mark is directed is part of the vast number of poverty-stricken peasants in the Roman Empire, who knew daily suffering. Mark could be aligning in solidarity the mission of the Christ with the reality of the poor.[12] That would explain why, in this Gospel, it is not glory but suffering that expresses the reality of God. However, there is also the instruction at the end of the gospel to "go to Galilee" (Mark 14:28 and 15:7), which suggests that following the Jewish War in the years 67–70 CE, when the Temple and city of Jerusalem were destroyed, the presence of the Christian movement in Jerusalem came to an end. The future involved reestablishing the early Jesus movement in Galilee and, from there, likely heading toward Antioch. Maybe the theme of necessary suffering in Mark relates to the aftermath of the Jewish War when the Jesus movement appeared to have no viable future. Perhaps suffering in Mark is a lament over a movement the writer thinks was a genuine failure.

Matthew and Luke present another picture of the tasks of Jesus as God's Anointed. In Matthew, the Christ is the fulfillment of the Torah and, in this way, is the new Israel. During the ministry of Jesus on earth, Matthew depicts the aim of the gospel to be directed solely to the lost sheep of the house of Israel

(Matt 10:6). Yet, following the resurrection, the commissioning of the disciples is to go out to the nations (gentiles). The Gospel of Matthew witnesses to the mix of Jews and gentiles involved in the early Christian movement, but Matthew is determined to show that this movement toward gentiles is indeed the right direction for Israel. It is a movement consistent with the witness of scripture. So, for Matthew, the mission of Jesus and the reason he is the Anointed is directly related to the re-birth of a new Israel among the nations after the fall of Jerusalem.

The Gospel of Luke is less concerned with demonstrating the continuity of the Jesus movement with the Torah of Israel except insofar as the Torah includes commandments to care for the poor. In Luke, the Anointed Jesus is explicitly the teller of good news to the poor. Indeed, the mission of Jesus in Luke is inaugurated exactly with these words from Isaiah: "The spirit of the Lord is upon me because God has anointed me to bring good news to the poor" (Luke 4:18).[13] To be a follower of Christ means not only to provide food, clothing, and shelter to the poor but also to see in this activity the reality of God. For Luke, Jesus is Christ because, in the activity of Jesus, the character of God as compassion for the poor is revealed.

The fourth of the Christian Gospels is John, who, unlike the other three, holds the identity of Christ so closely to the identity of Jesus that the proclamation of Jesus is pretty much about himself as the Christ. His task is to reveal himself. He is the one who comes from the Father, the one through whom the Father is known, and the one who takes away the sin of the world. The world is darkness in John, so the most significant thing about Jesus as Christ is that he calls his followers into the light. But only belief is necessary to hear the call and receive it. Those who hear his voice and obey bear witness to the light in the world. With John, the reader is invited to be among those of the light who receive in faith the Father's revelation of glory and by belief belong to the sheep of his fold.

It is possible to write extensive details about the use of Christ in the New Testament and the various theologies represented there. It is possible to do the same for the whole of Christian history. There are many resources to turn to for such a task.[14] The point here is to highlight some options that New Testament writers employed when articulating their understanding of Jesus as Christ. In this, it is clear that they followed no preset doctrine. They experimented freely with different ideas while trying to develop a theology related to the Anointed. The problem for us presently is twofold: the momentum created by the writers of the New Testament was not the momentum of the historical Jesus; secondly, of course, the historical Jesus had no idea he would be the Christ within a new religion. The momentum of the historical Jesus is wisdom, but what motivates the Christian movement is the confession of the Christ. The Christ is not the gospel of the historical Jesus, and this disjunction creates some genuine problems.

The church has historically used "Christ" as a synonym for the essential, or divine, quality of Jesus. This act is not even part of the New Testament, but it has become the central feature of the Christian tradition. The essence of a thing is its perfect and eternal form. It is what a thing is meant to be if its true identity is understood. Christ in Christianity is the perfect and eternal part of the human Jesus; it is his divine nature that exists with his human nature as a perfect form. The effort to explain how the human and the divine nature of Jesus could co-exist in the person of Jesus Christ occupied many centuries of Christian debate and continues in religious philosophy today. The problem from the historical Jesus perspective is that the Christ tradition has basically nothing to do with Jesus. The introduction of Christ in relation to Jesus converts the historical figure into an ideal who lies outside normal human life. Here, neither the context of his life nor the words of his teaching count. The focus is not on Jesus in existential reality but the essential reality of the Christ in Jesus. What matters is his essential form, which became the confession of faith. This first problem of the essential Christ transforming the historical Jesus to authoritative ideal is the first area of trouble a theologian of the historical Jesus encounters.

In addition, the title "Christ" holds a second problem. This consists of its imperial nature. As a teller of parables, Jesus mocked imperial ideas of God, particularly evident when associating the presence of God with a mustard plant or with yeast. Both are anti-imperial images where the divine glory is smothered with satire and associated with corruption. The gospel writers understood the point. Mark relates Jesus Christ to suffering, as we saw, and portrays the disciples as dim because they cannot make the connection. Luke explicitly relates the reality of God to the service of the poor. In Philippians, Paul explicitly associates the reality of God found in the Anointed with humility and emptiness (2:7–8). New Testament writers knew that to call someone who was crucified the Christ was ironically to offer an imperial title to a Roman criminal. The peasant Jesus who was confessed as the Christ brought an alternative parabolic reality in direct confrontation with the default reality of the Roman Empire. Dominic Crossan has made this remarkable point by indicating how Jesus as the Christ was an affront to Caesar as the Christ: parable reality set against empire reality. Still, from the historical Jesus perspective, it must be asked, is the anti-imperial intention of the title of Christ enough to save the historical Jesus?

The question returns us a final time to the apocalyptic nature of Christianity and the way in which, despite the irony that may have been originally intended, Christ works to turn Jesus into God's end-time envoy. As if he were Augustus Caesar who defeated his enemies in a bloody civil war, Jesus, too, will one day come back to earth to set things right. Like Caesar, he will acknowledge the faith of some and dispense the fate of others. In the Church, Jesus has become Caesar by another name. The historical person has been tragically lost in the competitions of power and anointing.

Learning to talk about Jesus without employing titles is the challenge of a historical Jesus community and historical Jesus theology. The difficulty is that the Christian tradition began with the Christ confession. The confession is the bedrock of Christianity. Yet the confession of Jesus as Christ is the central act that shifts the teller of parable from the peasant sage to the imperial guardian of heaven. Once the crown has been bestowed, there is no way back. What is left is a way around, which involves giving Jesus his demotion by dropping the title Christ.

In place of Christ, a historical Jesus community can emphasis compassion as the centerpiece of theology. The challenge of the historical Jesus is not to relate God to our nation, not to think of God as for or against other people, not to confine God within our religion, not to determine God in the acts of nature, and not to restrict God to correct beliefs. Indeed the challenge is to liberate God from being God and, in exchange, let God be the quality of life. These acts are the acts of compassion. They stretch our imagination; they ask us to overcome our narrow ego; they demand that we identify our common humanity with others. These acts rest on the momentum of parable, which directs us out of abstraction and into life. These acts also pose a third challenge to the Church from the historical Jesus: move theology from confession to practice.

In every opportunity I have had to speak of the historical Jesus and to talk about theology after the historical Jesus, I have always been asked whether a historical Jesus community that no longer confesses Jesus as Christ is it still Christianity? I usually point out, as I have done here, that even in the New Testament there are diverse ways to contemplate the meaning of Christ. The New Testament authors did not have a model. They wrote before the notion of Christian orthodoxy existed. The term Christ has always had an experimental nature to it. Christianity is a living process. Except in the minds of a few, it is not actually set anywhere for all time. If New Testament writers could experiment, surely it is permissible to engage this living religion like any other human phenomenon and to admit it has reached its time for change. Still, my questioner will usually persist, if a historical Jesus community drops the title Christ, is it still Christianity?

Notes

1. The four movements, as discussed in chapter 7, consist of the Gathering (Introductory Rite), the Word, the Table, and the Dismissal (Concluding Rite).

2. *Holzwege* is the German word Heidegger (1889–1976) used, which was translated as *Off the Beaten Track*.

3. Thomas Aquinas expressed the classical notion of simplicity by saying God's essence and being are one and the same (*On Being and Essence*, 61).

4. John Kloppenborg notes that ancient wisdom, in contrast to prophetic announcements, focused on the teacher and on the authority of the saying as instruction, not on God and the Word of God (*Formation of Q*, 321).

5. Don Cupitt, *Above Us Only Sky*.

6. Ludwig Feuerbach (1804–1872) identified the problem of God and the alienation of the self from the self most resolutely in his *The Essence of Christianity*, 28.

7. The book was written in 1965 but appeared for the first time in English in 1967 (London: SCM Press). It is not clear that Moltmann intended a trilogy, but the three books are seen in this light: *Theology of Hope*, *The Crucified God*, and *The Church in the Power of the Spirit*.

8. *Systematic Theology*, vol. II.

9. *Theology of Hope*, 40–42.

10. I do not interpret law in relation to gentiles to mean Torah. Paul means the law over gentiles, which is exactly not the Torah. Without the Torah and under their own law, the gentiles need Christ.

11. Lloyd Gaston, *Paul and the Torah*, 45–63.

12. This could mean Mark was fundamentally a political gospel. See Ched Myers, *Binding the Strong Man*.

13. Cf. Isa 42:1; 49:9; 61:1.

14. An excellent resource in this regard is Aloys Grillmeier's *Christ in Christian Tradition*.

9

Is It Still Christianity?

To work through the problem of the historical Jesus as a topic of discussion is an interesting and stimulating debate; to try to create a community experience based on the historical Jesus is quite another matter. While thousands of educated laity, clergy, and academic theologians enjoy engaging the question, the line is often drawn at taking the historical Jesus to church. This hesitation to move from private debates to public practices comes from a natural human conservatism. Community patterns are very hard to change because, especially in large communities, people are present based on the assumption that the practices that brought them there will remain. Even in the case of individuals, beliefs about life that we have either grown up with or decided upon, as long as we think they work, are difficult to question and change. To take the historical Jesus seriously means not only to open the door to debate about history, doctrine, and belief but also to put in practice features of the momentum of the historical Jesus that define a community pattern. Theoretically, as I hope this book has shown, it is not actually that difficult to do. The main obstacle to carrying out the project is often, ironically, Jesus and his traditional divine authority. Giving Jesus a demotion, as Bob Funk readily put it, can be experienced as uncomfortably irreverent. Jesus and his traditional authority can block the way to his own humanity.

193

Nevertheless, accepting Jesus as a human being and building a community experience in the momentum of this ancient wisdom teacher can be done. It is a question of identifying the barriers on the path and deconstructing their power.

If a community chooses to enter the way of the historical Jesus, there needs to be some frank discussion about how the traditional status of Jesus as God can function as an impasse that affects this decision. The first step involves understanding the roadblocks placed between a church community and the historical Jesus. Next, there is a need to address the question of what defines Christianity generally. Then, with this latter question satisfactorily addressed, there can be a discussion about whether or not a historical Jesus church is still part of Christianity. A community's choice for or against the path of the historical Jesus often depends on how that last question is answered.

The roadblocks to taking the historical Jesus to church are likely more than I am able to name, but the immediate task is not to imagine and then respond to every single question. At some point every individual or community who seeks to take the historical Jesus seriously must make their own decision about how it can be done. We can, however, identify at least three big roadblocks that hinder the question. These consist of academic hesitations, popular protestations, and the demand for mystery. Each one rests on the assumption that there is an aura of the authority around Jesus that makes him more than human.

In the first instance, academics often dismiss the question of the historical Jesus on the longstanding premise that Jesus was apocalyptic. His worldview is simply out of reach to our contemporary experience. There is, at this level, a built-in hesitation to consider alternatives to this traditional model. That model, however, and maybe too conveniently, also protects the authority of the Church and Jesus as the Christ.

Within the broad spectrum of Christianity, which I am calling the popular level, there is a second form of resistance to the historical Jesus. A purely human Jesus offers no miracle of instant salvation. Rather, reaching the historical Jesus requires time to study and to think in a context of open-ended dialogue. The impact the historical Jesus might have on one's life will take years. It is not a quick fix. This fact takes away the authority of Jesus as the panacea of spirituality.

A third roadblock lays in those efforts to define Jesus primarily in relation to the "mystery cults" of antiquity. That Jesus should be studied as a historical person who taught wisdom is unattractive. It is as if this detracts from the mystery of life and the ability of Jesus to be the ancient depository of divine enlightenment. Rather than a historical Jesus, there is a turn to Jesus as a divine allegory. This third roadblock is what I call the hidden mysteries approach to Jesus. Let's look at these roadblocks one at a time.

A significant number of scholars maintain that the historical Jesus was mainly, if not exclusively, an apocalyptic prophet who, to our time, is buried in the obscure fanaticism of first-century Palestine. This proposition defines a great divide between those scholars who place the historical Jesus mainly in the Jewish wisdom tradition and those who place Jesus mainly in the Jewish prophetic tradition (albeit as an extreme expression of the latter). The arguments in favor of the apocalyptic model were reviewed earlier, but here we can be reminded of some of the features. In the argument against the wisdom tradition, the historical Jesus is aligned with the Qumran community (the Dead Sea Scrolls), which seems to have held end-time beliefs, and John the Baptist, who seems to have pronounced end-time beliefs. Also, it is consistently pointed out that in first-century Palestine, there seemed to be an apocalyptic climate especially expressed among groups like the Zealots. There are problems with each proposition. For example, we don't really know that much about Qumran, and we can't even be sure if the scrolls found there originated from that location. John the Baptist is often placed by default into the apocalyptic camp, but this is based strictly on Christian sources.

Who John was and what he was up to apart from Christianity's interpretation of him still holds many questions. In addition, though the Zealot movement played an obviously key role in events prior to and during the Jewish War of 66 CE, the apocalyptic material related to Jesus does not have its source there. The sources of apocalypticism are the Church in Jerusalem, the Apostle Paul, and the deuteronomic theology evident in the Q-community. When each of these traditions is looked upon separately, however, two things stand out. One is that the apocalyptic material is confessional. It is about what to believe about Jesus either regarding his death or regarding his return. Secondly, the apocalyptic material always has wisdom material mixed in with it. Paul highly regards wisdom; the Jerusalem Church, despite relating Jesus to David, understands Jesus as the manifestation of the spirit; and the Q-community in its first stage is wisdom-centered. So, it is possible, even if one argued that the historical Jesus was primarily an apocalyptic prophet, to conclude nevertheless that the wisdom material is always co-present and remains the best way forward for the Church in our time. The question is, why do some scholars dismiss the wisdom material and insist that Jesus only be understood as an apocalyptic figure? Why is this roadblock placed in front of wisdom?

When looked at closely, the apocalyptic roadblock that is placed before the wisdom tradition is used to fabricate an extreme choice. As a politician might say, the apocalyptic Jesus creates a wedge issue. Learning in the academy about the analytical study of the Bible and, in this, learning that there was no one named Mark who wrote the Gospel of Mark or that the Christian gospels are confessional documents arranged at least two generations after the life of Jesus or that the New Testament has to be re-constructed through educated guesses that involve thousands of fragments from antiquity can lead a once determined Christian believer who picks up such studies honestly to atheism. If a once faithful individual follows this trail of hard and honest study only to arrive at atheism, there is a great shock involved in reaching this conclusion. The shock arises from the sense of having been betrayed all these years by the church and from the new liberty of being freed from longstanding confessional dogmas. The apocalyptic Jesus in this setting serves to promote the shock value and to justify the conclusion of atheism.[1] To promote Jesus strictly as an apocalyptic prophet also promotes the thinking that there is nothing to retrieve from him anymore and that, aside from being an interesting historical figure, there is no justification for holding religious beliefs in relation to him. The value of being shocked and being awakened to deep skepticism is, I think, one item that inspires the academic roadblock of apocalypticism set before the wisdom tradition of the historical Jesus. Yet this roadblock is still built on the assumption of a divine Jesus. A historical Jesus who is human like anyone cannot have the same shock value. A truly historical Jesus, even if thought an apocalyptic prophet, is a person to be understood and studied like any other figure from the past. To have shock value, Jesus and the Bible must first hold for the individual the status of divinity in order for disillusionment to follow. The apocalyptic Jesus can create disillusionment because it is a most obvious example of God (or the cosmic authority) being wrong. The world did not come to an end either in the lifetime of Jesus or shortly thereafter, and every time it doesn't, more reasons for disillusionment are present. An apocalyptic Jesus who is supposed to be God has shock-value that a Jesus who, from the start, is human like anyone does not carry. So, in some academic circles, we need an apocalyptic Jesus in order to have shock-value.

There is another side to the academic roadblock that also works to create a "wedge," though of a different nature, through the apocalyptic Jesus. If the first wedge is the use of apocalypticism to force atheism, the second kind of wedge is created when Christian orthodoxy or, more appropriately, neo-orthodoxy, uses apocalypticism to create crisis theology. Based on the same conclusion that the Jesus of history was an apocalyptic prophet who, as such, cannot realistically speak to our age, a neo-orthodox theologian can draw two conclusions. One is that only the "Christ" is of value to Christianity. The historical Jesus, on the other hand, is irrelevant to the gospel. The second conclusion is that the apocalyptic material belongs to the prophetic genre of theology, so the proclamation of the Christ is to be understood as a prophetic revelation that places the Word of God in transcendental (crisis) relationship to human history. God as the Christ is the breaking in of the Word from the outside as the voice of crisis or judgment upon the human situation. Thus, to uphold Jesus as an apocalyptic prophet is a good thing because it allows us to ignore the wisdom of the historical Jesus and focus on the Christ. When looked upon this way, the apocalyptic Jesus saves Christianity and the history of the Christian dogmatic tradition. The apocalyptic Jesus allows Jesus to be God, and, if I may state the case sarcastically, what more could a Christian want? An apocalyptic Jesus in this neo-orthodox form can be used as a roadblock to override and silence the humanistic wisdom of the historical Jesus in Christianity. Then, with this suppressive act completed, Jesus Christ can remain as the voice of a transcendental God and the authoritative foundation the Church. A strictly historical Jesus, on the other hand, cannot hold a candle to the neo-orthodox Christ.

The second roadblock I referred to above is the overwhelming popular appeal of a fast-paced, instant salvation form of Christianity. This is the Jesus we find in the great novel of Fyodor Dostoyevsky, *The Brothers Karamazov*. There, Dostoyevsky offers a parable called the Grand Inquisitor. Jesus comes back to earth in Seville during the time of the Inquisition. He causes a great stir, but is arrested and jailed. The Inquisitor comes to visit him in his cell and tells him to go back to the world of the dead and never return. The Inquisitor reasons that people do not want the freedom Jesus offers. What human beings need and want from their Jesus is miracle, mystery, and authority.[2] We are attracted to religion, Dostoyevsky thinks, because we need the certainties. It appeals to us to have a bishop dressed up in regal clothing, or a reverend bearing a preacher's scarf, or a televangelist walking around stage with open Bible in hand to assure us that what we believe or should believe is right. We need the gospel miracles that turn Jesus into God and make the church his dwelling place, the mystery that transforms religious rituals into magical salvation formulas, and the authority of television personalities or ecclesiastical offices to seal the deal. A strictly human Jesus who taught enigmatic wisdom that requires thoughtful reflection and personal engagement pales in comparison to this Jesus who comes from the sky with insider knowledge about heaven and the end of the world. A major roadblock to taking the historical Jesus to church is precisely that he comes with some assembly required and no miracles, no mystery, and no authority provided. The historical Jesus demands honesty: honest thinking about history and about life, and an honest encounter with the self and the world. On a popular level, this may not be appealing, but with the perspective of Christian history in mind, the historical Jesus may pose the most significant revision Christianity has faced in a very long time.

The third roadblock placed before the historical Jesus is Dostoyevsky's second element, mystery, in his trinity of human religious needs. This is what I am calling the hidden mysteries approach to Jesus. Sometimes the humanistic wisdom of the historical Jesus is not mysterious enough to be attractive. True wisdom is supposed to be of divine origin hidden inside sacred books and written in code. It must surely be "Egyptian,"[3] and it has to have secret initiation rites. No doubt it is somewhat of a downer to bring a "historical" Jesus, who demands actual scholarship to be understood, into the realm of obtuse mystery. On its own, an appeal to hidden mysteries is attractive because it feels like one has stumbled upon the pot of gold at the end of the rainbow. Something that is not common but cryptic has been decoded. The grand narrative of crucifixion, death, and resurrection of Jesus seem to parallel an omnipresent mythical cycle of death and resurrection found in the mystery cults like Dionysus of the ancient world. Indeed, the whole story of Jesus, which is reduced to death and resurrection, is an allegory about a hidden god inside us all. Jesus might be understood in the hidden mysteries approach as a literary creation of the ancient world who some wise person or community put together as an amalgam of mystery teaching, or he might be presented as a divine envoy from heaven who is available only to those who can break the code, or perhaps he did exist but his lessons are allegories about the hidden world of the soul. From this point of view, the question of the historical Jesus does not matter. Indeed, the question of the historical Jesus is actually a distraction. To engage the question of the historical Jesus is to invest of lot of time looking at trees and never seeing the forest.

The great objection to the hidden mysteries approach is its lack of foundational scholarship. I am not saying that only scholars should hold the privilege of interpretation. Far from it. Rather, if the hearing public does not have access to good scholarship, many ideas about Jesus that are not credible become freely disseminated as fact. True, work on the ancient mystery cults of the Roman Empire can cast a valuable light on the question of the origins of Christianity, but it is wrong to suppose that certain parallels between early Christianity and ancient mystery cults (like the cult of Dionysus or Isis) explain the origins of Christianity or express its true, if lost, theology. It is true that religious practices in antiquity, as much as today, influenced one another either distantly or intimately, and it is easy to find religious typologies like death and resurrection across cultures and around the world. But that does not explain anything. It only relays the general truth that human communities exist in relation to one another and that they always have. It is too easy to persuade public impressions with striking religious parallels that do not actually constitute the proof of something. Against this persuasive impression, the only avenue of protection for the public is religious literacy, which comes from familiarity with honest scholarship. The historical Jesus who had something to say on his own is unjustly silenced when he is converted into a mystery religion where his existence does not matter and where the parables and aphorisms are overwritten by the code of his death and resurrection. That act is a major roadblock to his wisdom.

Each roadblock that inhibits access to the historical Jesus expresses the broader problem of biblical literacy among Christians today. The roadblocks are there because of traditional assumptions about the authority of the Bible and the divinity of Jesus. Each one makes its impression either by a shocking rejection of this authority or by using it to augment the transcendental power associated with the Christ. Once these factors are humanized and neither Jesus nor the Bible carry such weight, the roadway is made clear. And the task of clearing the roadway involves biblical literacy.

Even though many scholars will stand against the historical Jesus and, in this, protect the authority of the church, in fact very few scholars have any problem with the analytical study of the Bible. The understanding that the Bible emerges from specific historical circumstances, that it was created and written by human beings, that it employs numerous sources, and that it expresses a writer's theological perspective and reflects cultural bias are all gains associated with the analytical study of the Bible. It is hard to find any well-trained scholar who rejects these fundamentals. The problem is that the riches of this study are not transmitted into the hands of the average church-goer. The lack of transmission creates biblical illiteracy, and biblical illiteracy creates a climate within the general church setting where many forms of belief, regardless what agenda is at work, sound sufficiently holy and authoritative. Biblical literacy, which

involves the teaching of biblical criticism from the pulpit and
the opening of the community to questions, is the antidote
to a Christianity driven by power but not founded on credible
beliefs. It is the task of a historical Jesus community to create
an atmosphere of learning where the general community is
empowered to make informed theological decisions on its own.
This means avoiding two things. One is the stress on believing
at all costs. The traditional stress on confessing Christ in order
to belong to church creates an imbalance between the Christian
identity and critical thinking. A historical Jesus community
holds identity through critical thinking such that confession is
not the power of inclusion. What is central is solidarity on the
path of wisdom. The second thing to avoid is fear. Sometimes
theological information that a leader has been taught in university or seminary is withheld from the people for fear of the response. This act restricts the church leader to only two options:
avoid telling the truth, or leave ministry. One gift of the historical Jesus is the overcoming of this "take it or leave it" dilemma.
Because the historical Jesus can only be reached through the
analytical study of the Bible, if a community chooses to establish
its identity here, the gate of permission for its trained leadership to think and speak honestly has been opened. It is hard to
believe, in our time, that Christianity could not benefit from
honesty in religion.

A historical Jesus community values honesty. This does not
mean that, on an academic level, the community is "right" about
one historical question or another and others are wrong; neither
does it suggest that the community is capable of addressing every
theological question out there. It does mean that such questions are welcomed and can be spoken in an open atmosphere.
Individuals or groups can feel betrayed by their communities,
and a historical Jesus community is not exempt from this possibility, but no one in a historical Jesus community should feel

betrayed on the basis of lack of access to questions about spirituality, the Bible, or theological queries.[4] The point is not to get the answer right. The point is to open the road of life honestly with the trust that people can make decisions for themselves.

However admirable a historical Jesus community may be with its turn to honesty, this still does not address the largest question and perhaps largest roadblock which lies before us now. Is a historical Jesus community still a Christian community? Such a central question is answered only against the background of what defines Christianity as a whole, and for this the Doctrine of the Trinity must be reviewed.

Christianity as the Doctrine of the Trinity

The principal definition of the Christian faith lies historically in the Doctrine of the Trinity. This is the doctrine that preserves Christianity in a monotheistic definition while holding to its proclamation that Jesus Christ is God incarnate. The Trinity, as it developed, intends to protect the notion of one, universal God in heaven even though God in Christ appeared on earth in human form. There were many different experiments in the history of Christianity designed to express the commitment to a monotheistic God held in tension with the reality of that God in the person of Jesus Christ. We might note here in passing some of those options, certainly not all, that remind us Christianity has always engaged in a struggle of self-definition.

Arianism was a fourth-century Christian movement named after Arius, who died circa 336 CE. It held that Jesus as the Son of God was the first born of all creation. That sounds impressive, but it meant for the Church a denial of the full divinity of Jesus, for to be fully divine, Jesus must be co-eternal with God and not a creature of God (even if the first one). In the Nicene Creed, we are reminded of this conclusion when it is confessed that Jesus was "begotten, not made." When Arianism defined Jesus in relation to God as the first creation, even though this was not acceptable to the church, it did mean that Jesus was a perfect creation. He was, in effect, the prototype, pristine and unequaled. Still, this thinking was rejected because it did not mean Jesus was fully divine.

Several other attempts to work out the relationship accordingly emerged. Apollinarianism (named after Bishop Apollonaris, who died around 390 CE) is the belief that Jesus held a human body but a divine mind. The explanation attempted to safeguard the unity of God while still allowing for God's appearance in human form, but the Western Church rejected this reasoning. If Jesus did not have a human mind then Jesus could not (also) be fully human and therefore did not fully participate in the human situation. Only a fully human Jesus could save human beings. Nestorianism (named after Bishiop Nestorius, who died around 451 CE) presented Jesus as two people, one fully human and one fully divine, in one body. This was a type of theological schizophrenia that the Western Church could not accept. The idea effectively canceled the incarnation because the divine and human person were disjointed, making the divine half of Jesus unrelated to the human situation. Surprisingly, though the church could not accept a two-persons Jesus, it could accept a two-natures Jesus. This is the orthodox position, which was defined at the Council of Chalcedon in 451 CE. It states that Jesus was one person with two natures, one nature fully human and other nature fully divine. This meant Jesus was fully united with God as a person of the Trinity, and he fully participated in human nature without corruption because his divine nature co-existed in full integration with him. This conclusion made the Christian form of monotheism a dynamic monotheism and not merely a transcendental monotheism. The Christian understanding of God has always included God's dynamic participation in history as a human subject, which is a unique expression that sets it apart from Judaism and Islam.[5]

The Trinity expressed this dynamism in the ancient formula of "Father, Son, and Holy Spirit." This is the economy, that is, relationship and function, of elements involved in Christian salvation. Human beings are "saved" purely by divine action directed toward and incorporating human history. The alienation between the corruption of the earthly world and the purity of the heavenly world is healed (reconstituted, or saved) through the divine offer of grace by means of Jesus who, while divine and without sin, participated fully in the human world. Human beings using earthly means cannot save themselves because any human action, by definition, is already corrupt. The act of salvation must come from above, but to be effective it must still fully include the reality of being human. This is the basic orthodox understanding of Christianity shared across many denominations, Catholic, Protestant, and Orthodox alike. Grace is an act of reconstituting, or even awakening, human reality to the original blessing of creation offered by God in person. In the reasoning of the Church, for grace to be in Christ, Jesus must be both human and divine. The Christian Trinity preserves this paradox without compromising the standard of monotheism.

Jesus Christ in Christianity can be understood as the full and sufficient paradox of saving faith. He is fully human, embracing the sin of the world, and fully divine, forgiving the sinner with the transforming power of new life. If Jesus does not hold the divine position in the Trinity as one who is fully God, then the grace offered through him is empty; if Jesus does not assume the full status of a human being, then the grace offered through him misses the mark. Christianity in its orthodox expression confesses the need for faith in Jesus Christ because it confesses separation from God, and it proclaims the power of the Trinity because it proclaims a gospel of salvation.

The Historical Jesus
as the New
Heart of Christianity

The historical Jesus community undermines the dogmatic history of the Trinity and even makes the doctrine impossible. It does so simply because the historical Jesus was a human being like anyone. There cannot be a controversy about his divinity since he was not divine. In the examples above, Christianity endured controversies and named heresies while it worked out a formula for the Trinity. With the historical Jesus, the initial trouble that created these controversies disappears. Jesus was not God incarnate who walked on earth and is not God the creator who dwells somewhere up in heaven. Like you and me, he was just a human being. His life was subject to the same limitations we all face everywhere and every day. On this basis alone, it would seem the answer to the question about whether or not a historical Jesus community is still a Christian community is simple. No.

But maybe such a sharp response needs a second look. The historical Jesus offers a credible, spiritual path of wisdom that has always been there with Christianity. Indeed, Christianity has been the keeper of the historical Jesus whether wittingly or not. The wisdom of the historical Jesus does not come from a foreign land. It remains possible to say that, in fact, it is the only surviving expression of a lost Jesus movement that failed to form the main face of Christianity. A community of the historical Jesus is, in some ways, merely emphasizing a place in the Christian tradition where some revitalizing energy remains that for so long has been left dormant. Additionally, at many points in its history, Christianity engaged the work of redefining itself due to changing circumstance and knowledge. Insofar as the historical Jesus might be controversial and pose a challenge to Christianity, it is worth remembering that controversies and challenges are the life of any living and vibrant tradition. Accepting the historical Jesus into Christianity certainly involves more than a few minor revisions. It involves reconstituting Christianity on a new foundation. Nevertheless, it does not have to involve the wholesale rejection of Christianity or Christian history. History is one of the few subjects from which human beings gain wisdom, since history is the story of life experience. The turn to the historical Jesus comes from the experience of Christianity, and without a solid understanding of that history, the turn to the historical Jesus will not achieve depth in wisdom.

In every era of Christian history, the Church was "true" for its time. This does not mean in a practical sense that the Church was always right. It was often wrong. On many occasions, it was even corrupt, prejudiced, and inhumane. In spite of this, in its theological reasoning a dialogue remained with the philosophy and science of the time. In the Middle Ages, Christianity absorbed Aristotelian physics and philosophical expression that was then the new knowledge, attained when the works of Aristotle, arriving in Europe from Muslim Spain, were translated into Latin. The revolution centered on Thomas Aquinas, who was initially regarded with suspicion but then became one of the most influential theologians in Christian history. When the Enlightenment came along in the seventeenth through the nineteenth centuries, Christianity on many occasions engaged the new science with great creativity. Even though the evolutionary theories of Charles Darwin in particular became a flashpoint of controversy, and continues to be so in some quarters, Darwin's ideas found theological defenders who sought to adapt and change Christianity in light of the new thinking.[6] Evolution, the Big Bang, Quantum Mechanics, Relatively, and other such theories have become the basis of our understanding of the world, and each insight has infused Christian theology with new expressions for the faith. New ways of thinking, in this sense, are nothing new to Christianity.

Christianity has never stood still. It has always been capable
of revision and restatement. Contrary to the impression extreme
fundamentalism makes today, on a historic scale Christianity
has never been anti-intellectual. It holds an impressive history
of learning in philosophy and general advancement in the arts.
The great challenge of the historical Jesus involves shifting
Christianity to a different ground of reasoning, and, against the
background of Christian history, it is not fair at all to say that it
cannot be done.

Taking the historical Jesus seriously, then, is not a rejection
of Christianity. Despite the way in which traditional Christian
beliefs have become increasingly unsustainable in our time,
there are things that can be retrieved from Christian history to
help think theology anew with the historical Jesus. This can be
demonstrated by retrieving some insight even from the primary
doctrine that defined Christianity, the Trinity. Despite the ancient metaphysics involved in the Trinity and its difficult way
of working out the status of Jesus, the doctrine need not be
thought of as something from which no serviceable learning is
available. The Trinity does supply the insight that humanity is
worth caring about, a quality that is valuable to a community
of the historical Jesus. The Trinity need not be the "confession"
of Christianity anymore, but it still can be a part of Christian
memory in which there remain some insights to wisdom.

The Trinity as a doctrine assumed that there once was a pristine form of human experience that was restored in Christ. This
part of its rationale is no longer credible. Yet, this was not all that
the doctrine assumed. It also assumed that, within us and in spite
of us, there remains some quality of interest. It assumed that
within the limitation of human life and in spite of the ignorance
of human beings, there remained a capacity to live beyond the
competitive drive for survival. We can, and are capable of, living
with graceful love and in solidarity with one another. Mixed in
the language of God becoming human is the inescapable reason-

ing that human beings are interesting to God. Otherwise, why would "God" bother with a human incarnation? Stripped of its divine metaphysics, at its base the Trinity is motivated with a deep and overwhelmingly cosmic love for humanity. It is not necessary to confess the Trinity or even to believe in God to see that our ancestors, through the Trinity, held a profound commitment to human life.

The Trinity also has within its metaphysics a certain hesitation that prevents exaggerated faith in the human enterprise. We could say it holds in its structure a theological safety hatch. Even though the Trinity reflects a commitment to human life, the fact that humanity should need to come under this grace in the first place implies the authors of the Trinity held caution about human potential. The human condition is not just a condition of ignorance. Ancient Christians also thought that human beings held an inexplicable will for self-destruction. So much is this the case that the only hope lay in God's intervention in human affairs. It is not necessary to believe in God to see that the composers of the Trinity were convinced humanity could not help but be self-indulgent. We might conclude that they were right, but in a historical Jesus community, the antidote is not a doctrine. It is, rather, found in sustaining a community of debate that necessitates a relationship to the other. The Christian Trinity holds the reminder of a necessary "outside" to otherwise insular human awareness. With the historical Jesus, the active community, and not the abstract doctrine, is the source of this reminder.

From the Trinity can be gained this double edge of insight. On the one hand, human beings hold a great potential for grace, but, on the other hand, this potential is never realized outside communal accountability. The historical Jesus brings to Christianity a deeper and more realistic confrontation with these two insights. If the Trinity is really about human beings finding the potential of their own compassion by means of accountability, then the community of the historical Jesus is not only Christian but a more direct form of honest Christian expression. It is exactly about a community holding its members accountable to the honesty of compassion. There may not be the Trinity in the historical Jesus community, but there is the heart of Christianity.

The Historical Jesus and the Absence of Christ

Is holding the heart of Christianity enough to keep a historical Jesus community inside the faith? For many it is not, because in the sayings material related to the historical Jesus, the content of the Christian faith is conspicuously absent. So far as scholars can tell, it is unlikely Jesus in his lifetime referred to himself as "Christ" or "Messiah." If he did think a figure like the "son of man" from the book of Daniel would arrive to close out the age, he was thinking of someone or something else. The earliest references to Jesus as Christ occur in the letters of Paul, but here we encounter not the sayings of Jesus but an early confession about the Christ who died, according to the scriptures, was buried and was raised, according to the scriptures (1 Cor 15:3–4). The phrase, "according to the scriptures," reveals that the belief about Jesus as Christ is as an early Christian interpretation, for early Christians searched the scriptures to find a meaningful way to speak about their belief in Jesus. The practice of searching through and reading back into scriptures what you already believe is a practice called *eisegesis*—the act of reading meaning into scripture. In ancient times, reading meaning into a text was quite common. Indeed, Christianity was born with this practice even though, today, it is frowned upon because it ignores the context in which scripture was written. Paul's form of *eisegesis* was to read into the life of Jesus the reality of Christ, but there were other possibilities. The Q gospel makes no use of Christ at all. For the Q people, the act of *eisegesis* consisted of interpreting Jesus in the tradition of the prophets. Neither act of *eisegesis* tells us anything about the historical Jesus. Instead, they reveal the Jesus the first and second generation of Christians created out of the fragmentary materials they actively redacted.

The problem for a historical Jesus community is that a word like Christ or status like a prophet are products of ancient *eisegesis* that do not add interpretive value when it comes to the parables and aphorisms. In fact, Christ is a distraction to the teaching of wisdom. Instead of encountering the parabolic world, "Christ" invariably projects a divine if secretive reality on the sayings. In place of allowing wisdom to impact our perception of life, the teaching is lifted to the authoritative status of God. Such authority ironically turns the liberating teaching of Jesus into a distant and sometimes oppressive set of moral dictums exempt from questions. This, as discussed in chapter 8, is one of the main reasons a historical Jesus community, in the name of Jesus, ceases to employ the word Christ.

Now we arrive at the problem! If the word Christ is not used as a title for the historical Jesus, how can the community based on him be considered "Christian" at all? Lloyd Geering has proposed Christianity without God, but is it really possible to have Christianity without Christ? The problem seems impossible to overcome but only insofar as Christ is strictly related to Jesus and only if Christianity is strictly the name to use. The earliest communities in Christian history did not have these restrictions. The names used were varied: "the Way," "the Nazoreans," and "the Poor." The word Christian appears only three times in the New Testament, and its use reflects the original derogatory intention. As Tacitus, a Roman historian of the early second century, reported, "Christian" (which he incorrectly spelled "Chrestian" after the Greek word *Chrestus,* or "good") was the name the populace used against this new and generally hated community.[7] Christianity was not a designation that emerged from the early movement but, rather like the modern word "queer," is an example of adopting an intended insult for self-identity.

Additionally, Christ is not always the title or even personal identity of Jesus. In early wisdom forms of Christianity, including those reflected in Pauline and Deutero-Pauline letters,[8] there is a cosmic sense to the word Christ. It is as if Christ is the universal reality and Jesus is only a participant. Col 1:15 can be read in this way, where Christ, like Wisdom (Prov 8:22), is the first born of the creation (as Arius thought). At the end of 1 Cor 15:28, Paul also shares the image of Jesus stepping down from the role of Son to be included in the fullness of God, and this suggests Jesus performs a role for Paul that concerns a reality to which Jesus, too, belongs along with everyone else. Christ, then, has a secondary sense in the type of Christianity often found in Christian mysticism, where Jesus is not the Christ but more like an ambassador for a Christ reality.[9]

A historical Jesus community can continue in Christianity on the basis of shifting the foundation from working out the doctrine of Christ's nature to using the concept of a Christ-nature to express the fullness of human life. That expression was worked out in chapter 6 as the five gospels of the historical Jesus. The Christ-nature—this fullness of life—is not intended to describe a spiritual essence only wise people can know. In philosophy, an essence is an eternal, unchanging, truth that persists unaffected by historical circumstance. In contrast, the five gospels that express the Christ-nature are existential dynamics but not essential truths. They are qualities that *can* awaken the Christ-nature in individuals and communities and that *appear* to be consistent with the parabolic vision of the world the historical Jesus sought to live. But every person and community has to live out those qualities for themselves in their own circumstances. This is what makes the qualities existential. I may be challenged to live in the parabolic world as the ego-less, anonymous self, but in the consumerist context of the Western world that meaning and challenge is vastly different from the context of starvation, oppression, and psychological slander suffered by a first-century

Galilean peasant. My ego relates to my sense of self-importance and destiny, but this has been ingrained in my psyche from birth through the constant persuasion of Western advertising and the promotion of wealth. To become an anonymous self in my life, I need to break free from those idealized definitions of success. I need to see how my life values have been constructed within this consumer context, and perhaps finally recognize that I am only one being, one configuration of awareness, in human form within the vast unfolding of the universe. To break from ego-centric consuming to ego-less living is the struggle offered in parable. It is the Christ-nature that can define my life and the context of my experience. It is the existential dynamic of the Christ that is my awareness.

The struggle to liberate oneself from consumerism is likely a contour of life most citizens of Western nations know. In as much as the West can be praised for its many technical advances, its commitment to the equality of citizens through democratic structures, its ability not only to tolerate but value difference, and its basic sense of human rights, the present cultural reality of Western nations remains one that rests on a history of consumption and exploitation. From the seventeenth century onward, the powerful economies created by Western nations have also created a default world where material resources are thought infinite, where human greed is an economic good, and where the world that is home for all living creatures can be bought and sold. As the leading nations of consumption, Western people in particular bear an onus of responsibility to change the world and to re-evaluate the current ideals of success that are slowly burying our planet.

The parable world that promotes the Christ-nature is not meant to be a fancy idea that is irrelevantly placed outside of these and other issues. The vision of the historical Jesus and his own struggle to realize the Christ-nature of himself was not ethereal idealism. A parable is, in fact, a critical complement to the world, for it offers the alternative to the default. Jesus spoke the parables, and in this act he held even the criticism of himself. A parable is not directed exclusively to an audience; it also comes back to haunt its creator. The speaker is simultaneously the hearer. A parable is a work of literary art, and an artist conceives a parable as a co-participant in the world. The critical edge of parables has no owner and no privileged interpreter. Jesus could not have composed the parable of the Good Samaritan if he did not know the enmity between Jews and Samaritans and if he was not also a participant in that enmity. The historical Jesus was a person like us who struggled in life to realize, through his own personality and situation in the world, the Christ of himself.

If Christianity is no longer conceived on the footing of the Trinity, where the problem is to work out the identity of Jesus but shifts from this to thinking about the historical Jesus as one who worked out the Christ-nature of himself, then indeed a historical Jesus community is still a Christian community. It is Christian in that it seeks the critical engagement of the self and reality with the parabolic vision of a differently reasoned world. It is possible, that is, to live differently, and this is the challenge of being the Christ you are.

Conclusions

Taking the historical Jesus to church changes both the contours and the sense of the church. It changes the reason why people gather as community, and, most significantly, it changes the status of Jesus in the tradition of Christianity. Over the course of these pages, many points have been made to highlight how understanding Jesus as a teacher and his movement as a school can be taken into the Christian church to center its language and practice. To hold all the information together and put it into practice requires an educated leadership, and, for the sake of biblical literacy, Christian churches need to affirm this truth more resolutely than ever. The change also requires liturgy, which I suggest is not nearly as radical an alteration as some might think.

To understand the historical Jesus is not just to clue into his words but also to be with and grow in a wisdom tradition. I have named the elements of the tradition as the five gospels of the historical Jesus: (1) the anonymous self, (2) the equilibrium of the world, (3) the comedy of existence, (4) the commitment to non-violence, and (5) the joy of life (see chapter 6). These emerge from the parables of Jesus, and they constitute what are, for now, fragmentary elements of a historical Jesus theology. But there should not be any pretense here. Many people have worked hard to understand the wisdom of the historical Jesus, and there are excellent books that I hope this work may complement.[10]

The five gospels of the historical Jesus are not doctrines but directives, or markers on a path. It remains for the student to master them, or something like them, to become the Christ of the self. The art of becoming can only happen in dialogue and association with others. It is impossible to learn about the self without others to engage us, to interpret our demeanor, and to clue us in to how we are perceived. This is why a community of compassionate honesty is so important. The reality of being human is being in relationship to others. The historical Jesus community, far more deliberately than traditional Christianity, names this the existential reality of human life. This marks the shift from belief to practice, from doctrine to wisdom, and from salvation to solidarity.

The central metaphor for the historical Jesus community is the banquet. It is so for two reasons. The first is that the banquet was a key practice in the life of Jesus. A banquet in antiquity was far more than a party. It was a forum for exchanging news, holding debate, and sharing food. It was part of the debt and debtor society. Especially among the poor, the banquet was good fortune. It could function as a moment of solidarity where an impoverished community, through collected goods, offered nourishment for all. Secondly, it is likely that the practice of a banquet in the life of Jesus created for him a medium of solidarity with social outcasts. In the historical Jesus community, the banquet is the symbolic act of openness and solidarity. It is free from the ecclesiastical restrictions placed upon communion or the Eucharist. It returns to common life the meal that marked the momentum of the Jesus school.

The last point I wish to make relates to the lifestyle of the school. Though we have spoken of the five gospels of the historical Jesus and outlined the parabolic world in contrast to the default world, there is no secret formula involved in these efforts. Too often, religious language breaks into mysterious sounding words with concepts only a few special folks can know about. Too often religion, despite efforts to the contrary, becomes once again a pretentiously supernatural phenomenon. The turn to the historical Jesus is a turn to life; there is nothing supernatural about it. The one difficulty involved in using the term "Christ-nature" is precisely that it can donate itself to elite expressions that invariably disrespect our common humanity. Special expressions can create a sacred status for people and things. I believe that a historical Jesus community is persistently about humanity. Great care needs to be taken to avoid another devolution into religious metaphysics. It is, I hope, in contrast to such devolution that a historical Jesus community expresses a new age of realism, an age where the most important lesson to ascertain is the fact that we are all only human and that this plain truth is our hope.

Notes

1. I would remind the reader that I am not a critic of atheism. In fact, I think we live in an era of post-atheism. We have to accept the conclusions of atheism and move forward with new forms of human spirituality that are not inconsistent with our best knowledge about the origins of life and the nature of the universe.

2. *The Brothers Karamazov*, book V, chap. 5, 636–82.

3. Here I jest, but it is very common in circles that want to argue the historical Jesus never existed to appeal to Egyptian sources for ancient mythical cycles. Timothy Freke and Peter Gandy's very popular *The Jesus Mysteries* is, I believe, a case in point.

4. I do not say this naively. No matter what community we speak of, people enter communities for a variety of reasons and people can feel betrayed for a variety of reasons. What I mean is that an honest community consists of providing the best information available through openness.

5. We could say, however, that Judaism and Islam express dynamic monotheism through the Torah and the Qur'an, whereas in Christianity it is expressly through the human incarnation.

6. For an interesting and surprising discussion, see *Darwin's Forgotten Defenders.*

7. See Tacitus, *Annals,* 15.44.

8. Deutero-Pauline letters are letters written in the name of Paul after his lifetime, like Ephesians, Colossians, and 2 Thessalonians.

9. For example, Hildegard of Bingen (1098–1179) held this theme. Pierre Teilhard de Chardin (1881–1955) is a more contemporary expression of a similar theme.

10. See *Suggested Reading.*

Appendix

1

The Original
Q Sayings Gospel

The Q Gospel is a sayings gospel that Matthew and Luke used in combination with the Gospel of Mark to compose their gospels. An independent copy of the Q Gospel does not exist. Q instead must be reconstructed from the parallel sayings and short narratives shared by Matthew and Luke, from traces of the Q tradition found in Mark, and from some Q parallels found in the Gospel of Thomas (the Q-Thomas parallels are called the Common Sayings Tradition).

It is not difficult to know generally what content the Q Gospel held, but it is difficult in some cases to know specific words and word order. Sometimes there are gaps in the Q material and an educated guess must be made.

Q is called a "sayings gospel" because, similar to the Gospel of Thomas, at its core it presents the sayings (*logoi*) of Jesus. The sayings are called *chreiae,* or pronouncements, and there is some but little narrative otherwise.

The Q Gospel does hold theology (beliefs) about Jesus even though many central features of the canonical gospels are missing. The baptism of Jesus by John and a temptation narrative compose the introduction to the Gospel, and there is "son of man" material that presents Jesus as an apocalyptic figure. Still, Q holds no Christ language, no crucifixion and resurrection narrative, and only a few hints of miracle lore associated with Jesus.

The Q1 material, which is presented below, is even more constrictive, holding only the sayings of Jesus with minimal evidence of redaction and no narrative or miracles at all.

It has been a favorite penchant of some scholars to deny the existence of the Q Gospel or emphasize with exaggerated vigor how Q is a hypothetical text. The argument is that, because the Q Gospel must be reconstructed mainly from Matthew and Luke, and because no independent copy of Q has ever been found, it is pure speculation to pose its existence. This criticism is a minority position, but it is worth answering in any case.

The evidence in favor of the Q Gospel consists mainly of two types: source evidence and (what we might call) genre evidence. Source criticism shows that the parallels between Matthew and Luke are too striking in word correspondence and at times exact sentences to deny a common source. Even if Q was not a written document, which is improbable because the Greek words match too exactly, a stable oral tradition would have to be supposed.

The second form of evidence is genre evidence, or what in German is the *gattung*, the type of literature to which the Q material belongs. Since the early 1800's, when the Q material was first identified with academic thoroughness, scholars have accepted that the Q-source was essentially a collection of wise sayings. Prior to the identification of the major Q1 and Q2 material, it was thought the sayings were lost "oracles" or lore about Jesus that had been written in Aramaic and translated into Greek. But since the 1900's scholars have placed the Q material in the broader context of ancient wisdom sayings that were collected and organized thematically. There are many examples in antiquity (Hebrew, Greek, Egyptian) of collected wise sayings. When, in 1945, the Gospel of Thomas was found, this confirmed that Sayings Gospels did exist in early Christianity, and, given the parallels between Q and Thomas (the common sayings tradition), we must suppose that the earliest developments of a Jesus tradition consisted of gathering and composing Jesus sayings. The activity of gathering and composing the sayings of outstanding schools around a principle teacher is absolutely common in human history, with many parallels in Judaism, Greek philosophy, Buddhism, Taoism, and so on. It seems unfeasible to deny that the origins of the Q material rest exactly on this practice.

Understanding the technical aspects of writing in antiquity help us imagine how the Q Gospel might have been transmitted and why it did not survive independently. It is an anachronism in our day to think that Q would have existed like a medieval manuscript that was faithfully copied in the setting of a monastery. Q was never the subject of such deliberate copying. Ancient texts were written on the knee, not at a desk, and were written either on papyrus (if available and affordable) or animal skins. But many records were simply scratched into wax tablets that could be erased and re-used. Wax was the ancient equivalent of a blackboard or, perhaps, an awkward memory stick. In addition, acquiring and using writing material was normally a benefit limited to the wealthier classes in antiquity. "Writing" was usually accomplished through dictation to a slave. Some of the greatest scholars of the ancient world could have been technically "illiterate" by our standards. They employed slaves to read texts to them and to record their dictations. The physical task of reading and writing for oneself was "labor" and beneath the dignity of the privileged. The Q Gospel existed in the cheapest forms available in antiquity. The transmission of its text was subject to repeated fluctuation. It could have been only available on wax tablets. Thousands of documents from antiquity were written on wax and, consequently, have perished forever. The Q Gospel could have had several different versions, and Matthew and Luke had similar but not necessarily identical versions. There is no way to know in what state or states the Q Gospel had existed.

It is worth remembering that many Christian texts did not survive antiquity. Like the Q Gospel, we know they existed only because some other document quotes from them or refers to them. The Q Gospel receives a lot of attention and criticism because of its importance to the Christian canonical gospels, but it is absolutely not alone in terms of being a document only known and available through reconstruction from other documents. Equally, it is worth remembering that no document from the first century has survived in Christianity: all first century gospels, letters, and theological tracts survive only as copies of copies. The Gospel of Mark as we have it today is not the original Gospel of Mark. It, like Q, is a reconstruction. In fact, in relation to all the Christian gospels, it is really not possible or sensible to talk about originals.

The Q Sayings Gospel is now commonly understood to consist of three layers, called Q1, Q2, and Q3. Each layer represents a stage of redaction. Thus, Q1 material was likely the first edition of Q. Then, an editor re-worked the Q1 Gospel by adding new material and casting the document in a new theological shape to produce the Q2 Gospel. Finally, Q3 is a third hand of redaction that re-worked the text in minor ways to produce the last detectable edition of the Q Gospel. The full Q Gospel, when reconstructed, is the Q3 edition.

The material below is the reconstructed Q1 Gospel. This is the *logoi*, or Sayings Gospel, of Jesus. The Q1 material also holds some redactional or editorial elements that mark the way the collector of the sayings organized the material and linked the sayings to each other. I have used *italics* to mark where the likely hand of the Q1 redactor was at work.

A *logoi* document in antiquity is a collection of anecdotes from a wise person's life using the repeated formula "Diogenes said . . ." or "Crates said . . ." or "Rabbi Hillel said . . . ." I have added in square brackets material like [Jesus said], [and he said], and [when asked] to indicate the state the Q1 document *may* have held strictly as collected sayings prior to its redaction into a more literary presentation.

Thus, below (1) the *italic* material is what I believe is early commentary and various edits used to gather the sayings of the Q1 material into a document, and (2) square brackets [ ] indicate what might have been present when the material was only a loose collection of sayings arranged either according to themes or catch words.

I have retained the saying "son of man" when I think it refers or relates to the figure from Daniel 11; but when the expression "son of man" is only a self reference (to me or I) I have translated it as "this mother's son." The expression occurs only once in the Q1 material, and its meaning is slightly ambiguous. The expression is in Q1 at 6:22, but Matthew took the term to refer to Jesus; thus, Matthew has "on my account" in place of "son of man." But it is also possible that the emphasis of the term falls not on the treatment of Jesus or his followers but on the prophets of Israel. In this case, "son of man" is used as a paradigm for those cast out and reviled. This latter interpretation is in line with the voice of the preceding beatitudes, where the poor are to be happy. Accordingly, at 6:22 I have italicized the phrase *son of man* to indicate that it is an editorial clarification offered by the unknown Q1 collector/redactor.

Though there is considerable consensus, the specific content of Q1 frequently varies from scholar to scholar. It depends on how one understands the theology of Q2, which is the formative layer of Q, and what sayings belong there. Some parables are considered Q1 and some Q2; I have included in Q1 wisdom parables that hold aphoristic characteristics typical of the Jesus voiceprint.

I have translated *basileia* (traditionally "kingdom") as "dominion." I have relied on the New Revised Standard Version of the Bible, the Scholars Version, *The Lost Gospel Q* (Berkeley: Ulysses Press, 1996), and *The Sayings Gospel of Q in Greek and English* (Minneapolis: Fortress Press, 2002) to help in the translation and presentation of the text below.

Proposed Q1 Gospel

6 ^{20b}[Jesus said] How happy are you who are poor, for yours is the dominion of God.

²¹How happy are you who are hungry, for you will be filled. How happy are you who weep, for you will laugh.

²²[And he said] What a privilege when people hate you, and when they exclude you, [and when they] revile you, *and defame you on account of the son of man.* ²³*Rejoice in that day and leap for joy, for surely your reward is great in heaven* for that is what their ancestors did to the prophets.

²⁷[Jesus said] love your enemies, do good to those who hate you, ²⁸bless those who curse you, pray for those who abuse you.³⁵You will be children of the Most High; *for* God causes the sun to rise on the evil and the good, and the rain to fall on the just and unjust *alike.*

²⁹[Jesus said] If anyone strikes you on the right cheek, offer the other also; and anyone who sues for your pants, give your underwear as well (Matt 5:41).¹ *And* if you are conscripted to go one mile, go a second mile.

³⁰[And he said] Give to everyone who begs from you; and if someone steals your goods, do not ask for them back.

³²[Jesus said] If you love those who love you, what credit is there in that? Even the worst among us love those who love them. ³⁴If you lend to those from whom you expect to receive, what credit is that to you? Even gentiles (i.e., the most unfaithful) do exactly the same thing. [And he said] ³⁶Be compassionate, as God is compassionate.

³⁷[Jesus said] Do not judge, and you will not be judged; for *the judgment you give is the judgment you'll get.* ³⁸*And* the measure you give will be measured out to you.

³⁹[Jesus said] Can a blind person guide a blind person? Will not both fall into a ditch?

⁴⁰[Jesus said] A disciple is not above the teacher, but every qualified disciple will be like the teacher.

⁴¹[Jesus said] Why do you see the sawdust in your neighbor's eye but do not notice the log in your own? ⁴²How can you say

to your neighbor, Friend, let me clear the sawdust from your eye, when you yourself do not see the log in your own eye? *Hypocrite! First, take the log out of your own eye and then you will see right to clear the sawdust from your neighbor's eye.*

⁴³[Jesus said] No good tree bears bad fruit, nor again does a bad tree bear good fruit; ⁴⁴*for from its fruit each tree is known.* Figs are not gathered from thorns; grapes are not picked from brambles.

⁴⁵[And he said] Out of good treasure the good produce good, and out of evil treasure the evil produce evil; *for it is* out of *the abundance of* the heart that the mouth speaks.

⁴⁶[When called Master, Jesus said] Why do you call me Master, Master, and do not do what I tell you?

⁴⁷[And he said] *I will show you what* someone *is like* who *comes to me,* hears *my words,* and acts *on them.* ⁴⁸*That one* is like someone who built a house on bedrock; when the rain poured down and the flood arose and burst against that house it did not collapse because it had been built on bedrock.

9⁵⁷*[When] someone said to him: I will follow you wherever you go.* ⁵⁸Jesus said *to him:* Foxes have holes, the birds of the air have nests, but this mother's son has no place to rest his head.

⁵⁹*And [when] another said to him: Master, permit me to go to bury my father.* ⁶⁰Jesus said *to him:* Leave the dead to bury the dead.

10²Jesus said *to his disciples,* The harvest is plentiful but the laborers are few, *so go ask the harvest Master to dispatch the laborers into the harvest.*

³[Jesus said,] *Be on your way!* Look, I am sending you out like sheep in the midst of wolves.

⁴[Jesus said] Carry no purse, nor knapsack, nor shoes, nor stick. Greet no one on the road.

⁵[Jesus said] Whenever you enter a house, say, Peace be upon this house. ⁶And [he said] if a child of peace lives at that house, your peace will be received, but if not your peace shall return

to you. [7]Stay at that house, eating and drinking whatever they provide.

[8]*And* [he said] whatever town you enter, if they take you in, eat what is set before you. [9]Cure the sick there and say to them, the dominion of God is here among you.

[16][Jesus said] *Whoever takes you in takes in me, and whoever takes in me takes in the one who sent me.*

11[2][Jesus said,] *When you pray, say,* Father, may your name be holy. May your dominion be here. [3]Give us a day's worth of bread. [4]Cancel our debts as we cancel the debts we hold. *And* do not put us to the test.

[9][Jesus said] *I tell you,* ask and it shall be given, seek and you shall find, knock and it shall be opened to you. [10]*For everyone who asks, receives, and who seeks, finds, and who knocks, it will be opened.*"

[11][Jesus said] *Who among you when a child asks for bread will give a stone?* [12]*Or, when a child asks for a fish will give a snake?* [13]*So if you, though evil, know how to give good things to your children, how much more will your Father in heaven give good things to you who ask.*

12[2][Jesus said] Nothing is covered up that will not be revealed, nothing hidden that will not be known. [3]*What I say to you in the dark, speak in the light, and what I whisper in your ear, proclaim on the housetops.*

[22b][Jesus said] *I tell you,* do not be anxious about your life. Don't worry about what you will eat or what you will wear. [23]Is not life more than food, and the body more than clothing?

[24][And he said] Consider the ravens. They do not sow or gather a harvest. They do not store food in barns, and yet God cares for them. Are you not better than birds?

[25][Jesus said] Who among you by being anxious is able to add one hour of length to your life?

[26]And [he said] why be anxious about clothing? [27]Look at the lilies, how they grow! They do not toil nor do they weave. Yet I

tell you, not even Solomon in all his glory was ever decked out like one of these. [28]If God dresses up the grass in the field, which is here today and tomorrow thrown into the oven, it is surely more likely that God cares for you.

[29]*So, do not be anxious about what to eat or what to drink or what to wear.*

[30]*These things the gentiles chase, and God knows that you need them.*

[31]*But seek first God's dominion and all these other things will be given to you.*

13 [18][Jesus said] With what am I to compare the dominion of God? [19]It is like a mustard seed that someone took and tossed into a garden. And it grew and developed into a tree, and the birds of the sky nested in its branches.

[20][And he said] With what am I to compare the dominion of God? [21]It is like yeast that a woman took and hid in three measures of flour until it was all leavened.

14 [16][Jesus said] A certain person prepared a great banquet and invited many. [17]When the time arrived he sent out his slave to accompany his guests, saying: Come, for everything is ready. [18]One declined because he had bought a farm and had not seen it. [19]Another declined because he had bought some oxen but had not tried them out. [20]Yet another declined because he had just gotten married. [21]And the slave returned alone to report these things to his Master. The Master was enraged and said to his slave: [23]Go out on the roads and invite whomever you find so that my house will be full.

[26][Jesus said] Whoever does not hate father and mother, son and daughter, cannot be my disciple.

[27][Jesus said] Whoever refuses to take up their cross and follow me cannot be my disciple.

17 [33][Jesus said] Whoever clings to life will lose it and whoever lets go of life will find it.

14 [superscript 34][Jesus said] If salt has lost its zing, then with what will it be seasoned? [superscript 35]It is good neither for the earth nor the dung heap but fit to be thrown out.

15 [superscript 4][Jesus said] Who among you, having a hundred sheep, upon losing one will not leave the ninety-nine on the hillside and go hunt for the lost one? [superscript 5]And if you should find it, will call your friends together and rejoice?

[superscript 8][And he said] What woman among you having ten coins, if you lose one will not light a lamp, sweep the house, and hunt for it until it is found? [superscript 9]And when you find it, will call your friends together and rejoice?

[superscript 20][Asked] when the dominion of God is coming, Jesus said: The dominion of God is not coming as a thing to see. [superscript 21]No one can say, look over here or look over there! The dominion of God is within you.

Note

1. The more exact translation would be "cloak" and "under-garment" in place of pants and underwear. However, since the saying comes from a two-garment society, it indeed means to stand naked before your accuser. It seems that "pants" and "underwear" make the point better for us today.

Appendix
2

Illustrated Layers
of the Q Gospel

This is the text of the Q Gospel according to the conclusions of the International Q Project (IQP). The results of the IQP's work and their translation is available in *The Sayings Gospel Q in Greek and English*. I have translated the text, as in appendix 1, with the help of the IQP translation, the Scholars Version (SV), the New Revised Standard Version (NRSV) of the Bible, and *The Lost Gospel Q* translation.

The Q1 material is given in plain text. The Q2 redaction, which is the main stage of composition for the Q Gospel, **is in bold**. The Q3 material, which is the last evident hand of redaction, *is in italics*. The italics I use in the full Q Gospel below is not to be confused with the italics used in the Q1 translation in appendix 1 above. In appendix 1 above, it refers to what I think is likely the Q1 collector; below, it refers to the work and additions of the Q3 redactor. It is important to remember that no one knows who were the hands or groups of hands that, over a few generations, collected and redacted the sayings of Jesus into the Q Gospel. For convenience, we call the document as a whole the product of the Q community that possibly resided in Galilee.

I have benefited tremendously from the work of John Kloppenborg, particularly two books: *The Formation of Q* (Philadelphia: Fortress Press, 1987) and *Excavating Q*

(Minneapolis: Fortress Press, 2000). With minor exception, I follow Kloppenborg's suggestions for the content of Q1, Q2, and Q3.

As I indicated above, "son of man" is used when the reference seems to relate to the figure from Daniel 11, otherwise I use "this mother's son." The expression is exclusive to Q2 and Q3 material, except for 6:22, where it is ambiguous. Even so, the reference at 6:22 is clearly not to Daniel.

The Q Gospel is numbered according to the verses of the Gospel of Luke, which is a standard practice. The location of material taken from Mark or sources other than Luke/Matthew (such as Matthew alone or Thomas) will have the source indicated in brackets.

Dividing the Q Gospel into the layers of Q1, Q2, and Q3 does not mean that Q1 material is historical Jesus material while all of Q2 and Q3 are not. No one can be certain about what Jesus may or may not have said. As a historical figure, Jesus is wrapped up so tightly in the Christian proclamation that certainty about what he said is impossible. The work of the Jesus Seminar marked those sayings that bear a distinctive voiceprint of a wisdom teacher, with the conviction that the wisdom tradition was the first, earliest, and most pervasive tradition to arise from the historical Jesus. Still, even the Jesus Seminar did not claim that the red and pink sayings in *The Five Gospels* are precisely what Jesus said (see chapter 3).

There are two traditions likely founded upon the life and activities of the historical Jesus. One tradition is the wisdom tradition of ancient Judaism, and it is clear that Q1 expresses this tradition firmly; the other is the apocalyptic (deuteronomic) tradition of ancient Judaism, and it is clear that Q2 both expresses and organizes the Gospel on this foundation. It is possible that the historical Jesus expressed both wisdom and apocalyptic traditions simultaneously. This might seem odd to modern people, but Jesus was not a modern person. Or it is possible Jesus was mostly situated in one tradition but sometimes reflected the other.

My opinion has been that the voiceprint of the historical Jesus is found mostly in the wisdom tradition, but I am not willing to say that his voiceprint is exclusively here. I do uphold, however, that the future of Christianity or of a historical Jesus community outside of Christianity can only go forward on the wisdom foundation. Apocalypticism, I hope, is self-evidently unsustainable. Equally, I hope that outside of the academic questions about the historical Jesus and his voiceprint, people of good faith everywhere can understand that the age of believing in transcendental beings who have agendas for world history needs to come to an end. Such beliefs are simply too dangerous for the social, political, economic, and environmental health of our planet.

To this extent, Q1 material is significant because it shows that within the ancient practices, and arguably the first practice, of Christianity is a wisdom movement. This movement is too elusive for apocalyptic expression but better suited to parable and aphorism, to twists of phrase and circumstance, that set an alternative vision of life and politics in contrast to business as usual.

In the layout of the Q Gospel below, we can see how both these gospels, that of wisdom and that of apocalypticism, where in competition for the identity of the historical Jesus. Historically, I would argue, it is a competition that wisdom lost. Perhaps the revival of historical Jesus studies and the new seriousness with which the Q Gospel is taken will inspire a revival of concern for wisdom and for a different understanding of Christianity.

The Q Sayings Gospel

John the Baptist appeared in the wilderness (Mark 1:4a), **and 3 [7]he said to the crowds that came out for baptism: You brood of Vipers! Who warned you to flee from the wrath to come? [8]Bear fruit worthy of repentance, and don't even think of telling yourselves, We have Abraham as our father. For**

I tell you, God can raise children of Abraham right out of these rocks. ⁹The axe is already aimed at the root of the trees. Every tree not bearing good fruit will be chopped down and thrown into the fire.

[16b]I baptize you in water but the one who is coming after me is even more powerful. I am not worthy of taking off his sandals. He will baptize you with the spirit and fire. [17]His pitchfork is in his hands, and he will clear away the threshing floor and gather the wheat into his granary, but the chaff he will burn in a fire that can never be put out.

[21]And when John had baptized Jesus, the heavens opened up and the spirit descended upon him.

4 [1]*And the spirit led Jesus into the wilderness* [2]*to be tempted by the devil. For forty days he ate nothing and became very hungry.* [3]*And the devil said to him, If you are the son of God, tell these stones to become loaves of bread.* [4]*And Jesus answered, It is written that a person cannot live on bread alone.* [9]*And the devil took him to Jerusalem and put him on the top of the temple and said, If you are the son of God, throw yourself down.* [10]*For it is written, He will command his angels around you* [11]*and they will carry you on their hands so that no stone will strike against your foot.* [12]*And Jesus answered, It is written, Do not put the Lord your God to the test.* [5]*And the devil took him to a very high mountain and showed him all the nations of the world* [6]*and said to him,* [6]*All this I will give you,* [7]*if you bow before me.* [8]*And Jesus answered him, It is written, Bow before the Lord your God and serve God only. Then the devil left him.*

And Jesus left that place and came with his disciples to his hometown (Mark 6:1).

6 [20b]*And raising his eyes to his disciples he said*: How happy are you who are poor, for yours is the dominion of God. [21]How happy are you who are hungry *now*, for you will be filled. How happy are you who weep *now*, for you will laugh. [22]What a privilege when people hate you, and when they exclude you, revile you, *and defame you on account of the son of man.* [23]Rejoice in that day and leap for joy, for surely your reward is great in heaven for that is what their ancestors did to the prophets.

²⁷But I say to you who listen, love your enemies, do good to those who hate you, ²⁸bless those who curse you, pray for those who abuse you ³⁵and you will be children of the Most High; for God causes the sun to rise on the evil and the good, and the rain to fall on the just and unjust alike.

²⁹If anyone strikes you on the right cheek, offer the other also; and anyone who sues for your pants give your underwear as well (Matt 5:41). And if you are conscripted to go one mile, go a second mile. ³⁰Give to everyone who begs from you; and if someone steals your goods, do not ask for them back. ³¹*Do to others, as you would have them do to you.*

³²If you love those who love you, what credit is there in that? For even the worst among us love those who love them. ³⁴And if you lend to those from whom you expect to receive, what credit is that to you? Even gentiles do exactly the same thing. ³⁶Be compassionate, as God is compassionate.

³⁷Do not judge, and you will not be judged; for the judgment you give is the judgment you'll get. ³⁸And the measure you give will be measured out to you.

³⁹Can a blind person guide a blind person? Will not both fall into a ditch?

⁴⁰A disciple is not above the teacher, but every *fully* qualified disciple will be like the teacher.

⁴¹Why do you see the sawdust in your neighbor's eye but do not notice the log in your own eye? ⁴²How can you say to your neighbor, Friend, let me clear the sawdust from your eye, when you yourself do not see the log in your own eye? Hypocrite! First, take the log out of your own eye and then you will see clear right to clear the sawdust from your neighbor's eye.

⁴³No good tree bears bad fruit, nor again does a bad tree bear good fruit; ⁴⁴for from its fruit each tree is known. Figs are not gathered from thorns; grapes are not picked from brambles. ⁴⁵Out of good treasure the good produce good, and out of evil treasure the evil produce evil; for it is out of the abundance of the heart that the mouth speaks.

⁴⁶Why do you call me Master, Master, and do not do what I tell you? ⁴⁷I will show you what someone is like who comes to

me, hears my words, and acts on them. [48]That one is like someone who built a house on bedrock; when the rain poured down and the flood arose and burst against that house it did not collapse because it had been built on bedrock.

7 [1]And when he finished these sayings he entered Capernaum. [3]There he met a centurion who pleaded with him and said, My slave is gravely ill. And Jesus said, Am I to come by your place to heal him? [6bc]And the centurion said to him, Master, I am not worthy to have you visit my home, [7]but say the word and my slave will be healed. [8]For I am someone under authority who has soldiers who answer to me. I say to one "Go!" and he goes, and to another "Come!" and he comes. And I say to my slave, "Do this!" and it is done. [9]On hearing this Jesus was amazed and said to those around him, Never have I found such faith even in Israel.

[18]And when John heard about these things, he sent his followers [19]to ask of him, Are you the one to come or shall we wait for another? [22]And in reply to them he said: Go tell John what you have heard and seen, the blind receive their sight, the lame walk, the lepers are cleansed, the deaf hear, the dead are raised, and the poor are told good news. [23]And how happy are those who are not offended by me.

[24]And after John's followers had left, he began to tell the crowds about John: What did you go into the wilderness to look at? A reed shaken by the wind? [25]If not, what did you go to see? A person arrayed in finery? Look, those wearing finery are in royal houses. [26]What then did you go out to see? A prophet? Yes, I tell you, even more than a prophet! [27]This is the one about whom it is written: Look, I am sending my messenger ahead of you who will prepare your path in front of you. [28]I tell you: There has not arisen among women's offspring anybody who comes close to John. Yet the least significant in the dominion of God is greater than he.

[31]To what shall I compare this generation; what is it like? [32]It is like children seated in the marketplace who address

each other, saying, We fluted for you but you would not dance; and, We wailed, but you would not cry. [33]For John came neither eating nor drinking, and you say, He has a demon! [34]This mother's son came eating and drinking, and you say, Look! A glutton and a drunk, a crony of tax collectors and sinners! [35]But Wisdom is vindicated by her children.

9 [57]And someone said to him: I will follow you wherever you go. [58]And Jesus said to him: Foxes have holes, the birds of the air have nests, but this mother's son has no place to rest his head. [59]And another said to him: Master, permit me to go to bury my father. [60]But Jesus said to him: Leave the dead to bury the dead.

10 [2]Jesus said to his disciples: The harvest is plentiful but the laborers are few, so go ask the harvest Master to dispatch the laborers into the harvest. [3]Be on your way! Look, I am sending you out like sheep in the midst of wolves. [4]Carry no purse, nor knapsack, nor shoes, nor stick. Greet no one on the road.

[5]Whenever you enter a house, say, Peace be upon this house. [6]And if a child of peace lives at that house, your peace will be received, but if not your peace shall return to you. [7]Stay at that house, eating and drinking whatever they provide.

[8]Whatever town you enter, if they take you in, eat what is set before you. [9]Cure the sick there and say to them, the dominion of God is here among you. [16]Whoever takes you in takes in me, and whoever takes in me takes in the one who sent me. [10]*And whatever town you enter, if they do not take you in, on leaving that town* [11]*shake the dust off your feet.* [12]*I tell you: it shall be more bearable for Sodom on that day than for that town.*

[13]*Woe to you, Chorazin! Woe to you, Bethsaida! If the wonders performed in you had taken place in Tyre and Sidon, they would have repented long ago in sackcloth and ashes.* [14]*Yet for Tyre and Sidon it shall be more bearable on the day of judgment than for you.* [15]*And you, Capernaum, do you think you will be exalted up to heaven? Rather, into Hades shall you come down!*

¹⁶*Whoever takes you in takes in me, and whoever takes in me takes in the one who sent me.*

²¹*At that time he said, I praise you, Father, the Master of heaven and earth, for you hid these things from sages and the academics and uncovered them for children. Yes, Father, for it has pleased you to do so.* ²²*My Father has handed everything over to me, and no one knows the son except the Father, and the Father does not know anyone except the son and whomever the son chooses to reveal him.*

^{23b}*How happy the eyes that see what you see.* ²⁴*I tell you: many prophets and kings wanted to see what you see but never saw it, and many wanted to hear what you hear but never heard it.*

11²When you pray, say, Father, may your name be holy. May your dominion be here. ³Give us a day's worth of bread. ⁴And cancel our debts as we cancel the debts we hold. And do not put us to the test.

⁹I tell you, ask and it shall be given, seek and you shall find, knock and it shall be opened to you. ¹⁰For everyone who asks, receives, and who seeks, finds, and who knocks, it will be opened. ¹¹Who among you when a child asks for bread will give a stone? ¹²Or, when a child asks for a fish will give a snake? ¹³So if you, though evil, know how to give good things to your children, how much more will your Father in heaven give good things to you who ask?"

11¹⁴**And he cast out a demon that had caused someone to be mute. And when the demon was cast out, the mute person spoke. And the crowds were astonished. ¹⁵But someone said, By Beelzebul, the head of demons, he casts out demons! ¹⁷Knowing their thoughts, he said to them, Every kingdom divided against itself collapses to nothing, and every household divided against itself cannot stand. ¹⁸If satan is divided against himself, how can his dominion stand? ¹⁹And if by Beelzebul I cast out demons, by whom do your followers cast them out? This is why they will be your judges. ²⁰But if I rely on the finger of God to cast out demons, then the dominion of God has come upon you.**

[21]No one can loot a strong person's house, [22]but if someone still stronger overpowers him, he does get looted. [23]Those not with me are against me, and those not gathering with me scatter.

[24]When an unclean spirit leaves a person, it wanders through waterless regions looking for a resting place but finds none. So it says: I will return to the house from which I came. [25]And upon arriving it finds everything clean and tidy. [26]So it goes and finds seven other spirits more evil than itself, and, moving in, they settle there. Now the person is worse off than ever before. [16]But some were demanding a sign from him. [29]And he said, This generation is an evil one, for it demands a sign, but no sign will be given except for the sign of Jonah. [30]Just as Jonah was a sign to the Ninevites, so shall the son of man be a sign to this generation.

[31]The queen of the South will arise on the day of judgment with this generation and condemn it. For she came from the ends of the earth to hear the wisdom of Solomon, and, look, something greater than Solomon is here!

[32]The Ninevites will arise on the day of judgment with this generation and condemn it. For they repented at the announcement of Jonah, and, look, something greater than Jonah is here!

[34]The eye is the lamp of the body. If your eye is sincere, your whole body is full of light; but if your eye is jaded, your whole body is dark. [35]So if the light within you is dark, how great that darkness must be!

[42]Woe to you, Pharisees, for you tithe mint and dill and cumin but give up justice and mercy and faithfulness. *It is these you ought to do without giving up the others.*

[39][Woe to you, Pharisees,] for you clean the outside of the cup and dish but inside they are full of greed and debauchery. [43]Woe to you, Pharisees, for you love the front seats in the synagogues,[1] and accolades in the markets. [44]Woe to you, Pharisees, for you like unmarked graves and people walking on top of them without knowing it.

^{46b}Woe to you, interpreters of the Law, for you load a burden on the backs of people but do not want to lift a finger to help them. ⁵²Woe to you interpreters of the Law, for you shut people out of the dominion of God, you stay out yourselves, and you do not let others try to get in. ⁴⁷Woe to you who build tombs for the prophets even though it was your ancestors who killed them. ⁴⁸Thus, as the children of your ancestors, you witness against yourselves.

⁴⁹*Therefore Wisdom said: I will send them prophets and sages, but some they will kill and persecute.* ⁵⁰*Thus the blood of all the prophets shed from the founding of the world will require this generation to settle the accounts.* ⁵¹*From the blood of Abel to the blood of Zechariah, murdered between the altar and the house, yes I tell you: this generation will be required to settle the accounts.*

12²Nothing is covered up that will not be revealed, nothing hidden that will not be known. ³What I say to you in the dark, speak in the light, and what I whisper in your ear, proclaim on the housetops.

⁴*And do not fear those who can kill the body but not the soul.* ⁵*Fear instead those who are able to kill both the soul and body in Gehenna.*

⁶*Are not five sparrows sold for a few cents? And yet not one of them will fall to earth without God's consent.* ⁷*Even the hairs on your head are counted, so do not be afraid since you are worth more than many sparrows.*

⁸*Anyone who speaks in favor of me in public, the son of man will speak in favor of before the angels.* ⁹*But whoever speaks against me in public will be denied before the angels.*

¹⁰*And whoever speaks against the son of man will be forgiven, but whoever speaks against the holy spirit will not be forgiven.*

¹¹*When they bring you before synagogues, do not be nervous about what you will say.* ¹²*The holy spirit will teach you in that hour what to say.*

³³*Do not value for yourselves treasures on the earth that moths and wear will deface and that robbers will dig through to steal;*

value instead treasures in heaven that moths and wear cannot deface and that robbers cannot dig through to steal. ³⁴*For where your treasure is, there your heart will be also.*

^{22b}I tell you, do not be anxious about your life. Don't worry about what you will eat or what you will wear. ²³Is not life more than food and the body more than clothing? ²⁴Consider the ravens. They do not sow or gather a harvest. They do not store food in barns, and yet God cares for them. Are you not better than birds? ²⁵And who among you by being anxious is able to add one hour of length to your life?

²⁶And why be anxious about clothing? ²⁷Look at the lilies, how they grow! They do not toil, nor do they weave. Yet I tell you, not even Solomon in all his glory was ever decked out like one of these. ²⁸If God dresses up the grass in the field, which is here today and tomorrow thrown into the oven, it is surely more likely that God cares for you.

²⁹So, do not be anxious about what to eat or what to drink or what to wear. ³⁰These things the Gentiles chase, and God knows that you need them.

³¹But seek first God's dominion, and all these other things will be given to you.

12 ³⁹**But know this: If the householder had known during which hour the robber was coming, he would not have let his house get dug into.** ⁴⁰**You also must be ready, for the son of man is coming at an hour you do not expect.**

⁴²**Who then is the faithful and wise slave whom the Master has set over his household to serve food on time?** ⁴³**How happy is that slave whose Master, upon returning, finds at work.** ⁴⁴**I tell you: The Master will appoint that slave over all his possessions.**

⁴⁵**But if the slave says in his heart: My master is delayed, and then begins to beat his fellow slaves, and eats and drinks with the crowd,** ⁴⁶**the Master of that slave will return on a day he does not expect and at an hour he does not know, and will cut that slave into pieces and give him the inheritance of the faithless.**

⁵⁴And he said to them, When evening has come, you say: **Great weather! For the sky is fiery red.** ⁵⁵**And at dawn you say: Today is wintry, for the lower sky is red.** ⁵⁶**You know how to interpret the sky, but you are not able to interpret the times.**

⁵⁸**While you travel with your opponent on the way to court, make an effort to settle things beforehand lest your opponent hand you over to the judge, and the judge to the officer, and the officer throws you in prison.** ⁵⁹**I say to you: You will not get out of there until you pay the last cent.**

13 ¹⁸With what am I to compare the dominion of God? ¹⁹It is like a mustard seed that someone took and tossed into a garden. And it grew and developed into a tree, and the birds of the sky nested in its branches.

²⁰With what am I to compare the dominion of God? ²¹It is like yeast that a woman took and hid in three measures of flour until it was all leavened.

²⁴*Enter through the narrow door, for many will seek entry but few will manage it.*

²⁵*When the owner of a house has got up and locked the door and you stand outside and knock, saying: Master, let us in. He will answer you, saying, I do not know you.* ²⁶*Then you will begin to say, We ate and drank in your presence, and you taught in our streets.* ²⁷*But he will say to you: I do not know you! Get away from me, you lawless people.*

²⁹*Many shall come from sunrise to sunset and recline* ²⁸*with Abraham and Isaac and Jacob in the dominion of God, but you will be thrown out into the darkness where there will be wailing and grinding of teeth.*

³⁴*O Jerusalem, Jerusalem, you who murders the prophets and stones those sent to you! How often I wanted to gather your children together, as a hen gathers her chicks under her wings, but you were not willing!* ³⁵*Look, your house is forsaken! I tell you: You will not see me until that time when you say: Blessed is the one who comes in the name of God.*

14 [11] *All self-promoters will be humbled, and all humbled ones will be exalted.*

[16]A certain person prepared a great banquet and invited many. [17]When the time arrived he sent out his slave to accompany his guests, saying: Come, for everything is ready. [18]One declined because he had bought a farm and had not seen it. [19]Another declined because he had bought some oxen but had not tried them out. [20]Yet another declined because he had just gotten married. [21]And the slave returned alone to report these things to his Master. The Master was enraged and said to his slave: [23]Go out on the roads and invite whomever you find so that my house will be full.

[26]Whoever does not hate father and mother, son and daughter, cannot be my disciple.

[27]Whoever refuses to take up their cross and follow me cannot be my disciple.

17 [33]Whoever clings to life will lose it and whoever lets go of life will find it.

[34]If salt is has lost its zing, then with what will it be seasoned? It is good neither for the earth nor the dung heap but fit to be thrown out.

16 [13] *No one can serve two masters, for either you hate the one and love the other or be devoted to the one and loathe the other. You cannot serve God and money.*

[16] *The law and the prophets were until John. Since then, the dominion of God is violated and the violent plunder it.* [17] *It is easier for heaven and earth to pass away than for one letter of the law to disappear.*

[18] *Everyone who divorces and marries another commits adultery; and whoever marries a divorced person commits adultery.*

17 [1] *It is necessary for temptations to come, but woe to those through whom they come!* [2] *It will be better for them if a millstone were put around their necks and they were thrown into the sea than that one of these little ones should be caused to stumble.*

15 ⁴Who among you, having a hundred sheep, upon losing one will not leave the ninety-nine on the hillside and go hunt for the lost one? ⁵And if you should find it, will call your friends together and rejoice.

⁸What woman among you having ten coins, if you lose one will not light a lamp, sweep the house, and hunt for it until it is found. ⁹And when you find it will call her friends together and rejoice.

17 ³*If your friend does harm against you, scold your friend; if your friend has a change of heart, forgive your friend.*

⁴*And if seven times a day your friend does you harm, then seven times forgive your friend.*

⁶*If you have faith like a mustard seed, you might say to this mulberry tree: Hey, be uprooted and plant yourself in the sea! And it would obey you.*

²⁰Asked when the dominion of God is coming, Jesus said: The dominion of God is not coming as a thing to see. ²¹No one can say, look over here or look over there! The dominion of God is within you.

²⁶*As it was in the days of Noah, so shall it be on the days of the son of man.* ²⁷*For as in those days, they were eating and drinking, marrying and being given in marriage, until the day Noah entered the ark and the flood came and washed them all away.* ³⁰*It will be like that on the day the son of man is revealed.* ³⁴*I tell you: There will be two men in the field; one is taken and one is left.* ³⁵*Two women will be grinding at the mill; one is taken and one is left.*

19 ¹²*A Master about to take a trip* ¹³*called his slaves together and gave each of them ten minas. He said them, Do business until I get back.* ¹⁵*After a long time the Master returned to settle accounts with those slaves. The first came to him, saying, Master, your ten minas have produced ten more.* ¹⁷*And the master said, Well done, good slave, you have been faithful over little, so I will set you over much.* ¹⁸*And the second came to the Master and said, Your minas have earned five more.* ¹⁹*The master said: Well done, good slave, you have been faithful over little, so I will set you over much.* ²⁰*And the other slave came before the Master and said, Sir,* ²¹*I knew that you are a* *hard person, reaping where you did not sow and gathering up from where you did not harvest; and I was afraid and hid your minas in the ground. Here is what belongs to you.* [22]*The Master said: Wicked slave. You knew that I reap from where I did not sow and gather up from where I did not harvest, did you?* [23]*Well, you should have invested my money with the moneychangers! Then upon my return I would have received what belongs to me plus interest.* [24]*So, take from him the minas and give them to the one who has ten.* [26]*For to those who have, more will be given, but as for those who have little, even what they have will be taken from them.*

22 [28]*You who have followed me* [30]*will sit on thrones to judge the twelve tribes of Israel.*

Note

1. The places of honor at banquets (Mark 12:39; Matt 23:7).

Appendix

3

Liturgy in the
Key of Q

As discussed in chapter 7, the liturgical form of historic Christianity need not be altered in light of the historical Jesus. The language and practice, however, do need to change.

When a community is dealing with approximately an hour or two for gathering time on a Sunday morning, the liturgy needs to be familiar, orderly, and hold a consistent motion. In this respect, there is nothing wrong with Christianity's traditional fourfold structure: Introductory Rite, Word, Table, Concluding Rite. That is what I like to call the basic chassis of the community order (see chapter 7). However, while the historical Jesus community can employ that chassis, it is the content that differs. First, the language must change from a focus upward on the divine gods, to immanent care for the earth and the human family. No god can make an individual more compassionate or more forgiving. Human beings must learn these acts from one another and through the collective understanding of our nature. They happen when we choose to love, and that gift does not fall from the sky, nor is it granted by a hidden monarch, somewhere. It comes only from the human heart, and it is under the care of individuals and communities. The language of immanence is the language of wisdom, and this must be the language of the historical Jesus community.

Such a shift from divine transcendence to human life is expressed in the liturgy that emphasizes Gathering, Learning, Banquet, and Parting. The community gathers in peace; it sings and it meditates; it learns and shares a banquet; then it parts with good wishes. It is the same order of traditional Christianity but not the same words, same spirit, or same intention. The theme is one of openness and honesty; the heart is one of compassion and understanding. These qualities come alive in the community but only if the community so desires. There is no magic to liturgy except for what is brought to the gathering by the people.

Below is the liturgical order used at the Quest Learning Centre, of which I am the director. I included a few comments in parentheses that might be helpful. Following the order, I have placed a few banquet liturgies used at the Centre.

I
A Gathering Order

GATHERING

GATHERING MUSIC
(Sometimes there is a band that plays contemporary music and sometimes there is a choir.)

GREETING:
Peace be upon all who enter this house
And also with you
(See Q 10:5.)

GATHERING SONG
ANNOUNCEMENTS AND CONCERNS
SOLIDARITY MEDITATION
(This is not a prayer but rather expresses a relationship with one another and the world. There are no petitioning words to God. The intention is to create a sense of dwelling with one another and in the world as a collective.)

THE LITURGY
OF LEARNING

READING

(Normally there is only one reading so that concentration and discussion can be focused.)

COMMUNITY SONG
REFLECTION ON THE READING
CONGREGATIONAL RESPONSES

(People freely share opinions and questions with responses from the speaker. It is a regulated yet informal time of learning that is normally about fifteen to twenty minutes.)

MUSIC OFFERING

(At the Quest Centre, this is either a choir or band.)

THE LITURGY
OF THE BANQUET

SHARING OF THE PEACE

May a heart of peace rest with you

And also with you

(The sharing of peace is not in the name of Christ. It is a gift each person can sincerely offer to another without a necessary seal of divine authority.)

OFFERING

(In the community, the call for an offering is usually issued as "From each according to ability" and the collective response is "To each according to need.")

CELEBRATION OF THE BANQUET

(See examples that follow.)

PARTING

CLOSING SONG
WORDS OF GOOD TIDING

(The words of good tiding are not offered as a blessing but as words of encouragement and hope. It is important to emphasize that the responsibility for life and its forms lie in the hands of people and what we do.)

II
Banquet Examples[1]

These banquet liturgies are written to celebrate the tradition of open meals associated with the historical Jesus. These are not Eucharistic prayers. The banquet expresses the symposium tradition of antiquity.

In the history of Christianity, the most sacred act of worship is the celebration of the Eucharist (or communion), in which bread and wine are used to symbolize the body and blood of Jesus Christ. In fact, the word "symbol" is too loose. The bread and wine either become (transform into) the body and blood of Jesus (Roman Catholic *transubstantiation*) or exist together with the body and blood of Jesus (Lutheran *consubstantiation*). Though the traditions used different words, both Protestants and Catholics speak of the real presence of Christ in the Eucharist.

The historical Jesus did not institute the Eucharist. The tradition of holding a meal to recognize the presence of the risen Jesus arose early in Christian history but took many forms. Paul relays in his first letter to the Corinthians (chapter 11)[2] that on the night Jesus was betrayed he took bread and broke it, poured wine and shared it. The Corinthians remembered this in their banquets, but they had full meals which, probably, were started with the memorial act of blessing the bread and wine.

As Christianity developed, the Eucharist became a separate act conducted in the context of formal worship. It developed the theological meaning of participation in the death and resurrection of Jesus Christ. The Eucharist in Christianity is normally the humble and contrite act of acknowledging that Jesus died and rose from the dead to forgive our sins. Many people do not feel worthy of receiving the bread and wine.

The Quest Learning Centre has returned to the banquet and turned away from the Eucharist. The banquet symbolically remembers that the historical Jesus used meal settings to express his teachings and to create an alternative community. Everybody is welcome at the banqueting table.

The historical Jesus, of course, had no idea his open banquets would become the Christian Eucharist. In keeping with the spirit of the historical Jesus, Quest banquet liturgies stress equality, justice, and community celebration.

This first banquet is called the Banquet of the Teacher because it is based on the teaching of the historical Jesus and employs both a translation of his peasant's prayer[3] (The Lord's Prayer) and a Jewish blessing for bread and wine that might have been a blessing familiar to Jesus. Finally, the liturgy acknowledges the historical Jesus as the teacher and initiator of the path the community follows. The server is a community member who assists in the sharing of the bread and wine; the "host" is either the speaker or the leader of the community. The "Abba" prayer is my own translation. The short verses sung below were written in the community to a tune not shared here.

1. Banquet of the Teacher

SERVER:

Welcome to this banqueting table. Enjoy the hospitality.
All human beings are equal. All life forms are to be respected.

We give thanks for the gifts of the earth, for its love, and for its sustaining energy.
The earth and all that is in it gives witness to the creativity of life.

HOST:

We give thanks for the life of Jesus, our teacher, and the memory of his loving kindness. Jesus taught that compassion is the heart of God; he practiced equality in the simple act of table friendship. When he blessed bread, he used his traditional Jewish prayers, saying, **Blessed is the Holy One of Israel, sovereign of all that is who brings forth the bread from the ground.** And when he blessed wine, he said,

Blessed is the Holy One of Israel, sovereign of all that is who brings forth the grape from the vine.

SERVER:

We share this act of friendship with millions of people around the world and with all faithful people of the past. With them and in celebration of our community we sing:
Gifts to share and sustaining memory
Bring people in hope together.
The banquet's joy and celebration
Mark the presence of light.

HOST:

May the bread we break speak of love; may the wine we pour speak of compassion; may our commitment to peace bear witness to the heart of this community. As one people who follow the path Jesus initiated, we share his memorable prayer.
Abba, may your name be respected among us. May your reality be alive in us. Help us to focus on what is really important. Let us affirm this each morning. The forgiveness of debt is your way of life; let it be ours, too. And when we are carried into evil schemes, let us have the strength to say no. Amen.
As a community of the historical Jesus we share bread and wine to acknowledge the bond of our common humanity. This is bread for our journey and wine for our life.

2. Banquet of Waiting on the Light

This banquet was written for use prior to the spring equinox. It was inspired by the common theme of light that is shared throughout history and around the world in many religious traditions.

HOST:

This time of year each day grows a little longer and, as each week passes, we move closer to the spring equinox.

SERVER:

Across time and throughout various cultures, the themes related to this season of waiting are consistent: anticipation, excitement, hope, rebirth, renewal, resurrection.

Egyptian or Hebrew, Christian or Pagan, members of First Nations or descendents of Europeans, indeed people all around the world share this one promise: the light is breaking forward; dawn is on its way.

The Hebrew Bible speaks of hope against hope and of waiting upon the light.

"Arise, shine, your light has come," proclaimed the prophet Isaiah. And in the Exodus story, Israel is led through the darkness with a fiery light.

HOST:

Early Gnostic movements spoke of the ocean of light above us from which we are in temporary exile, and the Apostle Paul described Christian people as the children of light.

In ancient Egypt, Horus was the sun god whose journey across the sky defeated the darkness of night. The Akkadian sun god Shamash was a being of justice and correct balance; and Sumer's Utu, the son of the moon, was the spirit of the law. **Jesus said, "Let your light shine" and "a city set on a hill cannot be hidden." He did not call his followers into depression and hopelessness but rather to vision and to light.**

SERVER:

During this season of waiting upon the light, may the practice of our daily lives reflect the anticipated light. May the gifts we offer the world share in those ancient notions of the balance of justice, the light of hope, and the peace of understanding.

HOST:

Welcome everyone to this banqueting time. We break bread as a community in solidarity, and we share wine to express our common bond. This is bread for your journey and wine for your life.

3. Banquet of the Justice Imperative

LEADER:

Welcome to this banqueting table. This is a table of hospitality, of sharing, and of celebration. We break bread and pour wine because these are the gifts that strengthen our journey together.

SERVER:

We remember and honour the justice imperative that is the biblical heritage: justice is not belief but action, not silence but voice, not tolerance but compassion. A banquet reminds us of our common humanity and our common need for just relationships.

PEOPLE:

Jesus said, "If you love those who love you, what merit is there in that? An outlaw can do the same thing. And if you give only to those who give back to you, do you really expect congratulations? Rather, love your enemies, do good, and lend without expecting anything in return."

LEADER:

The call to follow justice is easy to issue, but the resolve to follow justice is difficult to muster. Together, let us be a community that not only issues the word but follows the dictate.

SERVER:

May our community be one that holds the strength of compassion and the resolve to act. May we be a people who unites our words with our deeds.

PEOPLE:

For the dignity of life and the hope of humanity, may it be so.

LEADER:

We break bread as an act of solidarity. We pour wine as an act of sharing. Welcome to this banquet celebration. You are invited to participate.

4. Banquet for the House of Sophia

LEADER:

Welcome to this time of banqueting and to the house of Sophia.

SERVER:

Sophia is the ancient goddess who personifies wisdom. She was known by many names and celebrated in cultures internationally.

LEADER:

Ancient Israel knew her as "Hokmah," and the first Christians used her Greek name, "Sophia."

SERVER:

Wisdom is first instruction but it is also knowledge. Ancient people understood wisdom to be the force that ordered the universe.

LEADER:

Wisdom resides both in the world and in all human beings. In the Bible, Sophia calls human beings to share in a common dignity and to partake in the abundant gifts of the earth.

PEOPLE:

Like every other creature on earth, human beings, too, must learn to walk with Sophia. She is the gift of right judgment, the source of compassion, and the peace of understanding.

LEADER:

Wisdom also invites humanity to a common table, "Come, eat of my bread and drink of my wine". It is wisdom who presides at the banquet of life.

PEOPLE:

Jesus, too, knew of the invitation of wisdom and shared her promises in parable and practice.

LEADER:

The table is ready. Here is bread for our journey and wine for our life.

III
Solidarity Meditation

A solidarity meditation is not a prayer. The word prayer etymologically means, "to beg"; it is to petition or ask a favor from a superior. Prayers are offered to gods or to monarchs in the hope that they hear and grant the favor.

Meditation etymologically means, "to concentrate on a subject." Meditation is an attempt to connect with what has been brought into focus. An individual might practice meditation as a way to reach the quiet center of the self. In a public setting, the intention is to draw a gathered community together as a body of compassionate solidarity. This is why in place of "prayer," solidarity meditation is used, because the aim is to concentrate on concerns about life that all community members share and to relate these concerns to the world in which we live. It is like sharing in the energy of life, not for the purpose of mysteriously affecting an outcome of certain events but simply to remind the community of its fundamental relationship to all that is.

A solidarity meditation is normally stated out loud by the leader and is not written. Prior to the time of solidarity meditation, community members are invited to share news and express concerns.

The following is a sample of the style of meditation used. It is offered in a generic format, without reference to specific concerns or issues. The purpose of including it here is simply to give a basic impression of solidarity meditation.

As this community gathers, we unite by our presence here many different stories into one. We all know times of loneliness; we all know times of loss. We each have had great opportunities in life, great moments of laughter, and great memories of friendships. Everybody is different, yet everybody is the same. When we listen intently to one another, differences fade as we learn more about our shared experiences of life. It is possible to care for one another because it is possible to know how we are connected.

Life, however, is not just a story of good and bad things. There is more to our humanity than that. It cannot be ignored how both joyful and painful things affect our interpretation of the world. Those of us who have been fortunate to know mostly joy in life can sometimes find it difficult to concern ourselves with the tragedy of others. Tragedy in life can become distant to our experience, and when it does happen, it is as if we are undeserving. Equally, the reverse is true. Those of us unfortunate enough to know mostly tragedy in life can sometimes believe good things are only for others more deserving. In both these ways, we can lose track of a realistic understanding of life. In both ways, we can learn a certain type of self-indulgence that obscures the basic gift life is and that blocks our ability to grow in the maturity of understanding. Let us, then, be courageous enough to allow our stories to bring forward the gift of maturity and not to deliver us to self-indulgence.

Let us together also allow our stories to do one thing more. We are certainly privileged in a general sense as members of the Western world. We know and hold precious lifestyles filled with common opportunities for health, welfare, and education. But sometimes the privileges we assume also create distance between ourselves and the world. We see the problems of hunger, violence, intolerance, and injustice out there in the world, somewhere else, but fail to know how deeply connected we are to those problems. Sometimes what we buy contributes to the hunger of another; sometimes how we vote contributes violence to the world; sometimes our attitude about "them" creates divisions between cultures and nations that we pass on, through our comments, to our students or children or neighbors. We, too, are part of the problem of the world even when the problems that we see cast on our television are from lands we have never visited, involving people we will never know.

In this gathering, let us together remain determined not to allow division and distance to define our humanity or our place in the world. Let us work for understanding, knowing that we are not better than but part of all others. Let us add positively to the world in what we say and what we do. Let us be a community that makes a difference in the world we share with all life forms.

Notes

1. Section II of this appendix is used with the permission of The Quest Learning Centre of Hamilton, Ontario.

2. In the Christian Bible, Paul's correspondence with the people of Corinth appears as the books 1 Corinthians and 2 Corinthians. The

books, though, are a creation of the church, and the two letters are an amalgam of several letters of correspondence and the various inserts of a redactor.

3. We can think of the Lord's Prayer as a Peasant's Prayer because it reflects the concerns of poverty: food and debt. That it became in the church the sounds of austere and holy piety constitutes one of those instances where truth is stranger than fiction.

Selected Reading

Robert Funk set the agenda for the Quest for the Historical Jesus for a generation of scholars, both critics and admirers alike. His summary book is *Honest to Jesus*, which is listed in the bibliography below. I still consider this book to be the best introduction to the question since it gives a foundational view on the work of a biblical scholar. Nevertheless, some folks have complained to me that it is too difficult. Accordingly, some may prefer his shorter but equally stimulating commentary on the sayings of Jesus in *A Credible Jesus* (Santa Rosa: Polebridge Press, 2005).

For information on the Q Sayings Gospel and its significance, one must read *The Excavation of Q* or similar books by Kloppenborg (below). However, a book written in a popular style by James M. Robinson, one of the pioneers in Q research, is *The Gospel of Jesus: A Historical Search for the Original Good News* (New York: HarperSanFrancisco, 2005). Robinson's book depends upon the conclusions of Q scholarship and may be more accessible to the general reader.

There are many models employed for understanding the historical Jesus. In this specific work, I have chosen to focus on the wisdom of the historical Jesus. This does not mean wisdom is the only model; rather, I think it is the only one that allows us to go forward in the momentum of the historical Jesus in our time. Nevertheless, all the different models should be considered, and the best guide in this regard is David Boulton's *Who On Earth*

Was Jesus? The Modern Quest for the Jesus of History (Washington: O Books, 2008).

Another interesting and very accessible book is by journalist, writer, and ecologist Rex Weyler entitled, *The Jesus Sayings: The Quest for His Authentic Message.* Any study group or individual will find this to be a stimulating book that is sure to raise significant questions within Christian groups or in the general context of religious studies.

Finally, the reader may ask, aside from the particular presentation of this book, what impact has contemporary historical research and the context of our postmodern world had on the Christian faith and its future? To address this question further, readers may be interested in Lloyd Geering's *Christian Faith at the Crossroads: a Map of Modern Religious History* (Santa Rosa: Polebridge Press, 2001) and Don Cupitt's *The Meaning of the West* (listed below).

327174

CUSTOMER'S ORDER NO.				DATE		

NAME

ADDRESS

CITY, STATE, ZIP

SOLD BY	CASH	C.O.D.	CHARGE	ON. ACCT.	MDSE. RETD.	PAID OUT
			✓			

QUAN.	DESCRIPTION	PRICE	AMOUNT
1	Embracing Jesus		19
2			
3			
4			
5			
6			
7			
8			
9			
10			
11			
12			

General Bibliography

Allison, Dale. *Constructing Jesus: Memory, Imagination, and History.* Grand Rapids: Baker, 2010.

———. *Jesus of Nazareth: Millenarian Prophet.* Minneapolis: Augsburg Fortress Press, 1998.

Aquinas, Thomas. *On Being and Essence.* Translated by Armand Maurer. Toronto: Pontifical Institute of Medieval Studies, 1968.

Bacon, Francis. *The Works.* Edited by James Spedding, R. L. Ellis, and D. D. Heath. Vol. 8. London: Longmans & Co., 1862.

Bataille, George. *The Accursed Share.* Translated by Robert Hurley. 3 vols. New York: Zone Books, 1991.

Best, Thomas F., ed. *Hearing and Speaking the Word: Selections from the Works of James Muilenburg.* Chico, CA: Scholars Press, 1984.

Borg, Marcus, ed. *The Lost Gospel Q: The Original Sayings of Jesus.* Berkeley: Ulysses Press, 1996.

Buddharakkhita, Acharya, trans. *The Dhammapada: The Buddha's Path to Freedom.* Sri Lanka: Buddhist Publication Society, 1996.

Bultmann, Rudolf. *History of the Synoptic Tradition.* Translated by John Marsh. New York: Harper and Row, Publishers, 1963.

——— and Karl Kundsin. *Form Criticism: Two Essays on New Testament Research.* Translated by Frederick C. Grant. New York: Harper and Row, Publishers, 1962.

Chilton, Bruce. *Rabbi Jesus: An Intimate Biography.* New York: Image Books, 2000.

Crossan, John Dominic. *God and Empire: Jesus Against Rome, Then and Now.* New York: HarperSanFrancisco, 2007.

———. *The Historical Jesus: The Life of a Mediterranean Jewish Peasant.* New York: HarperSanFrancisco, 1992.

———. *Jesus: A Revolutionary Biography.* New York: HarperSanFrancisco, 1994.

——— and Jonathan L. Reed. *Excavating Jesus: Beneath the Stones, Behind the Texts.* New York: HarperSanFrancisco, 2001.

Cupitt, Don. *Above Us Only Sky: The Religion of Ordinary Life.* Santa Rosa: Polebridge Press, 2008.

———. *Creation out of Nothing.* London: SCM Press, 1990.

———. *The Meaning of the West: An Apologia for Secular Christianity.* London: SCM Press, 2008.

———. *The Old Creed and the New.* London: SCM Press, 2006.

Davies, Stevan L. *The New Testament: An Analytical Approach.* Salem: Polebridge Press, 2011.

Dibelius, Martin. *Gospel Criticism and Christology.* London: I. Nicholson & Watson, 1935.

De Mello, Anthony. *The Song of the Bird.* New York: Image Books, 1984.

Dostoyevski, Fyodor. *The Brother's Karamazov.* Translated by Constance Garnett. Revised by Ralph E. Matlaw. New York: Norton, 1976.

Ehrman, Bart D. *Jesus: Apocalyptic Prophet of the New Millennium.* New York: Oxford University Press, 1999.

Elliot, Susan. "Pseudo-Scholarship Illustrated," *The Fourth R.* May–June (2011).

Epstein, I., ed. *The Babylonian Talmud.* London: Soncino Press, 1961.

Evans, Craig A. *Fabricating Jesus: How Modern Scholars Distort the Gospels.* Downers Grove: InterVarsity Press, 2006.

Feuerbach, Ludwig. *The Essence of Christianity.* Translated by George Eliot. New York: Harper & Row, Publishers, 1957.

Freke, Timothy and Peter Gandy. *The Jesus Mysteries.* London: Element, 2003.

Funk, Robert W. *Honest to Jesus.* New York: HarperSanFrancisco, 1996.

——. *Jesus as Precursor.* Sonoma: Polebridge Press, 1994.

——. *Parables and Presence.* Philadelphia: Fortress Press, 1982.

Fredriksen, Paula. *Jesus of Nazereth, King of the Jews.* New York: Vintage Books, 1999.

Galilei, Galileo. *Dialogue Concerning the Two Chief World Systems - Ptolemaic & Copernican.* Translated by Stillman Drake. Berkley: University of California Press, 1967.

Galston, David. *Archives and the Event of God: The Impact of Michel Foucault on Philosophical Theology.* Montreal: McGill-Queens Press, 2010.

Gaston, Lloyd. *Paul and the Torah.* Vancouver: University of British Columbia Press, 1987.

Grillmeier, Aloys. *Christ in Christian Tradition.* Louisville: John Knox Press, 1996.

Harpur, Tom. *The Pagan Christ: Recovering the Lost Light.* Toronto: Thomas Allen Publishers, 2004.

Heidegger, Martin. *Off the Beaten Track.* Translated by Julian Young and Kenneth Haynes. Cambridge: Cambridge University Press, 2002.

Hoeller, Stephen A. *Gnosticism: New Light on the Ancient Tradition of Knowledge.* Wheaton: Quest Books, 2002.

Julicher, Adolf. *Die Gleisnisreden Jesu* [*The Parables of Jesus*]. Freiburg: J. C. B. Mohr (Paul Siebeck), 1888.

Kierkegaard, Søren. *The Concept of Irony.* Translated by Lee M. Capel. Bloomington: Indiana University Press, 1965.

Kirk, Alan. *The Composition of the Sayings Source: Genre, Synchrony, & Wisdom Redaction in Q.* Leiden: Brill, 1998.

Kloppenborg, John S. *Excavating Q: The History and Setting of the Sayings Gospel.* Minneapolis: Fortress Press, 2000.

———. *The Formation of Q.* Philadelphia: Fortress Press, 1987.

———, ed. *The Shape of Q: Signal Essays on the Sayings Gospel.* Minneapolis: Fortress Press, 1994.

Lightstone, Jack N. "Roman Diaspora Judaism." *A Companion to Roman Religion.* Edited by Jörg Rüphe. Malden, MA, Blackwell Publishing, 2007.

Livingston, David N. *Darwin's Forgotten Defenders.* Grand Rapids, MI: Eerdmans, and Edinburgh: Scottish Academic Press, 1987.

Laertius, Diogenes. *Lives of Eminent Philosophers.* Cambridge: Harvard University Press, 1958.

Lao-Tzu. *Tao Te Ching.* Translated by Stephen Mitchell. New York: Harper & Row, Publishers, 1988.

Mack, Burton L. *Who Wrote the New Testament? The Making of the Christian Myth.* New York: HarperSanFrancisco, 1995.

Meier, John. P. *A Marginal Jew: Rethinking the Historical Jesus.* Vol. 2. New York: DoubleDay, 1994.

Meyer, M. W. *From Quest to Q: Festschrift James M. Robinson.* Leuven: Leuven University Press, 1999.

Miller, Edward L., ed. "Tertullian, Athens or Jerusalem?" In *Believing in God: Readings on Faith and Reason.* New Jersey: Prentice Hall, 1996.

Miller, Robert, ed. *The Apocalyptic Jesus: A Debate.* Santa Rosa: Polebridge Press, 2001.

———. "Is the Apocalyptic Jesus History?" In *The Once and Future Faith.* Santa Rosa: Polebridge Press, 2001.

Moltmann, Jurgen. *The Church in the Power of the Spirit.* Translated by Margaret Kohl. London: SCM Press, 1977.

———. *The Crucified God.* Translated by R. A. Wilson and John Bowden. London: SCM Press, 1974.

———. *Theology of Hope.* Translated by James W. Leitch. London: SCM Press, 1967.

Myers, Ched. *Binding the Strong Man: A Political Reading of Mark's Story of Jesus.* Maryknoll: Orbis Books, 1988.

Plato. "The Republic." Translated by Paul Shorey. In *Plato: The Collected Dialogues.* Edited by Edith Hamilton and Huntington Cairns. Princeton: Princeton University Press, 1989.

Reed, Annette Yoshiko, "The Construction and Subversion of Patriarchal Perfection: Abraham and Exemplarity in Philo, Josephus, and the Testament of Abraham." *Journal for the Study of Judaism* 40, 2 (2009), 185-212.

Robbins, Vernon K, ed. *Ancient Quotes and Anecdotes.* Sonoma: Polebridge Press, 1989.

Robinson, James M., Paul Hoffman, and John S. Kloppenborg, eds. *The Sayings Gospel Q in Greek and English.* Minneapolis: Fortress Press, 2002.

Sanders. E. P. *Jesus and Judaism.* Philadelphia: Fortress Press, 1985.

Schweitzer, Albert. *The Kingdom of God and Primitive Christianity.* Translated by L.A. Garrard. London: Adam and Charles Black, 1968.

———. *The Quest of the Historical Jesus: A Critical Study of its Progress from Reimarus to Wrede.* Translated by W. Mongomery. New York: The Macmillan Company, 1968.

Scott, Bernard Brandon. *Hear Then the Parable: A Commentary on the Parables of Jesus.* Minneapolis: Fortress Press, 1989.

———. *Re-Imagine the World: An Introduction to the Parables of Jesus.* Santa Rosa: Polebridge Press, 2001.

———. *Trouble with Resurrection: From Paul to the Fourth Gospel.* Salem: Polebridge Press, 2010.

Spong, John Shelby. *Rescuing the Bible from Fundamentalism: A Bishop Rethinks the Meaning of Scripture.* San Francisco: HarperSanFrancisco, 1991.

———. *Why Christianity Must Change or Die: A Bishop Speaks to Believers in Exile.* San Francisco: HarperSanFrancisco, 1998.

Strauss, David Friedrich. *The Life of Jesus, Critically Examined.* Translated by George Eliot. Philadelphia: Fortress Press, 1972.

Tacitus, Cornelius. *The Annals of Tacitus.* Translated by D. R. Dudley. New York: New American Library, 1966.

Tillich, Paul. *Shaking the Foundations.* New York: Charles Scribner's Sons, 1948.

———. *Systematic Theology.* Vol 2. Chicago: The University of Chicago Press, 1957.

Vermes, Geza. *Jesus the Jew: A Historians Reading of the Gospels.* London: Collins, 1973.

Whitsett, Christopher G. "Son of God, Seed of David: Paul's Messianic Exegesis in Romans 2:2–3." *Journal of Biblical Literature,* 119/4 (2000), 661–681.

Wilson, Barrie. *How Jesus Became Christian.* Toronto: Random House Canada, 2008.

Wilde, Oscar. *Saturday Night Review.* November 17, 1894.

———. "Critic as Artist." In *Intentions.* New York: Prometheus Books, 2004.

Wink, Walter. *Engaging the Powers: Discernment and Resistance in a World of Domination.* Minneapolis: Fortress Press, 1992.

Wright, N. T. *The Original Jesus: The Life and Vision of a Revolutionary.* Grand Rapids: Eerdmans, 1996.

Index

CPSIA information can be obtained at www.ICGtesting.com
Printed in the USA
BVOW09s1031021014

369195BV00003B/3/P